How
to be a
Doll Detective

By Patsy Moyer

Published by A.D. Publishing
7325 Quivira Rd. # 238 Shawnee, Kansas 66216
Telephone: (913) 962-8533
Web Site: www.antiquesdetectives.com
Copyright © 2001 by Patsy Moyer

Dedicated with love and affection to
Dick and Marilyn

Special thanks to:
Southern Oregon Antique and Collectible Club - for their support and help in meeting collectors looking for answers and the following who shared photographs of their dolls.

June Allgeier
Sue Amidon
Taras Antonick
Nancy Baker
Lee Ann Beaumont
Elaine Beling
Irma Cook
Martha Cramer
Debbie Crume
Barbara DeBiddle
Sally DeSmet
Marie Emmerson
Darlene Foote
Cornelia Ford
Cherie Gervais
Angie Gonzales
Odis Gregg
Donna Hadley
Adrienne Hagey
Debbie Hamilton
Amanda Hash
Barbara Hilliker
Barbara Hull
Patricia Hunker

Maxine Jackson
Chantal Jeschien
Iva Mae Jones
Jeff Jones
Jaci Jueden
Andrea Kavanagh
Sue Kinkade
Rae Klenke
Sandra Kline
Sharon Kolibaba
Connie Lara
Marguerite Long
Michele Lyons
McMasters Doll
Auctions
Peggy Millhouse
Marcie Montgomery
Sarah Munsey
Faye Newberry
W. Harry Perzyk
Marian Pettygrove
Penny Pittsley
Stephanie Prince
Rachel Quigley

Inge Ramey
Marilyn Ramsey
Mary Sakraida
Jill Sanders
Nelda Shelton
Sandy Simonds
Carolyn Sisson
Timothy Smith
Harlene Soucy
Betty Strong
Elizabeth Surber
Linda Lee Sutton
Ruth Swalwell
Martha Sweeney
Jennifer Warren
Margie Welker
Kathryn Wolbers
Oleta Woodside
Patricia Wright
Allen Zimberoff

Table of Contents

Introduction

From the beginning of time, little girls have loved to play with dolls. It is shown as part of the feminine makeup - that nurturing, caring part of us that makes us be good mothers along with the physical attributes that make us unique. It is the way we are - and little girls demonstrate that by the way they name their dolls, endlessly talk to them, dress them and make them a part of the family.

Those dolls that we fondly remember with nostalgia may also have an intrinsic value. If you can't stand to throw your favorite baby into the Goodwill box, or discover Aunt Trudy or Grandma Gertrude's carefully wrapped doll in the cedar chest, you may want to know if it has attributes other than sentimental ones. If you are undecided whether to pass it on to be another little girls playmate, you need to identify your doll. Is it a treasure, a nostalgic family keepsake, or should it be a candidate for the Goodwill or the dumpster?

After identifying dolls at antique and doll shows for years, I realized that many people have no idea how to describe their doll and what features they need to be aware of when examining a doll. Just because your great-grandmother Margaret has a doll in her trunk does not mean that it is old. She might have bought it last year at a garage sale or maybe someone gave it to her for Christmas.

As the great sleuth Sherlock Holmes said, *"It is a capital mistake to theorize before one has data. Insensibly one begins to twist facts to suit theories, instead of theories to suit facts..."* With this book you can learn to gather clues to discover the identity of a doll. Then you will be able to make an educated decision whether to buy, keep or sell it. You will find how, as a Doll Detective, you can decide what has intrinsic value and what does not.

Holmes also said, *"They say that genius is an infinite capacity for taking pains. It's a very bad definition, but it does apply to detective work."* A good sleuth has to gather lots of details to arrive at a successful conclusion, but these are very simple steps and you can do it!

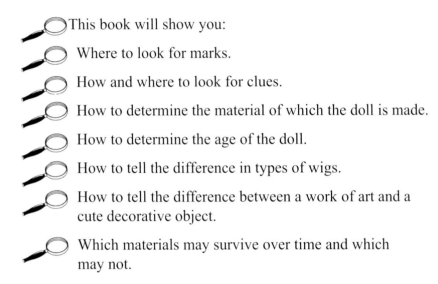

This book will show you:

Where to look for marks.

How and where to look for clues.

How to determine the material of which the doll is made.

How to determine the age of the doll.

How to tell the difference in types of wigs.

How to tell the difference between a work of art and a cute decorative object.

Which materials may survive over time and which may not.

You will learn that beautiful well-made objects are works of art and will always delight the viewer and be treasured. As real estate's top attributes are location, location, location, doll's desirable attributes are condition, condition and condition. A rare well-made beautiful doll in pristine condition is always more valuable than a doll of the same type that is scuffed, nude or flawed. A commonplace crudely-made doll mint-in-the-box may not have the appeal of a rare beautifully made doll that has flaws. This is the law of supply and demand. Later we will explore how this affects value.

Keep in mind that a deteriorating doll that is scuffed, cracked and soiled may not have the appeal or monetary value, but if it belonged to your mother or other dear relative, it will always be a priceless treasure. Value is relative; it may not always be based on intrinsic worth.

Some people believe they are buying a collectable treasure (and pay dearly for it). Yet, the doll may have been made in such huge quantities that it does not have the potential to increase in value. Cosequently, you may find it at reduced prices on the secondary (resale) market. Some extremely homely and well-played with cloth Raggedy Ann dolls from the early 1900s can have unexpectedly high values and a bright, clean example or rare example could bring $2,500.00 or more. Looks can be deceiving!

In all cases, knowledge is king. In order to recognize a treasure, you must begin to learn the differences in dolls. Like a detective you must learn how to keep track of the clues.

Maybe you will be as lucky as a lady who came into the Museum of History where I was conducting an identification clinic. She slyly opened her purse and pulled out a doll and laid it carefully on the cloth on my tabletop. With a slightly cautious look, she said "Twenty-five or more years ago, my mother bought this doll at a garage sale for a quarter. I am sure it is worth a lot more than that, now. What can you tell me about it?"

I was smiling as I gently examined the bisque doll. It was only 12" long and had an original leather body. The beautiful bisque head had paper weight eyes and it still had remnants of an old mohair wig. She was beautiful even without the original clothes.

I gently turned her over and on the back of her neck was the "Bru Jno" mark. Very collectible! Her mother's 25¢ purchase was worth $25,000.00.

It is our job as a "Doll Detective" to gain the knowledge to be able to recognize a work of art when we see it. Experience, study, research and patience can bring us the knowledge to solve the mysteries.This book will help you do that – by giving you the direction to start your research and where to look to find the answers to identify your own hidden treasures. A final note from Sherlock Holmes, "Education never ends, Watson." Happy detecting!

Chapter 1

Getting Started

While you may not need Sherlock Holmes' cap, pipe and cape, there are some handy tools that you will find helpful.

First, **a lighted magnifying glass** is a basic tool. Many doll makers marked their dolls to help identify the doll or parts of a certain model or mold number. With age the marks are sometimes very faint and a closer look may make it easier to identify them. It does not have to be big, but a lighted magnifying glass can be a great help especially if you are indoors where the lighting is not bright. In doll making, as the doll molds are used time and again, the fainter the mold marks become until sometimes you can barely tell there is a mark.

Second, **a tape measure** is an easy handy tool to help you measure the height of the doll. You can use a cloth one or a metal one or have several from which to choose. I found a small one that has a tape measure on one end and a small magnifying glass on the

other that just fits in my purse. Measurements are important because some dolls are known to be made in certain sizes and that is a clue to finding the name and age of the doll.

Third, you need **a notebook** to jot down notes and record them. You can use a simple three ring binder or your own personal computer. You might want to use a specially designed form. I made up my own to use to keep track of data for my projects and database. A sample that you may photocopy can be found on page 33.

An optional helpful item is **a combination fluorescent flashlight** to bring more light to the inside of the head or on the back of the neck of the doll. Sometimes if you do not have a black light, sometime this works to see inside the head of a bisque doll to check for flaws. More light can make those faint marks just a bit easier to read. (See page 206 for more info.)

A **black light** is another optional item that is helpful in several ways – to look inside a bisque head to see if it has flaws or to shine on the surface to see if it has been repainted. Battery operated, this lightweight lantern is small enough to fit in your pocket. It can also be carried with the convenient wrist strap. Under intense light, slight changes in texture on the painted surface are easier to detect.

A general **price guide** such as my Doll Values published by Collector Books can also be a good reference tool, if you need to check prices on your finds. Remember, however, that prices fluctuate with time, geographically, with demand and the whim of the buying public. No matter what type of doll you are curious about, chances are there is a price guide devoted to just that one subject – ie: Madame Alexander or Barbie dolls.

Now you have your sleuthing kit, and as Sherlock Holmes would say, *"Come, Watson, come! The game is afoot."* Happy hunting!

Chapter 2

Questioning the Suspect

First you need to physically examine the doll. You must give it an overall look to determine how tall it is, what material it is made from and if there are any maker's marks on it. Overall condition is also very important. Ask to undress the doll if it belongs to someone else, or they may wish to undress the doll and let you examine it. Be gentle about removing antique clothing. It may be very fragile. Look and see whether the doll is made of all one material or a combination of several.

Years ago, in nursing school, we were taught about "total patient care". Giggling college-age nursing students smiled about the "total" implications of meeting physical and mental needs, but the principal of viewing the whole patient is sound. We were asked to describe our patient from the top of the head down to his feet. This strategy is useful in describing your doll.

First, measure how tall the doll is from the bottom of its feet to the top of the head. I sometimes lay a terricloth towel down to provide a cushion for the doll. It also will catch any sawdust or filling that may be coming from a hole in the body. Gently straighten the legs and measure the doll with a tape measure or yardstick. If the doll is on a stand, note that the feet are straight and touching the bottom of the stand and measure up from the base of the stand. Do not let the tape sag and hold it straight to get an accurate measurement. Yardsticks are great, but awkward to put in your purse. Jot down these findings on a sheet of paper. The height of a doll is sometimes enough alone to tell us the name of the doll, but usually it is just one clue in your quest for the identity.

Next let's examine the head of the doll. The head can be a socket head, (fitting into the body or a shoulderplate) a shoulderhead, (where the head and shoulderplate are one piece) or the head and torso may be molded together. The doll may have a bald solid dome, molded hair, painted hair, or a wig.

The head determines how the doll is classified. The head is the most valuable part of the doll. A doll with a bisque head and a leather body is called a bisque doll. What is bisque? Bisque is a fired porcelain material. We call old dolls with an unglazed finish, "bisque" while newer dolls of porcelain material are just referred to as porcelain dolls even though they both are made of porcelain. A doll with a vinyl head and a hard plastic body is called a vinyl doll. There are many materials used in doll making and some have quite a history. We will look at these materials later one by one and the types of bodies that are used with them

Pate
The bisque doll may have an open crown in the top of its head, cut away during production so that the eyes could be inserted. This opening is generally covered with a plaster, cork or cardboard pate. This can be an identification tip as the only known company that used plaster for a pate in their bisque dolls was a German firm, J. D. Kestner. They made very high quality bisque dolls. French pates are usually made of cork, There are exceptions like Jules Steiners whose pates were made of pressed cardboard. Look on page 18 to see an open crown - that will be covered by a pate.

Eyes
The doll may have sleep eyes that open or close, set eyes that do not move, googly eyes that are oversize, flirty eyes that move from side-to-side, painted eyes, decal eyes or molded closed. If the eyes are painted, they may have an indentation and curve inward giving them depth. This is called an intaglio eye. You can seee a doll with googly eyes on page 34. The eyes can be glass and antique eyes can be hand-blown - some described with spiral threading. The more sought-after antique dolls have paperweight eyes that are hand-blown showing depth and detail. These are frequently found in French dolls. Before doll makers cut away the top of the head to

insert the eyes, some dolls had several holes in the top of the solid dome head to aid in stringing or for the eye mechanism to open or close. Antique bisque doll eyes may have been set into the head with plaster. With age this material can dry out or come loose causing the glass eyes to fall back into the head and break. For this reason it is wise to store a doll face down, especially when traveling. If you ship a doll somewhere, the head needs to have the pate removed from the crown opening and then packed with cotton.

Some eyes were made of celluloid over tin eyeballs. Another type of eyes had a celluloid iris and pupil. This type was called "glassine" and they were used on composition dolls until after World War II. Glassine eyes over time can dry out and "crack", "craze", or turn white. This mars the beauty of the doll. Some doll doctors can replace the iris with modern material making the doll more acceptable. However, the irises may not be the same size as in the old glassine version.

Mouth
Does the doll have an open mouth or closed? A basic doll will have an open mouth with upper or lower teeth and perhaps a tongue. (Some tongues quiver and they are called a "wobble" tongue.) It can have a closed mouth with no opening into the head cavity. It may have a closed mouth with the lips forming a curve. This is called a watermelon smile. It can have an open/closed mouth where the mouth is molded open and it may have teeth or tongue visible but there is no hole into the head cavity. It may have a round hole in mouth so that a bottle or pacifier can fit into the opening; this is called a "nurser". A doll with an open mouth and a bland expression is called a "dolly face". An example of a dolly face is the Japanese bisque Morimura Brothers child on page 38.

A doll with a definite expression is called a "character face". An example of a character face on a doll might have a closed frowning look, or a mouth wide open in a laugh. Character face dolls became more popular after a 1909 Berlin Exhibition that invited artists to participate. A few character face dolls were made during the 19th century, but they became popular after this time. This is a clue to help you date an antique doll. A color photos of Kämmer & Reinhardt "Max" character doll can be found on page 38.

Wigs

The wig can be made of human hair, mohair, synthetic, or some other fiber like embroidery floss, yarn, even seaweed. The doll may be bald - without painted, molded hair or a wig. Some china dolls are wigged and when one removes the wig, they find a solid dome underneath, some with a round black spot where a pate would be. These dolls are still erroneously called Biedermeier- circa 1820s-1840s, referring to the clean line German furniture. No accepted connection has been proven to tie in with the German furniture maker Biedermeier.

The wig is usually made of human hair, lamb's wool, mohair or synthetic materials. Human hair wigs are found on some antique dolls but generally, the wig is soft mohair - made from the goat. The human hair wig is sometimes taken from the owner's hair and this adds more sentimental value to a family doll. Human hair can range in texture from coarse to fine. An identification clue - human hair has a distinct odor when touched with a hot needle. Synthetic materials can be nylon, Saran and others and will melt when touched with a hot needle.

You will usually find that the wig is mohair (from goats) or human hair. Mohair wigs are very fragile and you should not try to comb or brush the mohair wig as it may all pull right out. You can use a toothpick to gently separate each strand of hair, one by one to untangle the hair, which then can be gently curled and restyled using plastic rollers or paper and permanent wave rods. Painstaking, but surprising how it nicely it can come back.

Human hair wigs should be treated gently also. Old wigs should be removed gently; excessive glue can be carefully moistened with a damp cloth to soften the glue so it can be removed. Do not rush this procedure! Remember the head is the most valuable part of the doll so take care in handling. Today you can buy commercially made human hair, mohair and synthetic material wigs, but original wigs are most desirable. If you substitute another one, you may want to retain the original. While an original wig may look a disaster, you may want to keep it - a worthy doll doctor can restore some mohair wigs or set a synthetic wig to get it back to its former glory.

A wig can be glued down so tight that you think nothing short of a bomb blast will separate it from the head. You can remove the wig from a bisque head doll by gently soaking the wig base with a damp cloth and then gently loosening the wig. This again, takes time and patience. Don't try this on composition dolls! The composition material used in doll making is glue-based and water will dissolve the glue and damage the surface of the doll.

Some hair was painted by combmarks where the comb was dipped in paint and used to decorate the head. The hair can be molded into curls or waves and may be described as deeply molded or lightly molded. The doll may have buns, braids, or topknots molded into the head. It may have combs, headbands, snoods or flowers molded into the hair. An example of these would be china dolls. Decorations in the hair add to the value. Some dolls have molded hats or bonnets and are called bonnet heads.

Bodies
Dolls with bent legs are described as baby dolls. Generally a baby doll will have a five-piece body, consisting of a torso, two arms and two legs. This body may be made of leather, bisque, composition, celluloid, cloth, wood, hard plastic or vinyl and may not be of the same material as the head. The bodies are usually attached to the head and held together by stringing them with elastic cord. Some dolls have other types of jointing - some using springs, or metal fasteners. Other dolls are molded in one piece with the head. Old wooden dolls had leather or peg joints and wooden limbs. Old

bisque dolls may have used composition bodies with five-pieces as a baby or they may have multi-jointed bodies for an adult or child. The multi-jointed bodies may have used wood balls to make the joints work smoothly and are termed "composition and wood jointed" bodies. The type of body combined with the material used can be an indication of the identity of the doll. Schoenhut used all wooden spring jointed bodies on their wooden dolls. The adult or

Above: 18 1/2" bisque Kammer & Reinhardt Mold 126 toddler. This shows the toddler composition and ball jointed body with the legs fitted diagonally to the body, courtesy McMasters Doll Auctions.

Above: 13" bisque Kestner, with child's body showing wooden ball joints with joints at knees, elbows, wrists, shoulders and hips, courtesy McMasters Doll Auctions.

Above: 24" bisque Simon & Halbig Mold 1159 with adult body showing a slimmer waist and slight bosom. This doll has straight wrists - no joints at the wrist, courtesy McMasters Doll Auctions.

fashion doll is defined as having an adult body - one with a smaller waist. Some antique fashion dolls have wooden bodies or leather covered wooden limbs - some had articulated padded metal armature.

Leather bodies were popular up until World War I and then declined in popularity. A toddler doll is jointed at the hips with straight

Above: 15" bisque Kestner solid dome baby. This shows the typical five-piece body with a torso, two arms and two bent legs that is typical of composition baby bodies, courtesy McMasters Doll Auctions.

Above: 25" bisque unmarked German shoulderhead with shoulder crease lines, glass eyes and leather body. Note the head is turned slightly and is joined with the shoulder in one piece. This is called a turned shoulder head, courtesy Debbie Crume.

Above: 20" bisque Kestner dolly face girl, has a leather body,with leather upper arms joined to bisque forarms with metal rivets. Note the Kestner logo crown and ribbons label on the front of the body, courtesy Nancy Baker.

chubby legs. A mama doll body is defined as being made of cloth, with a crier inside the torso and stitch jointed upper legs of cloth. The mama doll was invented by Georgene Averill in 1918 and has been used in one form or another on dolls since that time. New dolls can use leather, composition and other materials for dollmaking. Signs of wear, soil and construction can indicate if it is a new body or an old body.

Marks

Turn the doll over and check under the wig (if possible) and see if there are any marks on the back of the head. Sometimes the marks can be very faint and a collector will mistake the "Made in//Germany" mark for "Madeline". The novice can see a mark like "Simon & Halbig 117A" on the back of a dolls head and wonder why that mark is not listed as Simon & Halbig. They do not realize that the

Right 21-1/2" bisque Armand Marseille 11013 shows the cut-away piece of the head called the open crown . This opening was made to allow placement of the glass eyes. This particular open crown is fitted with a piece of wood and metal mechanism. There is also a round cut opening to hold the metal piece. Usually the open crown does not have the extra holes and metal mechanism.

The crown is covered with a pate of cork, plaster or cardboard and then with a mohair or human hair wig.

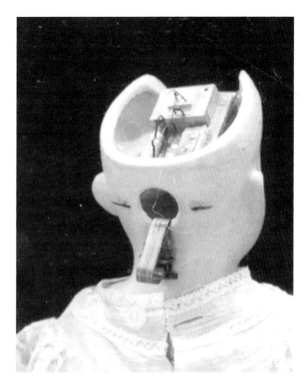

Marks are generally found incised or stamped on the back of the head below the open crown or lower down to the neck., courtesy Debbie Crume

top half of the mark that says "K (star) R" is covered up by the wig and this means it was made by Kammer and Reinhardt. Kammer & Reinhardt designed the mold and sent it out to a porcelain factory Simon & Halbig for production. The wig may be glued down tightly and you may hesitate to try to pry it up so that you can see all of the mark. It should be done gently as you do not want the head to break by using too much force. Antique wigs on bisque dolls sometimes can be loosened by patiently folding back as much of the wig as possible and applying a damp cloth to the stubborn glue. Don't try that on composition dolls though, as the water will melt the glue based finish on the doll. Fortunately, a lot of people have already had this learning experience and have identified many of the marks and numbers for us. Look in our Marks Section, beginning on page 66 and see if you can identify this mark, who made it and country of

Left: Example of back of neck of painted bisque doll, courtesy Sheryl Smidt. The mark reads:

A. 449. M.
Germany
0 1/2

This example is a clear easy to read mark on the back of the doll's head. Often the mark is covered with an old or original wig that has been glued down so tightly, you may think it will take dynamite to remove it.

origin!

Now, look and see if the back torso of the body is marked and note the marks. These are the two main places in which old dolls are marked, but there may be hangtags, brochures, boxes or other places on the body where you will find marks. Marks are one the most important ways to identify your doll and should be one of the first things you check. In the antique dolls, the marks are like a signature indicating who made what by their own particular marking system. Companies marked their dolls to assist in matching heads to bodies because dolls were mass produced and an efficient way to keep track of inventory was needed. A list of marks and mold numbers is included for your reference beginning on page 66.

Hangtags, brochures, boxes and labels
Note any separate pieces of paper with the doll. If there is a letter that states whose doll this was or any other information on the owner and origin of the doll, this is called a provenance and adds to the value of the doll. Hangtags, brochures, labels and boxes may contain information that helps you identify the company that made the doll. They can also give you the name of the doll or other important clues to its identity. You want to keep them. Certainly, hangtags, brochures, labels and boxes add value to your doll espe-

cially as time passes and these more fragile paper items are lost. Most modern collectible dolls - of the last thirty or forty years - are expected to have their boxes and complete tags, brochures and accessories to be considered collectible.

Some people are unaware that the paper, cardboard, accessories or even the fabric of the costume may affect the doll negatively by staining or emitting chemicals that can harm the doll body. One of the safest ways to wrap a doll to store is in a well rinsed white sheet or cotton towel. Museum quality acid free tissue paper is available at museum supply stores.

Costumes

Notice if the doll is dressed and if she has tagged clothing. Do not throw away the clothing even if it seems to be disintegrating. Old silk may "melt" when touched. Be careful! Original clothing adds to the value of the doll and rare or unusual costumes will add real value to the doll. Take care of the original clothing - sunlight, moisture, heat and pests are the biggest threats to the delicate fabrics and colors. A skilled doll costumer can recreate an acceptable costume using the old one as a pattern.

Dolls should be dressed to fit the era in which they were made. Antique dolls can be dressed according to the style of the era using only natural fiber materials. Dolls after World War II can be appropriately dressed in nylon laces and synthetic materials.

Costuming is very important in helping you date your doll - if she is wearing original clothes or clothes made in the era the doll was produced. A bisque, wax, papier mache, or wooden doll should be wearing natural fiber clothing, such as cotton, silk, wool or linen. Anything made after 1940s could be wearing nylon, polyesters and synthetics. Not only the material, but the color and pattern will help date a fabric. There is a particular color of green popular in the 1930s that you can quickly spot with a little practice. Trims also help date as they would be of natural materials on earlier dolls then after World War II could be made of synthetics. Many of the old

1930 -1940s patterned fabrics are being reproduced today, so you can find new fabric in the old color and style. This makes it great for costumers to dress their doll in the right blend of fabric in the correct pattern and colors.

What's it made of?

Bisque

Bisque is an unglazed fired porcelain material that was used in doll making circa 1860s. It was popular again in the 1930s and is still used today. The most well-known antique bisque dolls were made in either France or Germany from the middle of the last century up until the 1930s and later. Some bisques were made in Japan when World War I cut off the supply of dolls from Europe. Porcelain is also a current favorite material of many new doll makers. Old porcelain is called bisque; newer dolls are referred to as porcelain - it is still a similar material.

Porcelain dolls are breakable and should be handled gently. While at first glance, bisque may be thought to be an undesirable material for doll making, the fact is that many of the old bisque dolls have survived for years and continue to increase in value. The most common mold numbers are available at less cost than many modern dolls, while rare, unusual and beautifully made dolls continually increase in value.

Bisque dolls may be all-bisque with bisque bodies (on smaller dolls) or have bodies made of composition, leather or other types of material. The all bisque dolls that originally sold for pennies have become valuable. The German style have fat tummies and some have molded on clothing. Those with wire pin joints are presumably made before 1900. Later dolls were strung with elastic cording. When Rose O'Neill Kewpies became popular, they were soon made into dolls and they still remain charming. Those that are molded with cats, dogs, accessories like a gun or in unusual actions such as bursting out of an egg can be very valuable. The common Kewpie was one-piece or had jointed arms only. Nude, with blue wings,

Kewpie was made by the thousands and is still being made commercially today. Another type of all bisque dolls were the tiny "Snow Babies" named, so it is said, after Admiral Peary's daughter that was born in Iceland in 1893. These original Snow Babies were rolled in bits of porcelain to give a furry effect to their clothing. They too are still being made and sold commercially today - but the present "Dept. 56" revivals are much larger than the older antique ones.

Celluloid

Celluloid is an early material that was first patented in 1869 and is now used to refer to all dolls of this early plastic-type material. Some German bisque makers also made models of their bisque dolls in celluloid. Celluloid dolls were made in Germany, as well as England, France, Japan, the United States and other countries. While this may seem a lightweight flimsy material, it is not as fragile as you might think even though it does require delicate care. They should not be stored in plastic bags or where the temperature may get too warm. Celluloid dolls may have a mark on the back of the neck or on the back of the torso. A very common trademark is the turtlemark of the German firm, Rheinische Gummi und Celluloid Fabrik Co. later known as Schildkrote. Many Kewpies were made in celluloid. Caution - celluloid is highly flamable and it was eventually discontinued for safety reasons. Do not get it near a flame.

China

China is another porcelain material, but has been fired with a glaze and it looks shiny. There is a difference between the low-fired ceramic dolls, made at home and the older, more delicate porcelain dolls made in Germany. Look for the gentle, delicate painting of features. Since they were popular from the 1840s up until the 1930s, you can find a lot of chinas. They often have molded painted hair. The hairstyle may be one clue of the age of the doll, since it reflects the hairstyles generally of the era in which they were popular. The most common hair-style is called a "low-brow" from the

1890s and was made up through the 1930s. It has black curls coming down on the forehead and comes in a large variety of sizes. Chinas most often have a shoulderplate which will be glued to a leather body or with holes so that it can be sewn to a cloth body. The heads were sold as replacements when one broke or a mother could make her own cloth body instead of buying a leather one. Take care when examining china dolls that the china or bisque legs and arms do not swing against one another and break. A common sense approach to solving the leg problem is to attach a thread spool between the feet to keep them from banging against one another. The rarer Chinas are the older ones that have decorated hair-dos, pink skin tone, exposed ears, brown painted eyes and elaborate hair styles. Some have molded blouses on their shoulderplate.

Cloth

They made a wide range of dolls from different types of cloth material. Prior to 1900 some enterprising cloth dolls were made with flat faces and painted or molded and painted. Some cloth dolls from the 1900s were printed on fabric that was sold uncut, and then assembled. Raggedy Ann dolls were first made around 1915 and then commercially by P. J. Volland in 1920 through 1934. Lenci felt dolls were made starting in 1918. The charming cloth Käthe Kruse dolls were made from 1910. Because these soft cloth cuddly dolls were so appealing to children, they were well-played-with and fewer survived. Some cloth dolls in excellent condition such as the Volland Raggedy Ann of the1920s can be worth as much as $2,500 - $4,000.

Composition

Composition dolls have been made since the early 1900s up through the early 1950s. Because German bisque doll imports were not available during World War I, American manufacturers began producing composition dolls and advertised them as "unbreakable" or "hard-to-break". Early dolls were made by pressing "cold" glue-based material into molds. By the 1920s, the accepted formula was based on sawdust-type flour dough that was heated and "hot" pressed into molds. Upon drying, the composition heads and body parts were dipped in thinner composition to provide a smooth skin like finish. Then the features were hand-painted and later air-brushed on the face. Because the material was susceptible to changes in humidity, temperature and moisture, composition dolls may have deteriorated and be in varying declining conditions. They may have crazing where the thin painted finish has been affected and is starting to deteriorate. They may have cracks in the seams where too much tension from stringing has caused a break or around the molds' ends, where the dipped skin has curled back. They may have flaking where the paint finish is actually falling off. They may experience lifting where the surface paint is drying and lifting up from the surface.

Most composition dolls will have some of these flaws and even close examination of "excellent" dolls may show spidery fine craze lines forming. Dolls with heavy cracking, flaking, lifting and crazing are unacceptable for collectors and should only be considered for purchase when there are added incentives such as original clothing, tags, boxes, or rare costumes. Examples of composition were the Dionne Quintuplets, Patsy and Shirley Temple dolls.

Hard Plastic

Hard plastics were developed before World War II, but they came into accepted use during the war as production plants were converted for the defense effort. Some doll companies installed new equipment in their factories to supply needed parts for the war effort. After the war they returned to making dolls and used the new products. The hard plastic doll era was 1948 through the 1950s. At first, this rigid material was thought to be the perfect answer to doll production, but the material does require care as sunlight will cause it to fade, dry out and deteriorate. And some hard plastics will allow the growth of fungi that causes a white powder residue. Hard plastic examples are Toni, Ginny and Alexander's Nina Ballerina.

Magic Skin

This early 1940s and 1950s plastic was soft and pliable and thought to be another miracle material for producing dolls. Unfortunately with time, this "latex" may harden and, most often, change color from flesh to dark brown or black. Dipping molds in latex produced a one-piece body that was stuffed with cotton or Kapok through the neck opening. Although this made a soft doll, the latex dries out and splits. As yet, no one has found a way to mend it. Expect these dolls to continue to deteriorate. This condition cannot be reversed and some people have chosen to maintain their childhood doll by covering the body with cloth, replacing with another similar body of more stable material, or making a new cloth body. The value of keepsakes such as this is sentimental value only, but if it is your doll, you may delight to preserve it. Two unfortunate examples of magic skin are Baby Coos and Bonnie Braids.

Papier Mache

Papier-mâché is another form of composition material using paper as a main ingredient that is pressed and formed into molds. It is lighter than the other composition material with glue and sawdust bases. It was used as a material in Europe for dolls from the 1840s. A well-known American manufacturer was Greiner who made shoulderhead dolls with painted and molded features.

Rubber

Rubber was used as a material in the production of dolls during the 1930s and 1940s. World War II changed priorities causing shortages of this material and substitutions were made. Rubber limbs with a squeaker inside were used by Ideal on some of their Tickletoes dolls. Effanbee introduced their best selling Dy-Dee Baby in 1934 with a drink-and-wet mechanism that made great use of the rubber material. Unfortunately, the rubber material used cracked and split over time.

Experimental rubber types of materials transcended into the plastic era. It is very difficult to tell the difference in Dy-Dee Baby's head and hard plastic. Probably if the material was ever analyzed in a lab, we would not find true rubber or an exact plastic. When production methods embrace new materials and technology, the result is variations and Dy-Dee is an example. Soon rubber gave way to vinyl, that eventually would stay flexible over a longer period of time, was easily washable and not as easily affected by rough handling by children.

Vinyl
Vinyl is the new miracle plastic material thought to be the answer to doll production. It came into use around the end of the 1950s. Many variations of production methods and material caused some problems. The vinyl can be either soft or rigid and two major production methods were used. In the "rotational" method, molds filled with plastic are heated and rotated causing the material to be thrown against the sides of the molds. When the molds are cooled, the plastic material retains the shape of the molds. These first efforts were not successful because the material could become sticky or change color. Because a plasticizer ingredient was used, chemically these dolls may absorb some of the costume dyes and take on that color. It still was not the answer that doll makers had hoped for.

A new production method that used blow-molded vinyl and polyethylene pellets was tried. The materials were melted inside a tube, inserted into the molds, and then hot air was forced into the molds. This allowed the material to adhere to the molds shape. It proved to be the most successful.

Today vinyl can be hard or soft and painted to look like composition or other materials. It remains the accepted material used for doll production as we start the new millennium. After you have examined a group of dolls, it is usually easy to pick out the vinyl ones, because the costume materials are newer fabrics, the material is more flexible, and generally only vinyl has rooted hair. It is more difficult to distinguish rigid vinyl from hard plastic, but even here, the rigid vinyl seems to have a little give in flexing. Barbie, Cabbage Patch Kids and Chatty Cathy are examples of vinyl dolls.

Wax
Beeswax is another material used in doll making. It became popular during the 1850s to 1900s, especially in England. The obvious drawback was that waxes could melt from heat. Wax over papier-mâché made the doll more sturdy but there was a loss of fine detail and they were less attractive than the all-wax dolls. While modern doll artists sometimes use wax as a medium, very few are made. If you find any wax dolls, they will most likely be old and some of them can be very collectible - again those that have survived in excellent condition and are well made will be most collectible.

Wood
Wood has been a good source material for doll makers. Peg-wooden examples from England and Europe have been found dating as early as the 1600s to 1700s. An American doll firm, Schoenhut, made wonderful spring-jointed articulated wooden dolls circa 1911 to 1930. These continue to grow in value and are eagerly sought after by collectors who pay top prices for dolls in excellent condition and with original clothes.

Modern doll artists are carving small wooden replicas of "Hitty", a literary character from Rachel Field's children's book of 1929, "Hitty, Her First Hundred Years". This type of doll can be a fascinating collecting niche - a doll with a built in history. The story provides a series of escapades that Hitty faces and the small size, about 6 inches, makes it an easy "Travel Doll" (small dolls collectors take with them). Hitty is a simple doll to costume and a collector can buy a mass produced one, a hand-carved one, or learn to carve her own.

Others
There are various other materials used to make dolls – leather, soap, cornhusks, metal, and more. The same technique is used in assess-

ing your doll regardless of what material you find. Training your-
self to look at these important clues is the first step in solving the
mysteries of old dolls.

Clues to Condition

Perhaps one of the hardest concepts to grasp is condition. Condition
is vitally important in dolls. As a United Federation of Doll Club's
judge, you learn that "mint-in-box" means just that - as a doll might
be found on the shelf in a toy store during the year it was produced.
But in real life, time passes and with time, things like sunlight,
moisture, heat, cold, bacteria, fungus and pests can alter the condition of the doll. With each type of material used in doll making,
some or all of these things can affect the doll. When you come
upon a doll, you should expect to find them in various stages of
condition.

Bisque

With old bisque dolls, you can find them boxed in excellent condition. That is rare! Almost never will you find one "mint in box" with
the doll, wig, stringing material and costume in original unchanged
condition. With time, many fabrics deteriorate, melt or change color.
Bugs can invade the wigs or eat the leather. So bisque dolls in
original costume in excellent condition are highly prized and more
valuable than those that have replaced costumes and wigs. Any time
supply is limited and demand is great, values will rise.

Composition

With composition dolls, there is even more chance of deterioration
because this material can be affected by sunlight, heat, moisture,
soil and bacteria that could break down the finish. Even very fine
dolls may have a minute spidery crazing from age and exposure.
The value of these dolls will show a much greater variation in their
condition. There is a greater range from mint, to excellent, to good,
to poor, to a basket case whose only salvage might be as spare parts.
Even a doll in poor condition may have a redeeming quality, such as
a tagged original costume or clear eyes that can be salvaged to
replace a pair of eyes that have clouded over in another doll.

Hard Plastic

Hard plastic dolls present a smaller range again of condition. You can again have excellent, good, and poor condition as well as basket case examples that can only be used for parts. Hard plastic was at first thought to be the ideal doll making material, but time again has shown that plastic (with recipes and production methods for the plastic varying from manufacturer) can also fall victim to fungus and mold that destroys the beauty and sometimes presents an unpleasant odor.

Vinyl

Vinyl is another example that seems to be the ideal doll making material. However, early vinyls have turned sticky or discolored - the early Barbie faded. Fading is acceptable, but does affect value. Although vinyl has been around for at least 40 years and new types are being used every day, conditions affect its value and desirability as a collectible. Most collectors expect vinyl dolls to be mint-in-the-box and expect the box to be in perfect shape also. Vinyl dolls should be pristine, with all brochures, tags and accessories available for the doll to be most valuable. A rule of thumb is that newer dolls of the last 50 years should be mint-in-box to be the most collectible.

The only way to be aware of how condition greatly influences the value is to investigate and research the doll in question. Sherlock Holmes would advise the detective to learn all the facts before you make decisions and that holds true with dolls.

As you investigate you will learn also which dolls are rare. You will need to experience dolls at shows, on ebay, in books and magazines as well as through clubs and collections and the Internet. When you have seen enough examples, you will be able to make better decisions. Take every opportunity available to touch, feel and examine dolls. A mint-in-box composition doll of poor manufacture will be held less desirable than the excellent composition doll, that is well-made and a thing of beauty. Knowledge of the subject will help you to know the difference.

Chapter 3

Adding Up the Clues

Check the doll clue and record sheets on the following three pages to be sure that you have all your clues in order.

Have you:

Measured the height of the suspect?

Determined the material of the head and body?

Made note of makers marks, mold numbers or any other identifying factors?

If so the next step is to go to the "Marks" section that begins on page 66. Find the maker or makers mark that matches the one on the doll in question.

Next to the mark or makers name you will find the years that the company was in business and where the doll was "born". Many makers also include the exact years each model was produced.

Then if you want more information, just look for the 📖 icon with the individual numbers. The numbers correspond to the numbers next to the books listed in the Bibliography & Resources section that starts on page 183. For instance, any manufacturers listing that contains the number "46-47-48-49-50-51 or 52" will correspond to a book written by "yours truly". Number 46 refers to "Doll Values". This means that this book will provide prices for this type of doll.

This portion of the book should save you days, if not weeks in research time. Just make sure that you use your fact sheets so that you always compare "apples to apples". After researching your "suspect", don't forget to hone your detective skills by tackling the "cases" in our "Solve the Mystery" section. Happy Hunting!

Clue Sheet

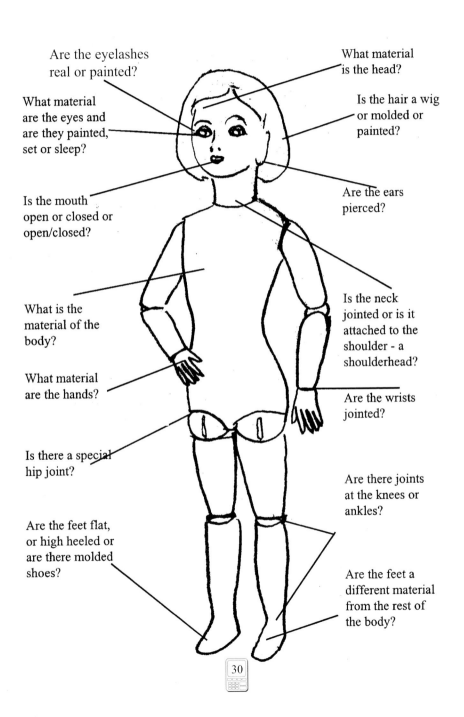

Are the eyelashes real or painted?

What material is the head?

What material are the eyes and are they painted, set or sleep?

Is the hair a wig or molded or painted?

Is the mouth open or closed or open/closed?

Are the ears pierced?

What is the material of the body?

Is the neck jointed or is it attached to the shoulder - a shoulderhead?

What material are the hands?

Are the wrists jointed?

Is there a special hip joint?

Are there joints at the knees or ankles?

Are the feet flat, or high heeled or are there molded shoes?

Are the feet a different material from the rest of the body?

Clue Sheet

How tall is your doll? Measure from the top of the head to the bottom of the feet.

Does it have an open crown?

What material is the pate that covers the open crown?

Are there marks on the neck or upper torso. Check under the wig for hidden marks that may tell mold number, maker or size.

Are the arms jointed at the elbows?

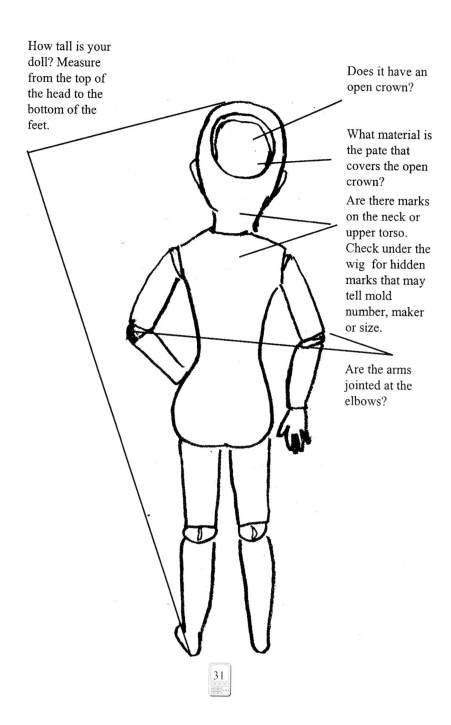

Doll Record Work Sheet

Height:_____

Measure from the bottom of the feet to the top of the head.
Straighten legs if necessary.

Material_____

Touch the head. What material is it?

Marks_____

Look on the back of the neck or back torso first - a clue to the maker.

Manufacturer_____

Who made it? (Check the mold number, letters or name in the Index.)

Age_____

What date was it made? Check when certain materials were used.

Name_____

Does it have a name on a label, wrist tag, box, or marked?

Eyes_____

Do they sleep, are they googly, glass, celluloid, plastic or painted?

Mouth_____

Is it open or closed or open/closed?

Ears_____

Are they molded with the head or applied, and are they pierced?

Wig_____

Is the wig synthetic, human hair or mohair? Is the hair rooted or glued
on? Or does it have molded, painted hair?

What is the body made of?_____

Is it cloth, leather, vinyl, composition, wood, bisque, hard plastic or
other material? Is it ball-jointed or does it have a five-piece construction or bent legs like a baby? Does it have a different construction?

Chapter 4
Rogues Gallery

MATERIALS

Whether it is the antique bisque Steiner above, the campy 1930s boudoir doll, the modern Tonner "Kitty Collier" or the lovable Kewpie Googly, photographs are helpful tools to help us identify dolls and the materials from which they are made.

Above: 17 1/2" bisque Jules Steiner Bébé, marked Flre A, open/closed mouth, dimple in chin, paperweight eyes, mohair wig, jointed wood and composition body, circa 1887+, courtesy Elizabeth Surber.
Top right: 31" cloth French unmarked Boudoir Doll, mask face, mohair wig, circa 1930s, private collection.
Center right: 18" hard vinyl Robert Tonner Doll Co. "Kitty Collier" red rooted hair, inset eyes, fashion type, circa 2000, courtesy Marilyn Ramsey.
Lower right: 10" bisque Kestner Kewpie Googly, circa 1920s, courtesy McMasters Doll Auction.

All- Bisque

Left: All-Bisque Bye-Lo displays round green sticker on torso, glass sleep eyes, painted pink shoes and white stockings, circa 1922-1930+s, courtesy Cherie Gervais.

Middle: 1/2" All-Bisque Snow Baby with top hat, and 3 1/2" Snow Baby lying down with arms out, circa 1900-1930s, courtesy Marguerite Long.

Right: 6 1/2" All-Bisque Kewpie, designed by Rose O'Neill, painted eyes to side, molded/painted tufts of hair, stiff neck, jointed arms, "starfish" hands; with seated All Bisque Kewpie holding cat on lap, both circa 1912 on, courtesy McMasters Doll Auctions.

All- Bisque

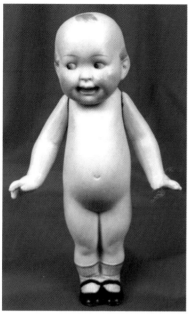

Above left: 6 1/2" All-Bisque, with painted blue side-glancing eyes, tufts of hair, jointed arms, stiff neck, molded blue socks, black shoes, circa 1910. All photos this page courtesy McMasters Doll Auctions.

Above right: 10 1/2" All-Bisque Kestner, mold 150, open mouth dolly face, stiff neck, sleep eyes, mohair wig, painted and molded stockings and shoes, circa 1897.

Left: 7 1/2" All-Bisque child, stiff neck, painted blue eyes, closed mouth, molded/painted blonde hair, molded-on clothing, socks and shoes, wire-jointed arms and hips, circa 1890.

Bisque

Above: 26" bisque portrait Jumeau on marked Jumeau body, closed mouth, paperweight eyes, pierced ears, circa 1877-1883, courtesy McMasters Doll Auctions.

Below: 23" bisque Schmitt & Fils socket head, marked SCH crossed hammers in a shield, open/closed mouth, compo/wood ball-jointed body, circa 1870s-1890, holds bisque Marotte, a twirling musical toy, courtesy McMasters Doll Auctions.

Above: 20" bisque Steiner "Le Parisien", with large glass paperweight eyes, open mouth, teeth, pierced ears, nicely dressed, circa 1885+, courtesy McMasters Doll Auctions.

Below: 12 1/2" bisque Kestner Googly, mold 221, closed watermelon mouth, nicely dressed, circa 1913, courtesy McMasters Doll Auctions.

Bisque

Above: 16" bisque character Kämmer & Reinhardt "Max" mold 123, character from German comics, original black flax wig and red and white print jumpsuit, circa 1913, courtesy McMasters Doll Auctions.
Below: 25" Kestner mold 245 "Hilda", glass sleep eyes, open mouth, mohair wig, nicely dressed, bent-leg baby body, circa 1914, courtesy McMasters Doll Auctions.

Above: 25" Japanese bisque "dolly face" Morimura Brothers child, open mouth, glass eyes, mohair wig, original in box, ball-jointed composition and wood body, circa 1918, courtesy McMasters Doll Auctions. Japanese dolls gained market share because of the ban on German dolls during World War I.

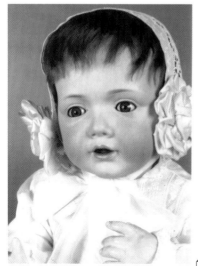

Bisque - Parian-type

Parian-type refers to the untinted white bisque material used to fill the head mold as opposed to bisque tinted to appear like flesh. This is just a descriptive term that many older collectors still used to describe dolls of this material.

Left and lower left: 21-1/2" Dornheim, Koch & Fischer Parian-type with untinted bisque shoulderhead, elaborate blonde hairdo, pink rose floral decorations shows in back view of hairstyle, painted eyes, molded necklace, nicely dressed, circa 1870s, courtesy Elizabeth Surber.

Above: 16" Parian-type untinted bisque shoulderhead, simple hairdo, blonde center part, glass eyes, bisque arms and black molded boots, old costume, circa 1860-1870s, courtesy Elizabeth Surber.

Celluloid

Celluloid was used as a doll making material by German doll makers who sometimes used bisque molds and poured the same head in celluloid. As its use became more accepted, celluloid was used by a wide range of manufactures for inexpensive dolls.

Above: 18" celluloid Kämmer & Reinhardt toddler mold 728, flirty eyes, open mouth, two teeth, original blonde mohair wig, five-piece composition toddler body, circa 1915, courtesy McMasters Doll Auctions.

Above left: 20 1/2" celluloid Buschow & Beck boy, marked "[helmet]//No. 7// 42//Germany" flange neck, painted molded brown hair, blue intaglio eyes, closed mouth, cloth body is flesh-colored cotton with disc joints, (missing hand), white shirt, blue print tie, brown suspenders, circa 1920s-1930s, courtesy Inge Ramey.

Lower left: 10" celluloid child with molded blue ribbon in molded hair, painted eyes, open/closed mouth with teeth, molded black shoes and brown socks, circa 1920s-1930s, courtesy Marilyn Ramsey.

China

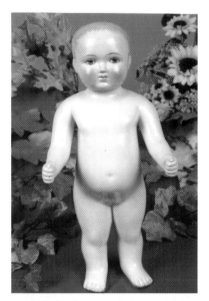

Left: 12 1/2" pink tint China "Frozen Charlie" no joints, blonde painted hair, circa 1860s+, courtesy McMasters Doll Auctions.

Below: 25" China shoulderplate, cobalt blue glass eyes, closed smiling mouth, high cheek color, human hair wig, cloth body, china lower limbs, circa 1850s+, courtesy McMasters Doll Auctions.

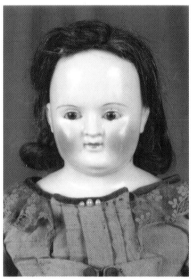

Above: 21 1/2" Alt, Beck & Gottschalck mold 1214 China shoulderhead, heavily molded painted hair, cloth body, china lower arms and legs, circa 1890+, courtesy McMasters Doll Auctions.

Right: 14 1/2" China Pet Name "Agnes" with molded blouse and name, black low brow hairstyle most common, cloth body, circa 1899-1930s, courtesy Elizabeth Surber

Cloth

Below: 23" cloth Alabama Indestructible baby, molded painted features, jointed shoulders and hips, monk's cap construction on head, large hands, made by Ella Gauntt Smith, circa 1900-1925, courtesy Cherie Gervais.

Right: 20 1/2" cloth Martha Chase boy, painted hair, features, cloth body and painted limbs, jointed elbow and knees, nicely dressed, some paint rubs, circa 1900-1920, courtesy Elizabeth Surber.

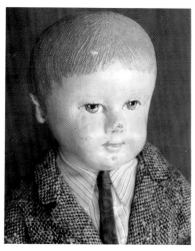

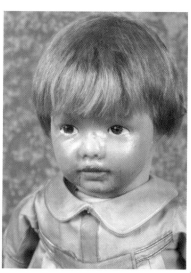

Above: 16" cloth Series 1 Käthe Kruse girl, painted green eyes, rosy cheeks, painted brown hair, wide hips, applied thumb, original costume, circa 1910-1930, courtesy Allan Zimberoff.

Left: 17" cloth Kamkins, oil painted swivel head, molded features, mohair wig, cloth body, circa 1919-1928, courtesy McMasters Doll Auctions.

Composition

Above: 13" composition Alexander Dr. Dafoe with gold hangtag and set of five 7 1/2" Alexander Dionne Quintuplets in multi-colored sunsuits, each Quint has her own color, in canvas topped swing, circa 1934+, courtesy McMasters Doll Auctions.

Right: 24" composition American Character Petite Mama Doll, blue sleep eyes, open mouth, four teeth, mohair wig, cloth body, composition arms, lower legs, original dress, boxed, circa 1923+ courtesy McMasters Doll Auctions.

Below: 14" composition Alexander "Scarlett" green velvet dress, feathered hat, wrist tag, boxed, circa 1941-1943, courtesy Harlene Soucy.

Below: Rare 8" Cameo composition "Scootles" all original, hangtag, circa 1925+, courtesy Sue Kinkade.

Composition

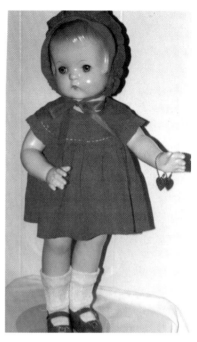

Above: 14" composition Mary Hoyer Skater, mohair wig, sleep eyes, eye shadow, knit/crochet costume, circa 1939-1946, private collection.
Right: 19" composition Effanbee Patsy Ann, in original tagged red silk dress, shoes, circa 1929, courtesy Marian Pettygrove.

Hard Plastic

Above: 14" hard plastic Madame Alexander Little Women "Amy" with loop curls, tagged dress, circa 1947-1956, courtesy Angie Gonzales.

Above: 7-1/2" vinyl American Character "Betsy McCall" marked "McCall//©//Corp" in circle on back, blonde wig with barrettes, sleep eyes, jointed knees, original pink dress with pink and white checked top, boxed, circa 1957-1963, courtesy Barbara Hull.

Hard Plastic

Above left: 9" hard plastic Alexander "Cissette", boxed, original lace teddy, circa 1957-1963, courtesy McMasters Doll Auctions.

Above right: 20" hard plastic Madame Alexander "Cissy", boxed, circa 1955-1959, courtesy McMasters Doll Auctions.

Above: 10" hard plastic R&B (Arranbee) "Littlest Angel" walker, original plaid taffeta dress, box, hangtag, circa 1956, courtesy Gay Smedes.

Above: 8" hard plastic strung Vogue Ginny, blue and white original dress, hat, painted lashes, circa 1950-1954, courtesy Sharon Kolibaba.

Hard Plastic

Above left: 22" Ideal's hard plastic Saucy Walker, box, braids, sleep eyes open mouth, upper teeth, tongue, circa 1951-1955, courtesy Sally DeSmet.

Lower right: 22" hard plastic American Character "Sweet Sue" walker, marked "Amer. Char. Doll.", Saran rooted "skull-cap", vinyl arms, jointed elbows, pink "Ding Dong School" sack hangtag, "Cotillion" costume, circa 1956, courtesy Cornelia Ford.

Above: 16" hard plastic Terri Lee, painted brown eyes, single-stroke brows, synthetic wig, in Hawaiian outfit, circa 1951-1962, courtesy Maxine Jackson.

Above: 14" hard plastic Ideal "Toni" marked "P-90", mint in box with beautiful cheek color, original dark blue and red trim play dress, play wave accessories, circa 1949, courtesy Rae Klenke.

Metal Head

Right: 15" metal shoulderhead marked with Helmet logo and "MINERVA" on front, painted and molded blonde hair, multi-stroked eyebrows, painted blue eyes, with red accents on inner eye, and red accent for lid, closed mouth, cloth body, circa 1900-1930, courtesy Martha Cramer.

Papier-Mâché

Right: 19 1/2" papier-mâché M & S Superior shoulderhead, cloth body, kid arms, paint rubs, normal wear, circa 1880+, courtesy McMasters Doll Auctions.

Above: 14 1/2" papier-mâché milliner's model with painted blue eyes, closed mouth, painted molded hair, unjointed kid body with wooden lower arms and legs with painted shoes, circa 1840s-1860s, courtesy McMasters Doll Auctions.

Above right: 17" German papier-mâché milliner's model with exposed ears, three curls on each side, bun in back, kid body, wooden arms, circa 1840s-1860s, courtesy McMasters Doll Auctions.

Rubber

Right: 15" hard rubber Effanbee Dy-Dee Baby with applied ears, sleep eyes, open mouth to receive bottle, molded and painted hair, softer rubber body, with labeled box, all accessories, circa 1940+, courtesy McMasters Doll Auctions. Set includes a pacifier, sponge, soap, bubble bath and "What every young doll mother should know" booklet by Aunt Patsy. Dy-Dee was a sensation at the time it was introduced in 1934 because of its drink-and-wet mechanism.

Vinyl

Left: 19" vinyl Mattel "Chatty Cathy" hard plastic body, pull string talker, blue sleep eyes, rooted hair, freckles, open/closed mouth, two teeth, circa 1962-1964, courtesy Darlene Foote.

Below: 18" vinyl Ideal Crissy, swivel waist, growing hair, boxed, circa 1969-1974, courtesy Angie Gonzales.

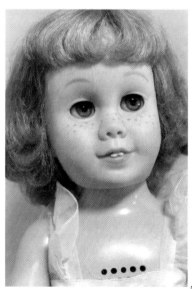

Vinyl

Above right: 12" vinyl Hasbro Jem outrageous fashion "Roxy" wearing Smashing Fashions "Just Misbehavin" and right, "There Ain't Nobody Better", circa 1985-1986, courtesy Linda Holton.
Above: 22" vinyl Ideal "Kissy", rooted Saran hair, jointed wrists, press hands together and mouth puckers up and makes a kiss with kissing sound, circa 1961-1964, courtesy Nelda Shelton.

The most accepted medium in today's market place is vinyl that manufacturers can finish to look like the old composition and hard plastic dolls of an earlier era. Chatty Cathie and Terri Lee are being reproduced to look like the earlier dolls.

Above: Set of four, vinyl Remco "Littlechap Family" 14 1/2" Dr. John, 13 1/2" Lisa, 12" Judy, 10 1/2" Libby, painted eyes, brown wigs on women, male has painted black hair, complete with brochures, mint-in-box, circa 1963, courtesy June Allgeier.

Vinyl

Above: 14" hard vinyl Robert Tonner Doll Co. "Betsy McCall" Limited Edition of 250 souvenir doll from 2000 Betsy Convention, courtesy Marilyn Ramsey.

Above right: 17" vinyl Ideal "Miss Revlon", pierced ears, high heels, tagged dress, in box, circa 1956-1959, courtesy Sally DeSmet.

Below bottom: 21" vinyl American Character Whimsie "Bessie the Bashful Bride" synthetic wig, one-piece stuffed vinyl body with molded head, circa 1960-1961, courtesy Amanda Hash.

Wax

Above: 21" poured wax baby, inserted human hair, wig, cloth body, wax lower arms and legs, old costume, circa 1850s+ courtesy McMasters Doll Auctions.

Above: 21" poured wax baby, with glass eyes, blonde mohair wig, nicely dressed, circa 1850-1870s, courtesy McMasters Doll Auctions.

Wood

Below: 16" wooden Schoenhut model 16/103, a early Graziano carved hair doll, circa 1911, courtesy McMasters Doll Auctions.
Right: 19" wooden, spring-jointed Schoenhut model 19/308, circa 1912-1924, courtesy McMasters Doll Auctions.

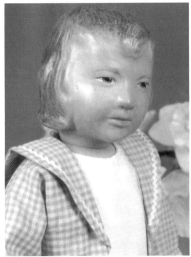

Advertising

Above: 12" composition Horsman Campbell Kids, Campbell soup paper label pinned to costume, molded painted hair, side-glancing eyes, molded socks and shoes, circa 1930s+ courtesy McMasters Doll Auctions.
Below: 17" vinyl Atlanta Novelty Company 1979 Anniversary Gerber Baby, molded features, flirty eyes, advertised Gerber Baby Food, courtesy Ruth Swalwell.

Advertising dolls are doubly collectible - as a doll and as memoriabilia of the product they represent.

Top: 13" hard plastic Buddy Lee engineer, advertises Buddy Lee workclothes, circa 1949-1962, courtesy McMasters Doll Auctions.
Above: 17" cloth Comfort Powder Doll, printed on muslin, shown with original framed fabric directions, circa 1915, courtesy Marian Pettygrove.

Advertising

Above: 20" hard plastic Hasbro Ronald McDonald with cloth body, plastic yellow hands, red boots, advertising McDonald fast food restaurants - with Golden Arches, circa 1978, courtesy Angie Gonzales.

Above: 11 1/2" vinyl Mattel Barbie Collectors Edition "Little Debbie" U.S. trademark of Mattel, Inc. except for Little Debbie which is the Trademark of McKee Baking Co. circa 1990s, courtesy Iva Mae Jones.

Right: 23" composition "Miss Curity", advertising Johnson & Johnson products, blue sleep eyes, blonde mohair wig, all original, circa 1940s-1951, courtesy Peggy Millhouse.

Artist Dolls

Artist Dolls can be a great collectible, particularly if you have the expertise to recognize great craftmanship and artistry that will propel the artist's work to become highly sought-after.

Right: 14" wooden artist doll, "Harriet Tubman" a black leader in the underground railroad who led 300 slaves to freedom. Hand-carved by LA teacher, Naida artist, Floyd Bell, cloth body, wire armature, wooden hands, signed on shoulderplate, "1994, Fred Bell", courtesy Cornelia Ford.
Below: 24" "Takeda Shingen" a warlord of the early 16th century is a wood carving sitting on his throne. Original and one of a kind, circa 1993-1996, courtesy W. Harry Perzyk.

Below: 6" wooden jointed "Hitty", a literary character from the Newberry award winning childrens' book, "Hitty, Her First Hundred Years" in Quaker costume, hand-carved and dressed by Janci doll artists, Nancy Elliot and Jill Sanders, circa 1997, photo courtesy Jill Sanders.

Artist Dolls

Above: 16" stone clay "Willie and the Spring Collection" by doll artist Sandy Simonds, one-of-a-kind, molded painted features, brown hair, canvas body stuffed with polyfill, wire armature, green suit, black felt hat, suede belt and shoes, holding cardboard boxes with fabric shoes and tissue, circa 1998, courtesy Sandy Simonds.

Above: 24" porcelain Linda Lee Sutton "Sara Jill" marked "Linda Lee Sutton Originals//©//1999" on back of head, big brown paperweight eyes, closed mouth, blonde human hair French braided wig, posable cloth body with porcelain arms and legs, coral silk dress, limited edition of 10, courtesy Linda Lee Sutton.

Automaton

Automatons are more desirable with multiple movements, tunes and actions and old unusual bisque examples in good working condition can range from $1,000.00 to $30,000.00 or more.

Right: 21" bisque Simon & Halbig mold 1300 fitted with key-wound mechanism to perform actions such as raising hand, playing instrument, waving fan or twirling on base. The more movements, the more highly prized. This is a "dolly face" example with open mouth, glass eyes, mohair wig, circa 1902, courtesy McMasters Doll Auctions.

Barbie

The highly collectible and valuable first Barbie brings highest prices in unplayed with condition.

Left: 11 1/2" heavy vinyl Mattel "Number One Ponytail Barbie" with skin color faded, white irises, pointed eyebrows, holes in feet, painted fingernails and toenails, in black and white striped swimsuit, mint-in-box, circa 1959, courtesy McMasters Doll Auctions.

Below: 11 1/2" vinyl Mattel "Number Two Ponytail Barbie", brunette, same as above except no holes in feet, circa 1959, courtesy McMasters Doll Auctions.

Above: 11 1/2" vinyl Mattel "Number Three Ponytail Barbie" with blue irses, red lips, gentle curved eyebrows, brown eyeliner, heavy solid body may have faded to white, black and white swim suit, stock No. 850, courtesy McMasters Doll Auctions.

Right: 11 1/2" vinyl Mattel Fashion Queen Barbie in box with three wigs, near mint, circa 1963-1964, courtesy McMasters Doll Auctions.

Black

Because fewer Black dolls were produced, they are considered more rare and highly collectible and often win ribbons in competition with other similar dolls as well as bring higher prices.

Above: 20" all vinyl, marked "©1967//Beatrice Wright" child with rooted hair, sleep eyes; re-dressed, courtesy Marcie Montgomery.

Right above: 13 1/2" vinyl Shindana baby, rooted hair, ethnically correct features, drink and wet doll rooted hair, first major manufacturer of black dolls, circa 1972, courtesy Marcie Montgomery.

Right: 7 1/2" black bisque Ernst Heubach, mold 399, solid dome, pupiless eyes, bent-limb baby body, circa 1930, courtesy McMasters Doll Auctions.

Bonnet Head

Bonnet Head dolls derive their name from the molded on hats and can be of any material, but generally refer to old bisque dolls.

Left: 17" bisque Bonnet Head doll with molded hair and leaf hat with floral decoration, painted eyes, old costume, bisque hands and 14" bisque Bonnet Head doll with Butterfly hat on blonde molded curls, blue painted eyes, closed mouth, bisque hands, circa 1890-1920, courtesy McMasters Doll Auctions.

Celebrity

Celebrity dolls must represent a real person alive or dead to be in this category. The cannot just be a literary character but can be an actress who plays the character.

Above: 4 1/2" vinyl Remco Beatle, John Lennon, with name on Guitar, oversize head, circa 1964, courtesy Sarah Munsey.
Right: 21" Ideal composition Deanna Durbin, movie star, unplayed-with condition, with box, circa 1938-1941, courtesy McMasters Doll Auctions.

Celebrity

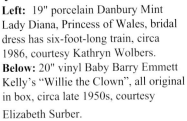

Left: 19" porcelain Danbury Mint Lady Diana, Princess of Wales, bridal dress has six-foot-long train, circa 1986, courtesy Kathryn Wolbers.
Below: 20" vinyl Baby Barry Emmett Kelly's "Willie the Clown", all original in box, circa late 1950s, courtesy Elizabeth Surber.

Above: 13" composition Ideal Shirley Temple, mohair wig, pinback button, tagged blue pleated party dress, circa 1934, courtesy Angie Gonzales.
Right: 18" composition Madame Alexander "Sonja Henie", marked "Sonja Henie", open mouth with teeth, dimples, tagged dress fur trim, ice skates, circa 1939-1942, courtesy Donna Hadley.

Comic

Dolls based on comic or cartoon characters bring back the childhood interest in comic strips, comic books or cartoons.

Left: 14" cloth Georgene Averill "Little Lulu" swivel head, mask face, cloth body, original costume, red plastic purse, excellent condition, circa 1944+, courtesy McMasters Doll Auctions.

Disney

Because Disney has created such beloved characters, this category of collecting can be enough to fill a collectors interest alone.

Above left: 12" cloth R. G. Krueger Dwarf "Bashful" circa 1930s-1940s, mint in box, courtesy Sharon Kolibaba.

Above: 11" cloth Knickerbocker Mickey Mouse Cowboy, circa 1936, courtesy McMasters Doll Auctions.

Ethnic

Above: 9" painted hard plastic Baitz "Luzern" girl, mohair wig, side-glancing eyes, felt-over-wire body, original regional outfit, Baitz heart tag, sticker "Made in Austria", circa 1970s, private collection.

Below: 11" composition Dream World Ethnic doll, Czechoslovakian costume, circa 1939, courtesy Carolyn Sisson.

Above: 9" bisque Israel "Bride of Bethlehem" marked "Germany//9" composition body, circa 1900+, private collection.

Ethnic dolls are dolls in regional or national dress. This category has dolls of a wide variety of materials and costumes and may be an overlooked collecting niche as more experienced collectors overlook these dolls that are generally priced less than others.

Ethnic

Above: 12 1/2" composition Squaw and 13" Skookum's Chief, "Bully Good" label on foot, circa 1920-1940, courtesy Timothy Smith.

Above: 15 1/2" cloth Ronnaug Petterssen boy, painted features, 1940s-1970s, courtesy Elaine Beling.

Below: 15" French celluloid, triangular tag marked "Poupee Reene D'Orior", circa 1950s, courtesy Irma Cook.

Some dolls can be collectibles in more than one category. The Skookum doll can be called Ethnic but may also appeal to someone who collects Western memorabilia or composition dolls. Ronnaug Petterssen dolls may appeal to cloth doll collectors as well as those who like Ethnic dolls. The French celluloid might appeal to celluloid collectors as well as those who like Ethnic.

Fashion-types

Left: 15" bisque French Fashion-type, unmarked, with painted blue eyes, pierced ears, closed mouth, kid body with stitched fingers, circa 1890s, courtesy McMasters Doll Auctions.

Below: 18" French Fashion-type, unmarked, closed mouth, feathered eyebrows, glass sleep eyes, kid body, circa 1880-1900, courtesy McMasters Doll Auctions.

The Fashion doll category does not stop with antique bisque dolls but contemporary dolls such as Barbie and Gene also fit the definition of a fashion type.

Left: 15 1/2" vinyl Fashion-type doll, circa 2000, is Ashton-Drake's Gene in navy blue "Moments to Remember" costume with painted eyes, closed mouth, rooted brunette wig, jointed at shoulders and hips, with small waist, a Limited Edition of 250, courtesy Marilyn Ramsey.

Oriental

Oriental dolls can be of many different materials from bisque to composition to cloth and vinyl.

Left: 13" bisque Kestner 243 Oriental baby in original romper, tunic, headpiece, circa 1914+, courtesy McMasters Doll Auctions.

Below: 14" bisque Simon & Halbig mold 1329 Oriental socket head, glass eyes, black mohair wig, pierced ears, circa 1910, courtesy Sharon Kolibaba.

Above: 11 1/2" wood Door of Hope "Manchu Lady" with colorful head-dress, carved features, pink original costume, circa 1930s, courtesy Elizabeth Surber.

Right: 8 1/2" composition Japanese Warrior, glass eyes, original costume, rides 10" papier-mâché horse, post WWII, courtesy Marie Emmerson.

Pincushion or Half-Dolls

Above left: 4 3/4" bisque marked Goebel half-doll, blonde mohair wig, hands away in graceful pose, circa 1900-1930, private collection.
Left: 5" china marked McDaniels Southwick Co. flapper half-doll, molded string beads around neck, one hand touching back of head, one arm away, circa 1920s, private collection.

Above: 5" marked Goebel China half-doll with fancy hairdo, arms away holding item close to body, circa 1915, courtesy Patricia Wright.

These fanciful dolls that were originally made to be pincushions, lamp shades, powder puffs and other decorative objects and are now collected for the beauty of the doll itself. Most desirable are the fragile ones with arms away from the body, because fewer will have survived breaking or dolls with decorative elements such as holding an object or with decorative accents on the hair or body.

Chapter 5
Makers and Marks

Manufacturers can hold many clues about the doll in question. This section includes notes, mold numbers and names, sizes and dates. 📖 See Bibliography

Henri Alexandre

1888-1892, Paris, France, made bisque children with paperweight eyes, no mold numbers, sizes: 17"- 23"
📖 **13, 14, 74**

Bébé Phénix

1889-1900, Phenix trade mark originated with Alexandre; Bébé Phénix used 1895 by Mme. Lafosse and later by Jules Mettais/Jules Steiner.

PHÉNIX
★ 95

Alexander Doll Company

1912+, New York. Made dolls in cloth, composition, hard plastic and vinyl.
📖 **16, 66, 67**

Cloth: Had flat faces in 1930s
Alice in Wonderland, 1930s,16"
Baby Genius, 1930s, 11"
Clarabel the Clown, 1951-53, 19", 29", 49"
David Copperfield, 1930s, 16"
Dionne Quintuplets, 1935-36, 16", 24"
Funny, 1963-77, 18"
Little Shaver, 1940-44, 7", 10", 15", 22"; 1941-1943, 12"
Little Women, 1930-36, 16"
Muffin, 1965-70, 14"
  1966 only, 19"
So Lite Baby, Toddler, 1930s, 1940s, 20"
Suzie Q, 1940-42, 8"
Teenie Twinkle, 1946 only, flirty eyes
Tiny Tim, 1930s, 16"
Composition:
Baby or Toddler
Baby Genius, 1930s, 1940s, 11", 16", 22"
Baby Jane, 1935, 16"
Dionne Quintuplets, 1935-39, 8", 11", 14", 20"
Pinky, 1937-40, 23"
Child or Adult
Alice in Wonderland, 1930s, 7", 9"; swivel waist, 13"

Often unmarked on body, but carries tag, brochures, cloth labels and marked boxes.

"Alexander Doll Co." and name of doll on cloth label.

Above: Types of Alexander Faces - Tiny or Little Betty 9" composition Madame Alexander "Chinese" girl, marked "Wendy-ann//Mme Alexander//New York " on back, sideglancing eyes, circa 1935-38, courtesy McMasters Doll Auctions.

Alexander used several face molds on many dolls - see examples of common faces.

Above: Types of Alexander Faces - Wendy Ann face, 14" composition, circa 1935-48, courtesy Rae Klenke.

Above: Types of Alexander Faces - Princess Elizabeth, 19" composition, sleep eyes, open mouth, 4 upper teeth, human hair wig, circa 1937-41, courtesy McMasters Doll Auctions.

1939-40, 14"
1948-49" 14 1/2", 18". 21"
Babs Skater, 1939-40, 18"
Bride and Bridesmaid, 1935-39, 7"
  1936-41, 11"
  1935-41, 13", 15",
  1935-43, 18", 21"
  1945-47, 21"
Butch, 1942-1946, 12";
  1949-51, 14", 16"
Carmen , 1938-43, 7", 11"
  1937-40, 14"
  1939-42, 17", 21"
Dr. Dafoe, 1937-39, 14"
Fairy Queen, 1940-46, 14", 18"
Flora McFlimsy , 1938-41, 9"
  1938-44, 14", 16", 22"
  1944, 12"
Jane Withers, 1937, 13", 21"
  1937-39, 15", 17", 20"
Jeanie Walker, 1940s, 13", 18"
Judy, 1945-47,   21"
Karen Ballerina, 1946-49, 15"
  1948-49 18"
Kate Greenaway, 1936-38, 9"
  1938-43, 7" 13", 15", 24"
Little Betty, 1935-43, 9"
Little Colonel, 1935, 9", 13", 17", 24", 26"
Little Genius, 1935-40, 12",
  1935-37, 1942-46, 16", 20"
  1942-46, 24"
Little Women, 1935-1944, 7"
  1937-40, 9"
  1937-46, 14"
Madelaine DuBain, 1937, 11"
  1938-39, 14"
  1939-41, 17", 21"
Marcella, 1936, 13", 16", 21", 23"
Margaret O'Brien, 1946, 14", 18", 21"
Marionettes by Tony Sarj 12"
McGuffey Ana, 1935-37, 15"
  1935-39, 7", 9",
  1937-39, 11"
  1937-42 21", 25"
  1937-44, 11", 13", 15",

1938, 13"
1948-49, 17"
Princess Elizabeth, 1937-39, 7"
1937-41, 9", 11", 13", 15", 18", 23", 28"
Scarlett, 1937-42, 7", 11"
1938-41, 9"
1939-46, 18"
1941-43, 14",
1945, 1947, 21"
Sleeping Beauty, 1938-40, 15"
1941-44, 7", 18", 21"
Snow White, 1937-1939, 13" painted eyes
1939-1940, 13" sleep eyes
1939-40, 12"
1939-40, 18"
1939-42, 16"

Above: Types of Alexander Faces - Maggie face, hard plastic, sleep eyes, closed mouth, synthetic hair, circa 1949-1953, courtesy Sally DeSmet.

Sonja Henie, 1939-41, 9"13", 15", 18", 21"
1939-42, 7"
Tiny Betty, 1935-42, 7"
W.A.A.C., 1943-44, 14"
W.A.A.F., 1943-44, 14"
W.A.V.E. 1943-44, 14"
Wendy Ann, 1935-48, 11", 13", 15"
1936-40, 9"
1938-41, 17", 21"
Hard Plastic & Vinyl:
Baby or Toddler
Baby Genius, 1949-50, hard plastic, 15", 18"
1952-55, hard plastic, 21"
1956-62, hard plastic, 8"
Child or Adult
Alexander-kins, 1953, hard plastic, straight leg, non-walker, 8"
1954-55, Straight leg walker, 8"
1956-65, Bent Knee walker (Alexander-kin renamed Wendy Ann in 1963)
Alice in Wonderland, 1949-50, 17", 23"
1950, 14"
1951-52, 15" 23"
1955-56, 1972-76,1990-92, 1997-98, 8"
1963, 12"
1966-92, 1996, 14"
1991, 10"
Binnie Walker, 1954-55, 15", 18", 25"
1964 only, 18" toddler

Above: Types of Alexander Faces - Cissy face, 20" hard plastic, eyeshadow over blue sleep eyes, closed mouth, dark blonde synthetic wig, vinyl arms, hard plastic body, yellow formal, circa 1955-1959, courtesy Mary Sakraida.

Above: Types of Alexander Faces - Margaret face, 14" hard plastic Cinderella, blonde synthetic wig, blue sleep eyes, circa 1950-51, courtesy Debbie Crume.

Above: Types of Alexander Faces - Jackie face, 21" vinyl Jacqueline, sleep eyes, closed mouth, eyeshadow, circa 1961-62, courtesy Sandra Kline.

Brenda Starr, 1964 only, 12"
Bride and Bridesmaid, 1949 on, 8"-25"
Butch, vinyl, 1950, 14"
       vinyl 1965-66, 12"
Carmen , hard plastic, 1983-86, 14"
       hard plastic, 1993, 10"
Caroline, 1961-62, 15"
       1992-93, 8"
Cinderella, 1955 on, 8", 10", 12", 14", 18"
Cissette ,1957-1963, 10"
Cissy,1955-59, 1996+, 20", 21"
Cynthia, 1952 only, 15", 18", 23"
Davy Crockett, 1955 only, 8"
Edith, The Lonely Doll, 1958 only, 8"
       1958-59, 16", 22"
Elise, 1957-64, 16 1/2", jointed ankles, knees
       1961-62, 1966-89, 17"
       1963, 18", jointed ankles, knees
       1977, 16"
First Ladies, (President's Ladies)
       1976-78, 1st set, 14", M. Washington, A. Adams, M. Randolph, D. Madison, E. Monroe, L. Adams.
       1979-81, 2nd set, 14", S. Jackson, A. Van Buren, J. Findlay, J. Tyler, S. Polk, B. Bliss.
       1982-84, 3rd set, 14" A. Fillmore, J. Pierce, H. Lane, M. T. Lincoln, M. Patterson, J. Grant.
       1985-87 4th set, 14"
       1988, 5th set, 14"
       1989-1990, 6th set, 14"
Fischer Quints, 1964, 7 1/4"
Flora McFlimsey, 1953, vinyl, 15"
       1955, 14"
Jacqueline, 1961-62, 1966-67, 21"
       1962, 10"
John R.Powers Model, 1952 only, 14", 18"
Karen Ballerina, 1949, 21"
Kate Greenaway, 1993, vinyl, 14"
Kelly, 1958, 18"
       1958-1959, 15", 16", 22"
       1959, 8", 12"
Leslie, 1965-72, 17"
Lissy, 1956-58, 11 1/2", 21"

Little Genius, 1956-62, 8"
    1993-95, 7" vinyl, painted eyes
Little Shaver, 1963-65, 12" painted eyes
Little Women, 1955, 7 1/2" straight leg, walker,
    1957-58, 11 1/2"jointed elbows, knees
    1956-59, # 609, 8" bent-knee walker
    1959-68, 11 1/2"
    1960-63, # 381, 8" bent knee walker
    1964-72, # 781, 8" bent knee-walker
    1969-89, 12"
    1973, #7811-#7815, 8" bent knee-
    walker
    1974-86, # 411-415, 8" straight leg
    1987-90, # 405-409, 8" straight leg
    1991-92, # 411-415, 8" straight leg
    1993 only, 12", no Marme
    1995, #14523-28, 8" straight leg
    1997-99, 16" Journal Series
Maggie, 1948-54, 15", 17", 21", 23"
Maggie Mixup, 1960 only, 16 1/2"
    1960-61, 8", freckles
    1961 only, 17"
    1997-98, 8", Post Office
Margaret O'Brien, 1947, 14", 18", 21"
Margot Ballerina, 1951-53, 15" 18"
Mary Martin, 1948-52, 14", 17"
Marybel, "The Doll That Gets Well", 1959-65
    1998, Marybel Returns, #12220
McGuffey Ana, 1948-50, 21"
    1949-50, 18"
    1955-56, 18", 25", 31"
    1956, 8" #616
    1963, 12"
    1963-65, 8"
    1968-69, 14", #1450
    1977-86, 14" #1525
    1987-88, 14" #1526
    1995, 14" #24622
Melanie, 1955-56, 8" #663
    1961, 21"
    1966- 71 21"
    1968-69, 10", #1173
    1970, 10", #1182
    1974, 21"
    1979-81, 21"

Above: Types of Alexander Faces - Lissy face, 12" hard plastic Lissy, blue sleep eyes, closed mouth, circa 1956-1958, courtesy Sally DeSmet.

Above: 30" hard plastic, Madame Alexander "MiMi" wearing tagged dress, marked "Alexander 19©61", sleep eyes, closed mouth, earrings, brown hair, jointed wrists, multi-jointed body, white dress with red rick-rack, circa 1961, courtesy Cornelia Ford.

Above: Types of Alexander Faces - Elise face, 1950s-60s, 15" hard plastic Elise blue sleep eyes, closed mouth, blonde synthetic wig, pierced ears, soft vinyl arms jointed above elbows, circa early 1950s, courtesy Mary Sakraida.

Above: Types of Alexander Faces - Elise face, 1960s-80s, 16-1/2" vinyl, sleep eyes, closed mouth, syntetic hair eyeshadow over eyes, earrings, hard plastic body with jointed elbows, ankles and knees, vinyl lower arms, circa 1957-1964, courtesy Jennifer Warren.

1987 only, 12" Portrait Children
1989, 10" #1101, Jubilee II; 21"
1990, 8", #627, Scarlett Series
1992, 8" peach gown/bonnet
1996, 10", #16555, Sewing Circle
Nancy Drew, 1967 only, 12" Literature Series
Nina Ballerina, 1949-50, 19"
1949-51, 14", 17"
1951, 15", 23"
Peter Pan, 1953-54, 8", 15"
1969 only, set of four, Peter, Michael 12", Wendy 14", Tinker Bell 10"
1991-93, 8"
Prince Charles, 1957 only, 8" #397
Princess Diana, 1998, 10" white satin gown
Princess Margaret Rose, 1949-53, 14", 18"
Quiz-Kin, 1953-54, 8", bald or wigged
Scarlett, 1950s, 14" 16", 20"
1953-54, 7 1/2" , 8"
1955, 8", #485 two tier dress; 21"
1957, 8" #431, bent-knee walker, white dress
1958, 21"
1961-62, 21"
1963, 8" bent-knee, #760; 12", 18"
1965, 8" bent-knee, white dress
1965-99, 21"
1966-72, 8" bent knee, #725
1968 - , 10"
1971, 8" only, bright pink floral
1973-91, #425, white gown
1976-86, #425, #426, straight leg, marked "Alexander".
1986-99, 8"
Sleeping Beauty
1959, 10". 16", 21" h.p., Disney
1971-85, 14", # 1495, Classic Series, gold gown, Mary Ann face
1986-1990, 14", Classic Series, Mary Ann face
1995, 8" #14543, Brothers Grimm Series
1996, 14" , # 87010, pink/gold gown
1997-99, 8" 13600, blue satin gown
Snow White

1952, h.p., 14", 18", 23" Margaret
face
1967-77, 14", Mary Ann face
1970-85, #1455, #1555, white gown
1972-77, 8", Wendy face
1986-92, 14", ecru, gold gown
1990-92, 8", #495, Storyland Series
1995, 8", # 14545, red bodice
1996, 14" #87013 Trunk set

Sound of Music, set includes, Brigitta, Friedrich,
Kurt, Liesl, Louisa, Maria, Marta,
1965-70, 10-17", seven dolls
1971-73, 8"-12", seven dolls
1992-93, 8"-12", seven dolls
1998, 8"- 10", seven dolls

Southern Belle
1953, 8" h.p. white dress,
1954, *" h.p., #370,
1956, 8", h.p., #437
1963, 8", #385, 12", h.p.
1965, 21" #2155, blue gown
1967, 21" #2170, white gown
1968-73, 10" #1170, #1185, white
gown

Timmy Toddler , 1960-61, 23"
1960 only, 30"

Tiny Tim, 1996, 8", # 18001, Dickens series

Wendy Ann, 1948-49, 14 1/2", 17", h.p.
1948-1950, 16", 22", h.p.
1949, 23", 25", h.p.
1995, 8", #79516, 100th anniversary

Winnie Walker
1953 only, 15", h.p., Cissy face
1953-54+, 18", 25"

**Types of Alexander
faces-** Caroline, 15"
vinyl rooted hair, blue
sleep eyes, inspired by
the daughter of John and
Jackie Kennedy and was
produced in 1961-1962
only, courtesy Iva Mae
Jones.

Alt, Beck & Gottschalck

1854-1940s+ Thüringia, Germany, made china and
bisque heads for dolls. Sizes may range from 14" -
28".

📖 12, 13, 14, 20, 46

Molds No: 630, 639, 698, 784, 870, 890, 911, 912,
915, 916, 990, 1000, 1008, 1028, 1032, 1044, 1046,
1064, 1123, 1127, 1142, 1210, 1234, 1235, 1254,
1304, 1322, 1342, 1346, 1352, 1357, 1358, 1361,
1362, 1367, 1368

L.A. & S.

Charlie Chaplin cloth
label on sleeve reads:

CHARLIE CHAPLIN DOLL
World's Greatest Comedian
Made exclusively by Louis Amberg
& Son, NY
By Special Arrangement with
Essamay Film Co.

Edwina mark:
AMBERG
PAT.PEN.
L.A. & S.

Mibs label:

L. A. & S.
Amberg Dolls
The World Standard
Created by
Hazel Drukker
Please Love Me
I'm MIBS

Vanta Baby marked:
Vanta Baby
Amberg
Paper Hangtag:

Vanta Baby
Known to Every
Woman Everywhere
Amberg Dolls
The World Standard

American Character
Marks:
A.C.
Petite
A Petite Doll
Petite Sally
AM//Character
Amer. Char. Doll Co.

Louis Amberg & Son

1878-1930s, Ohio and New York, imported bisque in
7"-20" sizes and later made composition dolls.
  📖 **1, 2, 7, 12, 13, 14, 31, 44, 46**
Molds No: 371, 886, 972, 973, 982, 983
Baby Peggy, 1923, 15", 18", 20",
Body Twists (also called Teenie Weenies, Tiny
Tots) circa 1929, 7 1/2". 8 1/2"
Charlie Chaplin, 1915, 14"
Edwina, (Sue or It) circa 1928, 14", swivel waist
Happiness, 1918+, 10"
MIBS, circa 1921, 16"
Sunny Orange Maid, 1924, 14 1/2"
Vanta Baby, 1927-1930, 18", 23"

American Character

1919-1963, New York City, made cloth, composi-
tion, hard plastic (some with skull cap)and vinyl
dolls.
  📖 **1, 2, 7, 14, 41, 30, 31, 44, 46, 47-51**
Betsy McCall, 1957-63, 8", hard plastic
Bottle Tot, 1926, 13", 18", composition
   1936-38, 11", 15" rubber drink/wet
   Marked: Petite//America's Wonder
   Baby Dolls
Campbell Kids, 1928+, 12" composition
Carol Ann Beery, 1935, 13", 16 1/2", 19 1/2",
   composition, celebrity daughter of
   Wallace Beery.
Chuckles, 1930s-40s, 20"
Eloise, 1950s, 21" cloth
Little Miss Echo, 1964, 30", vinyl talker
Mary Make Up, 1965-1966, 11 1/2", vinyl, no
mark
Puggy, 1928, 13" composition
Ricky Jr., 1954-1956, 13", 20", vinyl, celebrity son
of Lucille Ball and Desi Arnez.
Sally, 1930-34+, 12 1/2", 14", 16", 19", 24"
composition
Sweet Sue, 1953+, 15" 18", 22", 25" hard
plastic, some with vinyl skull cap
Sweet Sue Sophisticate, 1960s, 19", vinyl
Tiny Tears, 1950s, 11 1/2", 13 1/2", 16", 20"
   vinyl drink and wet
Toni, 1958+, 10 1/2", 20", vinyl, no mark

Toodles, circa 1950s-60s, 11", 21", 24" vinyl
Tressy, 1963-66, 11", high heel vinyl
Whimsie, 1960s, 19", 21", vinyl characters:
    Annie, the Astronaut
    Bessie, the Bashful Bride
    Dixie, the Pixie
    Fanny, the Flapper
    Fanny, the Fallen Angel
    Hedda-Get-Bedda (three faces)
    Hilda the Hillbilly
    Lena, the Cleaner
    Polly, the Lolly
    Simon, the Degree (graduate)
    Samson, the Strongman
    Suzie, the Snoozie
    Trixie, the Pixie (devil)
    Tillie the Talker
    Wheeler, the Dealer,
    Zack, the Sack (striped nightshirt, cap)
    Zero, the Hero (football player)

Annalee

1934 on, Meredith, NH, Annalee Davis Thorndike handmade decorative cloth dolls, early dolls unmarked, after 1930, used a cloth label, copyright marks were used in the 1960s, 1970s a satin label glued into the dolls, but usually they are folded and sewn. Tyvek labels used in 1976 with several variations. Since 1960s, patent date year included in some labels. Early dolls had cotton string or batting stuffing. Yarn hair was used 1935-1959. After 1960 also used synthetic fur. Dolls from 1951-54 have round dot eyes. Made mostly animals 1964-82, except for Santas. Now makes human form again. Made most figures in many sizes over years.
    📖 1, 2, 18, 29, 46, 47, 48, 49, 50, 51
Albert Einstein, 10"
Clown, 19"m 42"
Elves, 5", 10", 14", 22"
Pilgrims, 10",
Santa, 7", 10"12", 18", 30"
Skiers, 7, 10", 12", 18"
Uncle Sam, 25"
Witch, 7", 10", 12" 18"

Whimsie marked on head:

on back torso:
**AMER. DOLL &
TOY
1960**

Above: Circa 1930s-40s white label with black lettering.

Above: Circa early 1950s, pale green label with red script type lettering.

Above: Script type label from the latter 1950s was white satin with red lettering.

Above: Red and white 1990s tag, folded in half, sewn in to body seam.

Arnold Print Works
Incorporated
1876
North Adams, Mass.

ARRANBEE
R & B
KEWTY
NANCY

ART FABRIC MILLS
NY. PAT. FEB. 13TH, 1900
Mark on shoe
or bottom of foot

Max Oscar Arnold
1878-1925, Germany, made bisque dolls, some mechanicals, Baby, 12", 16", 19"
📖 **8, 12, 13**
Molds No: 150, 200, 201, 12", 15", 21", 32"

Arnold Print Works
1880-1925+, North Adams, MA, made printed fabric to be cut out for dolls.
📖 **13, 18, 29, 46**
Palmer Cox Brownies, 1892-1907, 7-1/2", twelve different figures include, Canadian, Chinaman, Dude, German, Highlander, Indian, Irishman, John Bull, Policeman, Sailor, Soldier and Uncle Sam. Produced by Arnold Print Works and/or Cocheco Manufacturing Company with circle marks.

Arranbee Doll Co.
1922-1958, New York, made bisque, composition, hard plastic and vinyl dolls
📖 **1, 2, 13, 28, 30, 31, 44, 46, 47-51**
Cinderella, circa 1952, 14", hard plastic
Debu' Teen, 1939-1940s, 14", 17", composition
Kewty, 1934-36, 14", composition
Littlest Angel, 1956+, 11", hard plastic
    1959, 11 1/2" vinyl
My Dream Baby, 1927, 14", 19", composition
Miss Coty , circa 1958, 10 1/2, vinyl
Nancy, 1930+, 12", 19", 21", composition
Nancy Lee, 1939+, 12", 17", composition
Nannette, 1939-40s, 20", 26", composition
    1949-59, 14", 17" hard plastic
Storybook Dolls, 1930s, composition
    Little Bo-Peep, 8 1/2"
    Little Boy Blue, 8 1/2"

Art Fabric Mills
1899-1910+, New York, New Haven (CT) London, lithographed cloth dolls
📖 **13, 18, 29, 46,**
Improved Life Size Doll, 20", 30"
Punch and Judy, 27"

Artisan Novelty Co.

Circa 1950s, Gardena, CA, made hard plastic dolls, open mouth, upper teeth, Dynel wigs, identifying clue, very wide crotch.

    📖 **1, 2, 33, 46, 47-51**

Little Miss Gadabout, 20"

Raving Beauty, 20"

No marks on doll;
box marked
"Artisan Doll"

Averill

1915+, New York, Georgene Averill, aka Madame Hendren, patented first Mama doll in 1918. Cloth doll I.D. clues, wide painted smile, bold painted lashes, also used real lashes, and hand-stitched back body seams, kinky yarn hair

    📖 **1,2, 30, 31, 44, 46, 47-51**

Bonnie Babe, 1926-1930s, Molds: 1005, 1368, 1402, 12", 14-15" bisque
    Celluloid, 10", 16"

Also made all bisque Bonnie Babe 4-7"

Baby Hendren, 1930, 16", 20", 26", composition

Becassine, 1950s, 13", cloth French cartoon character

Dolly Dingle, 1932, 12", 14" cloth, Grace Drayton design

Dolly Reckord. 1922 - 1928, 26", composition
    with record player in cloth torso.

Mama Doll, 1918+, 15", 18", 20", 24", composition, cloth body with crier, swing legs

Peaches, circa 1930s, 19" composition

Snookums, 1927, 14" composition, celebrity

Tear Drop Baby, 16", cloth, tear on cheek

Some times no marks

A. M. Co.
A. M© Co.
Madame Hendren Doll
Some cloth bodies stamped:
Madame Hendren
Life-like Doll
Patented June 11, 1918
or
Genuine
Madame Hendren
Doll
Made in U.S.A

Paper peach colored fuit hangtag:
Peaches
A
Madame Hendren
Doll
Everybody
Loves Her
I say Mama

Barbie®

Mattel, Inc., 1959 to present, Hawthorne, CA. 11 1/2" vinyl dolls, later special porcelain editions

    📖 **1, 2, 17, 34, 42, 46, 57-51**

No. 1 Ponytail Barbie, 1959, 11 1/.2" #850, heavy vinyl, pointed eyebrows, holes in feet, vinyl may have faded, black and white swimsuit, marked "Barbie™ //Pats. Pend. //©MCMLVIII//By//Mattel, Inc." (See photo at left).

No. 2 Ponytail Barbie 1959, 11 1/2", #850, heavy vinyl, pointed eyebrows, black/white swimsuit, marks same as No. 1, but no holes in feet

Above: No. 1 Ponytail Barbie, courtesy McMasters Doll Auctions.

1959:
No. 1, 2, 3, & 4
Ponytail Barbie
Barbie™
Pats. Pend.
©MCMLVIII
By
Mattel
Inc.
No. 5 Barbie:
Barbie®
Pats. Pend.
©MCMLVIII
by
Mattel
Inc.
No. 6 Barbie 1963
Midge™
©1962
Barbie®
©1958
by
Mattel Inc.
1963-1968:
Midge™©1962
Barbie ®
©1958
By
Mattel, Inc.
1964-1966:
©1958
Mattel, Inc. U.S.
Patented U.S. Pat.
Pend.
1966-1969
©1966//
Mattel, Inc. U.S.
Patented
U.S. Pat. Pend
Made in Japan

No. 3 Ponytail Barbie, 1960, 11 1/2", #850, heavy vinyl, gently curved eyebrows, no holes in feet, black/white swimsuit, same marks

No. 4 Ponytail Barbie, 1960, 11 1/2", #850, same as first two, blue irises, red lips, gentle eyebrows, blue eyeliner only, heavy body, vinyl does not fade, black/white swimsuit, same marks as first three

No. 5 Ponytail Barbie, 1961, 11 1/2", #850 less heavy, arm tag, black/white swimsuit, same marks as first four, but now Barbie ™

No. 6 Ponytail Barbie, 1962-64, 11 1/2", #850, same as #5, except more hair and lip colors, chubbier face, red jersey swimsuit, marked 1963, "Midge™// ©1962//Barbie®//©1958//by//Mattel,Inc."

Others:

Bendable leg, 1965-66, 11 1/2", #1070, bendable legs at knees, Dutch boy style hair, blue irises, gentle eyebrows, multi-striped top with aqua bottom swimsuit, marked 1965, "©1958//Mattel, Inc.//U.S. Patented// U. S. Pat. Pend."

Bubble Cut, 1961-1967, 11 1/2", #850, various hair colors, red lips in 1961, more colors 1962-67, gentle curve eyebrows, black/white (1961) or red (1962-1967) swimsuit, marked 1961-62, "Barbie®//Pats. Pend.//©MCMLVIII//by Mattel//Inc." Marked 1963-67, "Midge™// ©1962//Barbie®//©1958//by//Mattel, Inc.// Patented"

Color Magic, 1966-67, 11 1/2" #1150 blonde or black new hair that changes color, blue irises, heavy eye makeup, red or coral lips, gentle eyebrows, multicolored diamond print swimsuit, bendable legs, marked same as 1966

Fashion Queen, 1963-64, 11 1/2" #870, molded brown hair with blue vinyl headband, blue irises, coral lips, gentle curve eyebrows, gold lame striped swimsuit and turban, 3 extra wigs, marked 1963, "Midge™ ©1962 Barbie®//©1962// Barbie®//©1958//by//Mattel, Inc.//

Patented"

Twist and Turn, 1967-1968, 11 1/2", # 1160, bendable legs, new waist twists, new face with slightly open mouth, new rooted eyelashes, 4 hair colors, Summer Sand, Sun Kissed, GoGoCoCo, Choco late Bon Bon, hair long, blue irises, more rounded eyebrows, orange 2-piece swimsuit with white fishnet cover-up. Marked, "©1966//Mattel, Inc.//U.S. Patented//U.S. Pat Pend.//Made in Japan"

Friends:

Above: Color Magic Barbie, 11 1/2" vinyl, bendable leg, blue painted side-glancing eyes, molded painted eyelashes, blue eyeshadow, multicolor print swimsuit, circa 1967, courtesy McMasters Doll Auctions.

Allan, 1964-1967, 11 ½", molded painted hair, painted eyes, closed mouth. Marked: "© 1960//by//Mattel, Inc.//Hawthorn//Calif U.S.A."

Brad, 1970, 12" Black vinyl, painted/molded black hair, brown eyes, black brows, closed mouth. marked on head, "© 1968 Mattel", on body "© 1968//Mattel, Inc.//Inc.//U.S. & For Patd//Other Pats//Pending//Hong Kong".

Casey, 1967-1975, 11 ½", vinyl.

Christie, 1968-1973, 11 ½" vinyl. Marked: "© 1968 Mattel, Inc.//U.S. & Foreign Patented//Patented in Canada 1967//Other Patents pending//Taiwan"

Curtis, 1975, 11 ½" vinyl.

Fluff, 1971

Francie, 1966-1975, 11 ½", vinyl. Marked: "© 1966//Mattel, Inc.//U.S. Patented//U.S. Pat. Pend//Made in//Japan"

Ken, 1961-1976, 12", vinyl, #1, straight leg, blue eyes, hard plastic hollow body, flocked hair. Marked: "Ken®MCMLX//by//Mattel//Inc." Also molded hair, bendable legs on later dolls.

Midge, 1963-1965, 11 ½", vinyl, some with freckles. Marked: "b/l Midge" on head; "© 1958//Mattel, Inc.//U.S. Pat Pend//Made in//Japan" on body.

P.J., 1969-1978, 11 1/2"

Ricky, 1965, 9"

Skipper, 1964-1975, 9 ¼", vinyl. Marked:

Above: Bubble cut Barbie, 11 1/2" vinyl, straight leg, blue painted side-glancing eyes, blue eyeshadow, molded eyelashes, red swimsuit, circa 1961, courtesy McMasters Doll Auctions.

"© 1969 Mattel, Inc.//Taiwan//U.S. & For. Patd.//Other"

Skooter, 1965-1966, 9", vinyl.

Stacey, 1968-1970, 11 ½", vinyl. Marked: "© 1967//Mattel, Inc.//U.S. & Foreign// Pats.Pend.//Mexico."

Todd, 1967, 6 ¼", vinyl.

Tutti, 1966, 6 ¼", vinyl. Marked: "© 1965//Mattel, Inc.//Japan".

Bähr & Pröschild

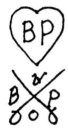

1871-1930, Thüringia, Germany. Bisque dolls, sizes range from 9" - 26" or larger.

📖 **12, 14, 46**

Molds: 204, 224, 239, 246, 247, 252, 273, 274, 275, 277, 286, 289, 293, 297, 309, 325, 332, 340, 379, 394, 520, 585, 586, 587, 602, 604, 619, 624, 630, 641, 642, 678

E. Barrois

E. B.

Circa 1844-1877, Paris, France, made bisque and china dolls.   Children and Fashion-types and range in sizes from 12" - 17", perhaps others.

📖 **14, 46, 72**

Beecher, Julia Jones

Marks not known

1893-1910, Elmira, New York, made all cloth dolls with stockinette oil painted faces, ranging in sizes from 16" to 23" and larger. Aided by sewing circle of Park Congregation Church of Elmira, NY, proceeds went to missions, these were called Missionary Rag or Beecher Babies.

📖 **14, 18, 46**

C. M. Bergmann

C.M. Bergmann
Waltershausen
Made in Germany

1889-1930, Thüringia, Germany, bisque dolls, also used heads by Simon & Halbig and others.

📖 **12, 14, 46**

Molds: 612, 1916, 10"-42"

Eleonore, 18" 25" and others

Flapper, 12", 16"

Carl Bergner

1860 -1930, Sonneberg, Germany, made multi-faced doll.

📖 **12, 14, 46**
Molds: 450, 12", 15"

Designed by
Carl Bergner

Bing Art Dolls

1921-1932, Germany, made cloth, felt and composition dolls, oil painted features, molded face, seams down front of legs, mitt hands.

📖 **14, 18, 46**
Painted hair, 13-15" and others.
Wigged, 10"-16" and others
Composition, 8", 12", 16"

BING
on shoes

George Borgfeldt & Co.

1881-1930, New York, assembled and distributed dolls, used designers such as Rose O'Neill

📖 **1, 2, 12, 14, 46**
Molds: 250, 251, 325, 327, 328, 329
sizes may range from 10"-27"
Baby BoKaye, 1926+, mold 1394, 11"-18"
Babykins, circa 1931, designed by G. S. Putnam
Hug Me, circa 1930s, 9" composition
My Girlie, 1910-1922, 10"-25"
Pansy, 1910-1922, 10"- 25"

G. B.

Bru

1867-1899, Paris, France, made bisque dolls, hand pressed, succeeded by SFBJ. Identification clue, metal spring screw type mechanism in neck

📖 **14, 72, 73**
Bébé Automate, 1892, 19-25", breather, talker, key type mechanism
Bébé Baiser, 1892, 11", kiss-thrower, pull string
Bébé Breveté, 1879-1880, 14"-20"
Bébé Gourmand, 1880, 16", eater, open mouth to accept food, discharged in foot
Bébé Marchant, 1892, 17"-25", walker, key wound mechanism
Bébé Modele, 1880, 19", wooden body
Bébé Teteur, 1879, 14"-20", nurser, key wound
Bru Jne, 1880-1891, 12"-27"
Bru Jne R., 1891-1899, 11"-21"
Circle Dot Bebe, 1879-1883, 12"-26"

Bru Jne

Bru Jun R.

Circle-dot Bebe

⊙
⌣

Poupee (Fashion type, some may have smile) 1867-1877, kid or wood body, 13-21"

Albert Bruckner
1901-1930+, made cloth dolls for Horsman
📖 **14, 18, 46**
Topsy-Turvy, 13" mask face, painted eyes

Bucherer
1921-1930+, Amriswil, Switzerland, made dolls with composition head with metal armature limbs
📖 **14, 46**
Charlie Chaplin, 6 1/2"
Mutt & Jeff, 6 1/2"
Other comic characters, 6 1/2" - 7 1/2"

Buschow & Beck
Circa 1890-1930s, Germany, made metal and celluloid heads for dolls. Minerva refers to metal head dolls, painted or glass eyes, cloth, kid or metal body. Sizes range from 11"- 21" or larger.
📖 **14, 46**

Buddy Lee

Buddy Lee
Some unmarked

1920-1963, Kansas City, MO, made composition and hard plastic dolls to display work clothes, all 13"   tall.
📖 **1, 2, 31, 46, 47-51, 5, 60**
Buddy Lee as:
   Cowboy
   Engineer
   Coca Cola Driver
   Gas Station Attendant

Butler Bros.
B. B.
1877-1935, New York, Germany, made and distributed dolls, various sizes
📖 **1, 2, 10, 12, 14, 46**
Baby Betty, 1913
Miss Millionaire, 1914
Dolly Dimple, 1914
Baby Bud, 1915

Pet Name Chinas,

1899-1930, Agatha, Bertha, Daisy, Dorothy, Edith, Esther, Ethel, Florence, Helen, Mabel, Marion, Pauline or Ruth embossed on molded bodice shoulderplate., 9"-21", often with alphabet bodies.

Bye-Lo Baby

1922-1952, designed by Grace Storey Putnam, distributed by George Borgfeldt & Co. of N.Y. All bisque versions made by Kestner have dark green circular sticker on chest.
📖 **1, 2, 12, 14, 44, 46, 65**
Bye-Lo Baby, 10"-21", Bisque, or composition cloth frog-style body may be stamped "Bye-Lo Baby".
Fly-Lo Baby, 1926-1930, 11-14", ceramic, bisque or composition head, cloth body, satin wings.
All Bisque, 3"-5"

Cabbage Patch Kids

1978+, Babyland General Hospital, Cleveland GA, later Coleco until 1989, then Hasbro, vinyl dolls with cloth bodies.
📖 **40, 46**

Cameo Doll Co.

1922-1930, New York, Joseph L. Kallus, founder, made bisque, composition, celluloid, hard plastic and vinyl dolls.
📖 **1,2, 14, 30, 31, 46, 47-51**
Baby Blossom, 1927, 19", composition head, cloth body,
Baby BoKaye, (see George Borgfeldt)
Bandy, 1929, 18 1/2" composition head, wood segmented body, Kallus design, marked on hat, "GE// General Electric Radio".
Betty Boop, 1932, 11", 13 1/2", composition head, wood segmented body, label on torso.
Champ, 1942, 16" composition, freckles
Giggles, 1946, 12", 14", composition, molded hair loop, hangtag reads, "Giggles Doll, by Rose O'Neill, A Cameo Doll".
Ho-Ho, 1940, 5 1/2", painted plaster, laughing mouth
Jeep, 7", 9", 12 1/2", yellow composition, wood segmented tail, Popeye's comic strip dog.

AGATHA

©**1923 by
Grace S. Putnam
Made in Germany
7372/45**

Above, All bisque sticker in dark green

Signature stamped on on lower back, differnt color for each year on early dolls

BETTY BOOP
DES. & COPYRIGHT
By Fleischer
Studios

MARGIE
DES & COPYRIGHT
By Jos. Kallus

JOY
DES. & COPYR.
J.L. KALLUS

CAMEO©

Little Annie Rooney,
label on sleeve reads:
Little
Annie Rooney
Trademark
Copyright 1925 by Jack
Collins
Pat./ Applied For

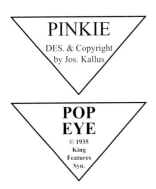

PETE
DES. & Copyright by Jos. Kallus

PINKIE
DES. & Copyright
by Jos. Kallus

**POP
EYE**
© 1935
King
Features
Syn.

Joy, 1933, 11", 15", composition head, wooded segmented body, label on torso.

Kewpie, 1930s-40s, 8"-13", 1960s-70s, 13-18", vinyl

Little Annie Rooney, 1926, 12", 17", cartoon character by Jack Collins, molded shoes,

Margie, 1929, 5 1/2", 9 1/2", 15", composition, wood segmented body, label on torso.

Miss Peep, 1969-1973, 14-18", vinyl, pin-jointed shoulders and hips.

Pete the Pup, 1930-1935, 9", composition head, wood segmented body, label on torso.

Pinkie, 1930-1935, 10", composition head, wood segmented body, label on torso

Popeye, 1935, 4 1/2", 14", composition head and body, wood segmented limbs, comic strip character created by E. C. Segar.

Radiotron, 1930, 15 1/2" composition, wood segmented body, tall molded hat, red banner across chest: "RCA Radiotron", Slits in hands.

Scootles, 1937+, 7 1/2", 12", 16", 20", composition, molded hair, no marks., cloth label on sunsuit, "Scootles//Reg. U.S. Pat. Off.//Copyright by Rose O'Neill//M'fd. By Cameo Doll Co.//Port Allegany, PA."

**C. P.
or
Catterfelder
Puppenfabrik**

Catterfelder Puppenfabrik
1894-1930, Thüringia, Germany, used Kestner bisque heads, celluloid dolls from Kammer & Reinhardt, also papier mache. Various sizes.
📖 **12, 14, 46**
Molds: 200, 201, 207, 208, 209,210, 212, 215, 218, 219, 220, ,262, 263, 264, 270, 1100, 1200, 1357

Century Doll Co.
Kestner Germany

Century Doll Co.
1909-1930, New York, used head made by others
📖 **12, 14, 46**
Molds: 275, 285, 11"-23" or larger
Chuckles, 1927-29, 16", composition head and limbs,, cloth body with crier

Chad Valley

1917-1954+, Harbourne, England, made cloth dolls, molded face, glass or painted eyes, after WWII, made rubber (vinyl) dolls.

📖 1, 2, 18, 29, 46, 47-51

Bambina, 18", 1927-1930, felt/velvet, glass eyes
Bonz, 1924+5 1/2", 14", velvet dog from cartoon
Captain Blye, 18", 20", glass or painted eye
Fisherman, various sizes
Ghandi, 13"
Mabel Lucie Attwell design, 1927-1930+, 14 1/2", 16", 18", painted side glancing eyes
Pirate, various sizes
Policeman, various sizes
Princess Elizabeth, 16", 18", glass eyes
Princess Margaret Rose, 16", 18" glass eyes
Red Riding Hood, various sizes
Snow White, 1928, 11", 16 1/2", 18" and **Dwarfs,** 6 1/2", 9 1/2" and 10"
Train Conductor, various sizes

Label on foot, 1938+:

THE CHAD VALLEY CO. LTD.
BRITISH ROYAL COAT OF ARMS
TOYMAKER TO
H.M.

Martha Chase

1889-1930s, Pawtucket, RI, made cloth dolls, molded faces, painted features, sometimes nostrils, weighted.

📖 1,2, 14, 18, 29, 46

Babies, 16-24"
Children, 12"-22"
Hospital mannequins, 20-29"
Alice in Wonderland characters, 1905, 12"
 Alice
 Duchess
 Frog Footman
 Mad Hatter
 Tweedledee and Tweedledum
Benjamin Franklin, 15"

Chase Stockinet Doll
on left leg or under left arm.
Paper label reads:
Chase
Hospital Doll
Trademark
Pawtucket, RI
Made in USA

Columbian Rag Doll

Circa 1890s, Oswego, NY, Emma Adams, made cloth dolls, flat faces, hand painted features, stitched fingers, and toes.

📖 14, 18, 46

Columbian Baby, Boy or girl, 15", 19", 23", 29"

COLUMBIAN DOLL
EMMA ADAMS
OSWEGO, NY

No marks on hard plastic
doll. Boxes marked
**"Cosmopolitan
Ginger"**
Vinyl Ginger marked
"Ginger"
on head.
Ginger clothes are tagged
**Fashions for Ginger
Cosmopolitan Doll
& Toy Corp.
Jackson Heights, NY**
or
**Richmond Hill, NY
® Trademark**

Label, 1920s-30s:

HYGENIC TOYS
MADE IN ENGLAND BY
CHAD VALLEY CO. LTD.

**Dean's Hygenic
Doll - Toys
Plush Animals**

**PAN
G.D.
H. D. & X**

Cosmopolitan Doll & Toy Corp.

Circa 1950s, New York , hard plastic dolls, similar to
Vogue's Ginny and Ideal's Little Miss Revlon.
Identification clue, molded arm hook, dimple on
chin, dimples for knuckles, dimples above toes.
Also made other dolls, Baby Emily, Gloria, Jeanette,
and Pam Baby.
📖 **1,2, 33, 46**
Ginger, circa 1956 7 1/2", 8 1/2" , hard plastic, later
vinyl
Little Miss Ginger, 1957-58, 8", vinyl, high heels
Miss Ginger, circa 1957, 10 1/2", vinyl, high heels

Dean's Rag Book Co.

1908, London, England, made first printed rag dolls
until 1930s, 1920s made cloth dolls with molded
faces, velvet faces in 1926, rubber faces, 1948
📖 **1,2, 14, 18, 29, 46**
Alice in Wonderland, 1931, 19", 27" cloth
Dormouse, 12 1/2", cloth
Mad Hatter, 15", 25", cloth
March Hare, 13", 25", cloth
White Rabbit, 13" 25", cloth
Charlie Chaplin, 1920, 11 1/2", cloth
Girl Guide, 1938, 20" cloth
Golliwog, 11-16"
Lillibet, 1938, 1949, 17", 18 1/2" cloth Princess
Lupino Lane, 1939, 9-1/2"- 28", cloth music hall
star
Margaret, 1938, 42" holds Scotty dog
Mickey and Minnie Mouse, 1930, 6-21", cloth
Peter Pan and Wendy, 1939, 17" felt face
Pollyanna, 1953, 1960, 19" rubber
Popeye, 1936, 9-36" , cloth
Yeoman of the Guard, 1953, 42" , Limited Ed. for
Queen Elizabeth's coronation

Henri Delcroix

1865-1867, Seine, France, made bisque dolls, closed
mouth, pierced ears, paperwieght eyes, socket head
📖 **14, 46**
Bébés, 13" and other sizes

Deluxe Reading

Circa 1955-1972, Also known as Deluxe Premium, Deluxe Toy, Topper Toys and Topper Corp., made hard plastic and vinyl dolls, some battery operated

📖 1, 2, 34, 46, 47-51

Baby Boo, 1965 21", vinyl, battery operated
Baby Catch A Ball, 1969, 18", battery operated
Baby Magic, 1966-68, 10 1/2" 18", vinyl rooted Saran hair, magic wand opens and closes eyes
Baby Peek 'N Play, 1969, 18", battery operated
Baby Tickle Tears, 1960s, 14"
Betty Bride, 30", stuffed one piece vinyl
Candy Fashion, 1960s, 22" with four outfits
Darling Debbie, circa 1957, 30", blue formal, has clear plastic royal Coach jewelry box
Dawn Series, by Topper Toys, 1970-73, 6"-6 1/2" Dawn and "Dawn Modeling Agency": Daphne, Denise, Dinah, Maureen and Melanie.
GoGos, 1965, 6 1/2" vinyl, posable, comes with plastic dome, base: Slick Chick, Brenda Brush, Hot Canary, Tomboy, Yeah Yeah, Swinger, Private Ida, Cool Cat
Little Miss Fussy 1960s, 18", battery operated
Little Red Riding Hood, 1955, 23", stuffed vinyl, book, basket.
Party Time, 1967, 18", battery operated
Penny Brite, 1963, 8" vinyl, rooted blonde hair, painted eyes,
Smarty Pants, 19", 1971, batter operated
Suzy Cute, 1964-65, 7" vinyl drink/wet dolls, came with yellow plastic crib, advertised in 1965 Wards Catalog.
Suzy Homemaker, 1964, 21", jointed knees
Suzy Smart, 1962, 25" vinyl, rooted ponytail, plaid skirt, comes with desk, chair, easel blackboard, sold in grocery markets.
Sweet Amy, 1957, 17", 25" vinyl, one piece body
Sweet Judy, 1957, 17", 25" stuffed one piece vinyl body

Domec Toys Inc.

1924-1925+, New York, made composition carnival and premium dolls

📖 14, 44

Kradle Babe, 13"composition head, cloth body

Dawn marked:

© **1970**
TOPPER CORP.
HONG KONG

DELUXE READING CORP.

DELUXE PREMIUM

DELUXE TOPPER TOYS

TOPPER CORP.

Above: 8 1/2" vinyl Deluxe Reading "Penny Brite" rooted blonde hair, painted eyes, with blue rigid plastic see through case, missing shoe, original dress, Marked "Deluxe Reading Corp, © 1963" circa 1963, courtesy Michele Lyons

Domec Dolls
Walk
Talk
Sleep

Door of Hope

1901-1950, Shanghai, China, Door of Hope Mission dressed wooden carved dolls showing 26 classes of Chinese society. Identification clues, hand carved pearwood heads, finely sewn silk costumes

No marks

📖 **14, 46, 47-51**

Bride and Groom, 11-12"
Amah with Baby, 11"
Manchu Lady or Man, 12"
Mourner, 12"
Schoolchild, 8"

Cuno & Otto Dressel

1873 - 1945, Thüringia, Germany, made wood, wax, composition, papier mâché, china and bisque dolls

📖 **12, 14, 46**

Molds: 1912, 1914, 1348, 1349, 1469 in various sizes.

C. O. D.

Admiral Byrd, 8", 12", bisque
Admiral Dewey, 8", 12" bisque
Buffalo Bill, 10", bisque
Farmer, 8", 12", bisque, character
Father Christmas, 12" bisque, character
Holz-Masse, 1875+, composition shoulderhead with molded hair or wigged, 13"-24"
Jutta, 8"-29", came as baby, toddler or child, bisque
Old Rip, 8", 12", bisque character
Uncle Sam, 13", 15 1/2", bisque character
Witch, 8", 12", bisque character

Duchess Doll Corp.

1948-50s, New York, made inexpensive hard plastic dolls, clothes stapled to doll, sleep eyes, jointed arms only, boxed dolls given as premiums.

📖 **1,2, 33, 46**

Mrked on back:

DUCHESS DOLL CORP.
DESIGN COPYRIGHT
1948

Alice in Wonderland, 1951, 7 1/2", 12 1/2", sleep eyes, Doll of all Nations box.
Cinderella, 1951, 7 1/2", 12 1/2", sleep eyes, jointed neck, arms, hips, Doll of All Nations box.
Dale Evans, 1948, 8", white cowgirl outfit
Dream Girl, 1952, 13", brunette wig, red satin skin, white apron, scarf, basket with chick, box.
Martha Washington, circa 1950s, 7", white wig, yellow and purple dress, Dolls of All Nations box.

Miss Valentine of 1951, 7 1/2", red and white rayon long dress, in box with cellophane window.
Peter Pan and **Tinkerbell**, 1953, 7", boxed together.

EeGee

1917-1935+, Brooklyn, NY, E.G. Goldberger made composition and cloth dolls, imported bisque heads from Armand Marseille, later made hard plastic and vinyl dolls.

📖 **1, 2, 14, 30, 31, 44, 46, 63**

Baby Carrie, 24" 1970, 24", vinyl, drink/wet doll with carriage or carry seat.

Baby Luv, 1973, 14", vinyl, rooted hair, marked "B.T. Eegee" cloth body, sewn on pants.

Baby Tandy Talks, 1963, 14", 20", vinyl pull string talker, rooted hair, sleep eyes, cotton body.

Beverly Hillbillies, 1960s, 14" Grannie, vinyl, gray rooted hair, Clampett family from TV sitcom, also car.

Fields, W.C., 1980, 30" vinyl ventriloquist doll by Juro, division of Goldberger.

Flowerkins, 1963, 16" vinyl, marked "F-2" on head, seven dolls in series.

Gemmette, 1963, 15 1/2", vinyl, rooted hair, sleep eyes, dressed in gem colored dresses, with jeweled ring, includes Misses Amethyst, Diamond, Emerald, Ruby Sapphire and Topaz.

Miss Charming, 1936, 14", 17" all composition walker Shirley Temple look-alike, open mouth, six upper teeth, blonde mohair wig, green sleep eyes, no marks on doll, wears oval metal pinback button that reads, "Miss Charming//Everybody Loves Me"

Parton, Dolly, 1978, 11 1/2", 18", vinyl, fashion-type celebrity country singer.

Susan Stroller, circa 1955, 20", 23", 26", vinyl head, hard plastic walker body, rooted hair, closed mouth.

Tandy Talks, 1961, 20" vinyl head, hard plastic body, freckles, pull string talker.

Effanbee Doll Company

1910+, New York, made bisque, cloth, composition, hard plastic and vinyl dolls, used metal heart bracelets circa 1932+.

📖 **1,2, 6, 7, 14, 31-32, 44, 46, 47-51, 62, 63, 64**

EEGEE

TRADEMARK
EEGEE
Dolls
MADE IN USA

E.G.

Oval metal pinback buton reads:
Miss Charming
Everybody Loves Me

Above: Early Bluebird pin used by Effanbee circa 1920s.

American Children
marked on head:
EFFANBEE
AMERICAN
CHILDREN
on back:
EFFANBEE
ANNE SHIRLEY

FLEISCHAKER & BAUM   45 East 17th Street
NEW YORK, N.Y.

Above: Effanbee copyrighted "The Doll with the Golden Heart" in 1924, Playthings magazine.

Above: Baby Grumpy advertised in Playthings, circa 1924.

Abraham Lincoln, 1983, 18" vinyl, painted features
American Children - 1937-1939+, composition, painted or sleep eyes (boxes marked "Portrait Doll" or "American Children"), hard rubber arms allow well formed fingers to wear gloves.

    Barbara Joan, 15", open mouth
    Barbara Ann, 17", open mouth
    Barbara Lou, 21" , open mouth
    Betty Jane, 15", closed mouth
    Gloria Ann, 18" closed mouth
    Peggy Lou, 21" closed mouth

Anne Shirley, 1936-1940, 14", 21", 27", composition, marked on back, "EFFANBEE//ANNE//SHIRLEY" used same mold for Little Lady dolls.

Baby Bud, 1918+, 6", composition, jointed arms only, marked on back Effanbee.

Baby Dainty, 1912, 12-16", composition, cloth body, marked on shoulderplate: "EFFANBEE//BABY DAINTY" or "EFFANBEE//DOLLS//WALK, TALK, SLEEP"

Baby Grumpy, 1915+, 11 1/2-23", composition, cloth body, intaglio eyes, frowning expression, marked mold numbers 172, 174, 176 and "EFFANBEE//BABY GRUMPY"

Baby Lisa, 1980, 11", vinyl, designed by Astry Campbell, a three-month old baby, came with pillow.

Baby Lisa Grows Up, 1983, 11" vinyl toddler

Betty Bounce, 1932, 19", composition, used Lovums marked head on Patsy Ann marked body.

Betty Brite, 1932, 16", composition, tousel wig, sleep eyes, some marked "Effanbee//Betty Brite" on body; others; "©Mary Lee" on head, "Effanbee Patsy Joan" on body.

Bubbles, 1924+, 16"-25" or larger, composition shoulderhead, open/closed mouth, painted teeth, sleep eyes, cloth body, bent cloth legs, some with composition toddler legs, wore heart necklace. Various marks: "Effanbee//Bubbles//Copr.1924//Made in U.S.A."

Butin-Nose, 1936+, 8" all composition, painted features, small nose, button misspelled to "Butin" on box or tag.

Candy Kid, 1946, 13 1/2", all composition, sleep eyes, toddler body, molded painted hair. Made later in vinyl.

Charlie McCarthy, 1937, 15", 17", 19", composition head, cloth body, tag: "Edgar Bergen's Charlie McCarthy//An Effanbee Product."

Dy-Dee family: 1934+, Hard rubber head, sleep eyes, jointed rubber bent leg body, drink/wet mechanism. Pre-1940 had molded ears; after 1940 had applied ears. Marked on back, "Effanbee//Dy-Dee Baby" with four patent numbers. Later made in vinyl.

> **Dy-Dee Wee,** 9"
> **Dy-Dee Ellen (Dy-Dee-ette),** 11"
> **Dy-Dee Kin,** 13"
> **Dy-Dee (Dy-Dee Jane),** 15"
> **Dy-Dee Lou (Dy-Dee Louise),** 20"

Eleonor Roosevelt, 1985, 14 1/2" vinyl, Great Moments in History Series

Franklin Roosevelt, 1985, 17" vinyl, President's Series.

George Washington , 1976, 11" vinyl (with 11" Martha); 1984, 16" vinyl

Groucho Marx, 1983, 17" vinyl, painted black hair, moustache, © Grouch Marx Prod. Inc.

Harmonica Joe, 1923, 15", cloth body, metal harmonica fits open mouth.

Historical Replicas, 1939+, 14", all composition, painted eyes, human hair wigs, set of 30 dolls depicting history of apparel 1492-1939, replicas of original three sets of Historical dolls, 21" marked "Effanbee//American//Children" on head, "Effanbee//Anne Shirley" on body.

Honey, 1947-48, 18"-27", composition, human hair wig, sleep eyes, closed mouth, full cheeks. 1949-1955, 14"-17", hard plastic, also as a walker in 1952.

Howdy-Doody, 1947-1949, 19", 23", character from TV children's show, composition head, cloth body, cowboy shirt, jeans, boots, hat, scarf marked, "Howdy-Doody", gold paper heart tag reads: "I AM AN//EFFANBEE//DURABLE DOLL//THE DOLL//SATIN-SMOOTH//SKIN".

John Wayne, 1981, 1982, 17" vinyl, molded hair, issued as cowboy in 1981, as a calvary soldier in 1982, marked on head and back, "WAYNE//ENT//19©81", Legend Series.

Judy Garland as Dorothy 1984, 15", vinyl, Legend Series

Above: Effanbee advertised their dolls could walk, talk and sleep circa 1924.

Above, Effanbee's golden metal heart necklace, circa 1924.

Above: 1924 Ad for Harmonica Joe from Playthings.

Above: Gold paper heart tag for Betty Brite.

EFFANBEE

The PATSYTOWN *News*
A Newspaper for Your Doll

VOL. II, No. 6   EFFANBEE DOLL CO., PUBLISHERS   NEW YORK, N.Y.

THE NEW DY-DEE DOLLS

ARE AMERICA'S GLAMOUR BABIES!

Their Adorable Beauty, Life-like Flexible Ears and Cute Turned-up Noses Endear Them To All.

Photograph of the new Dy-Dee showing the flexible ears which can be cleaned.

Such excitement and delight as greeted the arrival of the Dy-Dee doll babies has seldom been equalled in Dolldom. Not only are the new Dy-Dee Dolls heart-capturing and appealingly lovely . . . they also have new play features which make them a truly-human baby doll.

For example, the new Dy-Dees have soft flexible ears just like a little baby sister. These ears need cleaning with cotton-tipped Q-Tip! Why that is exactly what your mother does with a real infant.

And the new Dy-Dee Dolls have the cutest turned-up noses with nostrils that are open and need cleaning, too.

So you see that the new Dy-Dees will not only capture your heart with their glamorous charm — they also give you more fun in bathing and caring for them.

Aunt Patsy is just thrilled and hopes that you, too, will love the new Dy-Dees as much as she does.

Above: Effanbee, circa 1940, sent their in-house promotional newsletter, "The Patsytown News" to little girls.

THE PATSYTOWN NEWS

THE NEW DY-DEE DOLL BABY PHOTOGRAPHED IN ALL HER GLAMOUR

The Dy-Dee family is pleased to welcome the beautiful new Dy-Dee Baby pictured above. There are really three new Dy-Dee doll sisters—Dy-Dee Ellen is 11 inches tall, Dy-Dee Jane is 15 inches tall, and Dy-Dee Louise is 20 inches tall. They will capture your heart when you see them, and will give you lots of fun when you take care of their daily needs.

Above, Effanbee's new Dy-Dee in 1940 had applied rubber ears, announced in The Patsytown News.

Lamkin (Lambkin) 1930, 16", composition head, cloth body, feet turned in, chubby legs, sleep eyes, open mouth. Identification clue: molded gold ring on finger.

Liberace, 1986, 17", vinyl, molded hair, painted features, glittery costume, cape.

Little Lady, 1939+, 15"-27", used Anne Shirley mold, but gold paper hang tag had Little Lady name like Gaye or Carole.

Louis Armstrong, 1984, 15 1/2" vinyl, Great Moments Series, Black musician.

Lovums, composition, baby and toddler

Lucille Ball, 1985, vinyl, TV, Movie comedian, Legend Series.

Mae Starr, 1928, 16"-20", composition shoulderhead, open mouth, four teeth, cloth body holding cylinder records. Marked "Mae Starr//Doll".

Mae West, 1983, vinyl, actress, gold paper hangtag reads: "Mae West//The 'Come Up and See Me//Sometime' Gal// the Fourth of the //Effanbee//Legend Series".

Marilee, circa 1924, 24", 27", composition shoulderhead mama doll, cloth body with crier, marked on shoulderplate, "Effanbee//Marilee//Copyr.//Doll" in oval.

Mary Ann, 1932, 19", composition, sleep eyes, wigged, open mouth. Marked on head, "Mary Ann"; marked on body, "Effanbee//Patsy Ann//©//Pat. #1283558".

Mary Lee, 1932+, 16 1/2" composition, sleep eyes, wigged, open mouth. Marked "©//Mary Lee" on head; "Effanbee //Patsy Joan" on body.

Mary Jane, circa 1920, 20", some with bisque heads, others composition. Bisque heads made by Lennox Pottery, NJ, sleep eyes, composition body, wooden arms and legs, wears Bluebird pin.

MiMi, 1927, 14" all composition, prototype of Patsy, name changed indicates copyright name conflicts, very few made, marked on body" Effanbee//MiMi//Pat. Pend//Doll".

Pat-O-Pat, 1925+, 13",15", composition head, cloth body with mechanism allowing stomach pressure to make hands move together, name pinback button.

Patsy family: 1928+ patented neck joint allowed dolls to stand and pose. Later made in vinyl.

Patsy Baby, 1931, composition, or cloth body, sleep or painted eyes, marked on head and body: "Effanbee//Patsy Baby"

Patsy Babyette, 1932, 9", composition, sleep eyes, marked on head: "Effanbee"; on back, "Effanbee//Patsy Babyette"

Patsy Baby Tinyette, 1934, 6 1/2", painted eyes, bent leg composition body, marked "Effanbee" on head, "Effanbee//Baby//Tinyette" on body. Also was made as a toddler.

Wee Patsy, 1935, 5 3/4", head molded to torso, molded painted shoes and socks, advertised as "Fairy Princess" only, marked on back, "Effanbee// Wee Patsy" came with Fairy Castle box or trousseau cases.

Patsyette, 1931, 9 1/2" all composition, painted eyes, marked "Effanbee//Patsyette" on body.

Patsy, 1928, 13 1/2", all composition, painted, later sleep eyes, molded headband on red molded bobbed hair, bent right arm, gold paper hang tag, gold metal heart bracelet. Marked on body, "Effanbee//Patsy//Pat. Pend.//Doll"

Patsy Jr., 1931, 11 1/2", composition, advertised at Patsykins, marked "Effanbee//Patsy Jr.// Doll"

Patsy Joan, 1931, 16", composition, sleep eyes, marked "Effanbee//Patsy Joan"

1946, 17" composition, marked on back "Effandbee" with extra "d"

Patsy Ann, 1929, 19", composition, sleep eyes, molded hair or wigged, marked on body, "Effanbee//Patsy Ann//©//Pat. #1283558

1959, 15" vinyl with freckles

1959, 15" vinyl, limited edition, white dress, pink hair ribbon, marked "Effanbee//Patsy Ann//©// 1959" on head, "Effanbee" on body

Patsy Lou, 1930, 22", composition, molded red hair, or wigged, sleep eyes, marked, "Effanbee// Patsy Lou" on body

Patsy Ruth, 1934, 26", composition mama doll, wigged, cloth body, crier, marked "Effanbee// Patsy Ruth" on head, "Effanbee//Lovums//©Pat. No. 1283448" on shoulderplate

Patsy Mae , 1934, 29", wigged, composition mama doll, cloth body, crier, marked: "Effanbee//Patsy Mae" on head, "Effanbee//Lovums//©Pat. No.

Above: Advertisement in 1935 Toys and Novelties magazine announces company move.

Above: Diagram from early Effanbee advertisement shows placement of marks on Patsy family dolls.

Above: Effanbee invited little girls to join the Patsy Club and then would mail them a pinback button, certificate and "The Patsytown News" magazine.

1283448" on shoulderplate

Above: Gold paper heart tag for Patsy reads: "This is Patsy The Lovable Imp with tiltable head and movable limb an Effanbee Doll"

Above: Gold metal heart bracelet reads "Effanbee// Patsy//Lou" is called a name bracelet. After 1932, Effanbee used name bracelets on Patsy family dolls - but most read "Effanbee// Durable//Dolls".

Above: Red, yellow, white and black Patsy Doll Club pinback button.

Patricia family: 1935, composition, advertised as the older sister of Patsy with slimmer body of 12-year-old. Later some models made in vinyl. Effanbee combined bodies to make variants.

Patricia-Kin, 1935, 11 1/2" wigged, all composition, marked "Patricia-Kin" on head, "Effanbee//Patsy Jr." on body.

Patricia, 1935, 15", all composition, wigged, sleep eyes, marked "Effanbee//Patricia" on body.

Patricia Joan, 1935, 16", all composition, slimmer legs, marks unknown.

Patricia Lou, 1935, 22", all composition, wigged, sleep eyes, marks unknown.

Patricia Ruth, 1935, 27", all composition, wigged, marked: "Effanbee//Patsy Ruth" on head.

Polka Dottie, 1954, 21' vinyl head with molded pigtail, cloth or hard plastic body, 11" had latex body.

Quints, 1934+, 6 1/2", composition, used Patsy Baby Tinyette in groups of five to represent Dionne Quintuplets.

Rosemary, 1926, 18", 24", composition, sleep eyes, mama doll, marked: "Effanbee//Rosemary//Walk// Talk//Sleep in oval and "Made in USA"

Sherlock Holmes, 1983, 18", vinyl, Limited Edition Doll Club series, wears plaid "Deerstalker" hat and cape-coat.

Skippy , 1929, 14", advertised as Patsy's boyfriend, marked on head, "Effanbee//Skippy//©//P.L. Crosby", on body, "Effanbee//Patsy//Pat. Pend.//Doll" sometimes used cloth body.

1979, 14", limited edition in vinyl

Suzanne, ca. 1940, 14", all composition, sleep eyes, wigged, closed mouth, some with magnets in hands to hold accessories.

Suzette circa 1939, 11", composition painted sideglancing eyes, closed mouth, wigged.

Sweetie Pie, 1939+, 16", 20", 24" also known as Baby Bright Eyes, Tommy Tucker, Mickey, Noma - the Electric Doll, composition bent limbs, sleep eyes, caracul wig, cloth body, crier. Reissued in 1952, 27" in hard plastic, 1960, 22", 1969-1986, in vinyl.

Tintair, 1951, 14", hard plastic, hair color set.

NEW! "Tintair" Glamor Girl Doll
You can shampoo, curl, change hair color of Tintair Doll! A real glamor girl and it's fun to change color of her hair. Your little "hairdresser" can color it chestnut brown one day, carrot top red the next or change it back to natural blonde! Coloring kit has 3 bottles of non-toxic coloring, 7 applicators, plastic dish, curlers. Plastic body; fully jointed. She has rayon dress and panties; socks, shoes. 49 N 3670—14 inches tall. Shipping weight 2 pounds. $11.45

Above: Effanbee Tintair advertised in 1951 Sears catalog.

Elektra T. N.C. NY Copyright

FARNELL'S ALPHA TOYS MADE IN ENGLAND

No Marks

W. C. Fields, 1980, 15 1/2", all vinyl, Centennial Doll, marked "W/C/ Fields//Effambee//19©80" on head.

Whistling Jim, 1916, 15", composition head, intaglio eyes, hole in mouth, cork stuffed cloth body, label reads: "Effanbee//Whistling Jim//Trade Mark, red striped shirt, blue overalls.

Winston Churchill, 1984, 16 1/2", Great Moments in History Series, holds two fingers in "V" for victory sign.

Elektra Toy & Novelty

1912-1920, New York City, made composition carnival-type dolls, cloth body stuffed with excelsior, short arms.

📖 **14, 44**

Dutch Girl, 1915, 32", marked Elektra T. NC. // Copyright

Jockey, 1913, 29", marked Elektra T. NC NY. // Copyright 1913.

Rosy-Posy, 1917, 11" marked on base, "Made by Elektra Toy & Novelty Co//Rosy-Posy Copyright 1917//New York U.S.A.

Uncle Sam, 30"

J. K. Farnell & Co. Ltd.

Circa 1871-1974, London, England, made cloth, plastic dolls, circa 1960s-70s. Cloth identification clue, applied ear with double seam.

📖 **14, 41 29, 33, 46**

Alpha Cherub Dolls, Trademark

Joy Day, Trademark

Portrait dolls

George VI, 1937-39, 13", felt

Baby, 10 1/2" and various sizes

Scottish Guards, 1930s, 8" **felt**

Welsh Girls, various sizes

Soldiers, various sizes

Ralph A. Freundlich

1929-1945, New York, Massachusetts, made composition dolls.

📖 **7, 14, 44, 46, 47-51**

Baby Sandy , 1939, 8", 12", 16", marked on head, "Baby Sandy" composition, painted or sleep eyes, open or closed mouth, pinback button, celebrity doll of child star, Sandy Henville.

Dummy Clown, 1938, 14" no marks, white face, stuffed straw body and limbs. Venriloquist doll with hinged pull string jaw.

Dummy Don, 1937, 10", all composition, tagged "Dummy//Don//Made in USA" same face as Dummy Clown, but jaw not hinged.

General MacArthur, 1942, 18", molded hats, painted hair, features, in tan uniform, paper tag.

Goo Goo, 1937, 19", 27" composition head tag reads "Goo Goo//Doll" plastic eyes with floating pupils, cloth body and legs of floral fabric.

Little Orphan Annie and Sandy, 1936, 10" Annie, 7" dog, no marks, all composition, molded painted yellow hair, big blue painted eyes, comic strip character by Harold Gray, 1894-1968.

Puss in Boots, 1930s, 9 1/2", felt clothing

Rabbit , 1930s, 12", pink composition head

Red Riding Hood, Grandma & Wolf, 1934, 9 1/2"

Three Little Pigs, 1930s, 10"

WAVE, circa 1942, 15", molded cap, uniform

WAAC, circa 1942, 15", molded cap, uniform

Sailor circa 1942, 15", uniform, paper tag

Soldier, circa 1942, 15", molded cap, uniform

Above: Advertisement for Red Riding Hood, Wolf and Grandma from 1934 Sears catalog.

Fortune Toys Inc.

Circa 1950s, New York, made hard plastic dolls, no marks on doll, box marked.

📖 33

Blue Ribbon Classics, 1950s, 12"

Ninette, 1955, 8" walker

Pam, 1950s, 8" walker, molded t-strap shoe.

No marks on doll, box marked: Fortune Toy Inc.

Fulper Pottery Co.

1918-1921, Flemington, NJ, made bisque dolls

📖 14, 46

Babies and Toddlers 14-26"

Fulper Mark

Furga

1870s+, Italy, made hard plastic and vinyl dolls after WWII.

33, 46

Furga Italy

Gabriel

Children
Ca. 1970s, Made vinyl action figures.

📖 **7, 46**

Butch Cavendish, 1981, 3 3/4" molded clothing
Lone Ranger, 1973, 9 3/4" vinyl head, plastic body, marked on back, "©1973 Lone Ranger//Tel. Inc.//Made in Hong Kong//For Gabriel Ind. Inc."
Tonto, 1981, 3 3/4", vinyl, molded clothing

F. G.

Gans & Seyfarth

1908-1922, Watershausen, Germany

📖 **12, 14, 46**

Babies and Children, 16"-28"

Gaultier

1860-1899, France, later part of S.F.B.J.
F.G. (Block letters) 1879-1887 (Scroll Letters) 1887-1900

📖 **14, 46**

Bébés (children) and Fashion-type dolls various sizes, 11"-28".

GEM
or no marks
on doll, may
have paper
tag

Gem Toy Co.

1913-30+, New York, made composition dolls

📖 **14, 44**

Babies and children

Gene ™//
© 1995 Mel Odom
on head

Gene (Ashton-Drake)

1995+, Niles, IL, designed by Mel Odom, a 15 ½" vinyl fashion doll, rooted hair, painted eyes, jointed arms and legs.
Gene is a fashion type doll with a story; she is a movie star from the 1930s-50s era and stars in Hollywood. Ashton Drake
Madra , 15 1/2", introduced in 2000 is Gene's archenemy.

📖 **15, 46, 50,51**

Gesland

1860-1928, Paris, made, distributed dolls, patented a doll body with metal articulated arms.

📖 **14, 46**

Bébés, (children) and Fashion-type dolls.

E. GESLAND
BTE S.G.D.G.
PARIS

Ruth Gibbs

Circa 1940s+, Flemington, NJ, made and dressed china, porcelain and hard plastic dolls.

📖 46

Godey Lady Book dolls

R G
on doll
GODEY LITTLE
LADY DOLLS
on box

Gilbert Toys

Circa 1960s, made vinyl celebrity dolls.

📖 7, 46

Honey West, 1965, 11 3/4" vinyl, rooted blonde hair, painted eyes, comes with locked fur leopard, sexy detective portrayed by Anne Francis on T.V.
James Bond, Agent 007, 1965, 12 1/2" played by Sean Connery in Thunderball movie.
Napoleon Solo - Man from UNCLE, 1965, 12 1/2", vinyl head, rigid vinyl arms, spring mechanism raises gun, portrayed by Robert Vaughn on T.V.

Mark on head like
K 73 (Honey West)
K 45 (Napoleon Solo)
Used some marked Ideal
bodies (James Bond)

F. & W. Goebel

1871-1930 on, Bavaria, made porcelain, china, Hummel figurines, latex and vinyl dolls.

📖 12, 14, 46

Molds 120, 521, various sizes from 12-20"
Vinyl dolls patterned after Hummel figures, circa 1970s-80s+, 9"-11"or larger, marked, "M.I. Hummel//©W. Goebel"

Ludwig Greiner

1840-1874, Philadelphia, PA, made papier-mâché shoulder head dolls with molded painted hair, painted eyes. Paper labels on body:

📖 14, 46

Children and adults in sizes 13"-38"

**GREINER'S
PATENT HEADS**
No. 0
Pat. March 30th, '58
**GREINER'S
PATENT DOLL HEADS**
No. 7
Pat. Mar. 30'68 Ext. 72

Gund

Circa 1898 on, Connecticut & New York Made cloth, composition, plush and vinyl dolls

📖 1, 2, 29, 44, 46, 50

Mary Lou, 1940s, 18" cloth, floating celluloid googly eyes, identifying pinback button.
Disney Characters, 1950s, 19", tagged, yarn hair, cloth body.

**"A Gund Product,
A Toy of Quality and
Distinction"**
From World War II on, stylized "G" in GUND with rabbit ears and whiskers.
Mid 1960s-70s, Bear head above the letter "U" in GUND.

No marks on doll;
had silver and navy tag
reading:
Quality//
Halco//
Brand//
Made in U.S.A."

Halco (J. Halpern Co

Circa 1950s, New York, made composition and hard
plastic dolls.

📖 **33, 46, 50**

Baby Fluffee, circa 1951, 24", hard plastic, magic
skin body, no marks,
Bride, circa 1951, 29" hard plastic
Nurse, circa 1940s, 16" composition, blue plastic
sleep eyes, eye shadow, open mouth, four upper teeth,
blonde mohair wig, no marks on body, blue and silver
hangtag.

H

A. Halopeau

📖 **14, 46**

Circa 1881-1889, Paris, France, made pressed bisque
dolls, 15-16" - little information available.

Made in Germany
Viola
H & Co.

5777
Dep
Dolly Dimple
H
Germany

Hamburger & Co.

1889-1909, New York, Germany, made and distributed composition and bisque dolls, some hair stuffed
bodies.

📖 **12, 14, 46**

Dolly Dimple, 1907, various sizes (Made by
Gebruder Heubach)
Imperial, 1901, various sizes
Santa, 1900, various sizes
Viola, 1903, various sizes

Hch H Germany
119 - 13
HANDWERCK 5 GERMANY

Bodies stamped
"Handwerck" in red
lower back torso.

Heinrich Handwerck

1876-1930, Germany, bisque heads made by Simon
and Halbig to Handwerck design,

📖 **12, 14, 22, 46**

Molds: 69, 79, 89, 99, 109, 119, 139, 189, 199
Trademark names:
Bébé Cosmopolite, 1895
Bébé de Reclame, 1898
Bébé Superior, 1913
Various sizes 18-25"

283/28,3
MAX
HANDWERCK
GERMANY
2 1/4

Max Handwerck

1899-1930, Waltherhausen, Germany, made bisque
dolls.

📖 **12, 14, 46**

Molds: 283, 286, 287, 291, 307
Trademark: Bébé Elite

Globe Baby
DEP
Germany
C 3 H

30

꒡ꀗ꒡

HASBRO

Hong Kong

Above: 11 1/2" hard plastic Hasbro G.I. Joe mint with box, dogtags, brochure, circa 1964-79, courtesy Jeff Jones.

Carl Hartmann

1889-1930, Neustadt, Germany, made bisque and celluloid dolls.

📖 **12, 14, 46**

Globe Baby, 1898+, 8"- 12" and others

Karl Hartmann

1911-1926, Stockheim, Germany, made and exported bisque dolls.

📖 **12, 14, 46**

Baby and Child, various sizes including 24", 26"

Hasbro

Hassenfeld Bro., Pawtucket, RI. Circa 1960s+, makes hard plastic and vinyl dolls.

📖 **1, 2, 7, 33, 46**

Adam, 1971, 9" vinyl, marked "Hasbro//U.S. Pat. Pend//Made in //Hong Kong" World of Love Series which included Flower, Love, Peace, Music and Soul.

Aimee, 1972, 18", rooted hair, amber sleep eyes, vinyl, long dress, sandals, marked "HASBRO INC// ©1972" on head.

Dolly Darling, 1965, 4", marked "©1965 (or 1967) HASBRO©//JAPAN" on back, molded hair or rooted, came in round hatbox cases or boxed, many variations, accessories.

Flying Nun, 1967, 4", Sally Field, played Sister Bertrille on ABC TV show, all vinyl, rooted brown hair, open closed mouth with one painted tooth, wears white habit, marked "©1967//HASBRO©// HONG KONG" on back - a Dolly Darling

10 1/2", Sally Field played part on TV1967-70, rooted brown hair, painted brown eyes, closed mouth, wears white habit with "winged" headdress.

G.I. Joe, 1964, 11 1/2" marked G.I. JOE ™ // COPYRIGHT 1964//BY HASBRO®//PATENT PENDING//MADE IN U.S.A.//G.I. JOE®.

Jem, 1985-1988, 12 1/2", vinyl, marked on head, "HASBRO, INC." on back, "COPYRIGHT 1985 (or 1986, or 1987)HASBRO, INC. followed by "CHINA' or "MADE IN HONG KONG". Not all are marked on head. There were 27 dolls in this line, including Rio, Jerrica, Aja, Kimber, Shana, Danse, Video, Raya and the Starlight Girls, Ashley, Krissie, Banee,

Pizzazz, Stormer, Roxy, Clash and Jetta. Their fashions were "Truly Outrageous".

Leggie, 1972, 10" long legged vinyl dolls, marked ©1972©//HASBRO//HONG KONG"on back. Kate, redhead; Nan, brunette; Sue, Afro-American; Jill, blonde.

Little Miss No Name, 1965, 15", vinyl, tear on cheek, marked on head "©1965 Hasbro©" wears burlap dress, blonde hair, big brown eyes, barefoot.

Mamas and Papas, 1967, 4 1/2" Show Biz Babies, Denny Doherty, John Phillips, Michelle Phillips, Cass Elliot, all vinyl, jointed heads, painted features, open mouth with molded teeth, rooted hair, first hippy band, comes with 33 1/3 rpm record.

Monkees, 1967, 4" vinyl Show Biz Babies, Mickey Dolenz, Peter Tork, Davy Jones and Mike Nesmith, wired bendable bodies, rooted brown hair, painted brown eyes, comes with 33 1/3 rpm record.

Real Baby, 1984, 18", vinyl, cloth body.

Sweet Cookie, 1972, 18" vinyl , with rooted blonde hair, freckles, open closed mouth, with teeth, jointed elbows, comes with mixer, cookbook, apron, yellow, dishes, Black version advertised in Wards catalog, marked, "©HASBRO IND.//PAT.PEND.1972" on head.

Above, 15 1/2" vinyl Little Miss No Name, 1965, 15", vinyl, tear on cheek, marked on head "©1965 Hasbro©" wears burlap dress, blonde center part hair, oversize brown eyes, barefoot, private collection.

Hertel, Schwab & Co.

1910-1930+, Stutzhaus, Germany, made china, bisque and all-bisque.

📖 12, 14, 46

Molds: 127, 131, 134. 136, 140, 141, 142, 149, 150, 151, 152, 154, 159, 167

Various sizes from 9"-24" and others.

Made in Germany 151/0

Ernst Heubach

1886-1930+, Köppelsdorf, Germany, made bisque dolls.

📖 12, 14, 46

Molds: 250, 251, 267, 275, 300, 302, 320, 321, 338, 339, 340, 342, 348, 349, 399, 444, 1900

Various sizes, 9-36"

Gebrüder Heubach

1820-1945, Thüringia, Germany, made bisque dolls,

after 1910 with character face. Used several marks, including square mark and sunburst. Most dolls have square mark with "HEUBACH".

📖 **12, 14, 46, 59**

Baby Stuart , circa 1912, 8"-13"

Dolly Dimple, circa 1913, mold 5777 for Hamberger & Co.

Santa , circa 1912, mold 5730 for Hamberger & Co.

Tiss Me, mold 11173

Molds: 5636, 5689, 5730, 5777, 6688, 6692, 6736, 6894, 6897, 6969, 6970, 6971, 7246, 7247, 7248, 7268, 7345, 7407, 7602, 7603, 7604, 7622, 7623, 7644, 7681, 7711, 7759, 7847, 7850, 7911, 7925, 7926, 7972, 7975, 7977, 8191, 8192, 8221, 8226, 8316, 8413, 8420, 8429, 8686, 8724, 8774, 8819, 8950, 9027, 9055, 9355, 9457, 9746, 10532, 11010, 11173

Various sizes

Hollywood Doll

Above: Dark blue Hollwood Doll Manufacturing logo on white box with dark blue stars.

Hollywood Doll Manufacturing Co.

Circa 1940s-50s, Glendale, CA, made composition and hard plastic dolls, 5", 6", 8" and vinyl dolls.

📖 **1, 2, 33, 46**

Ballerina, 1940s, 1950s, 5"

Bedtime Dolly, 1940s, 1950s, 5"

Bridegroom, 1950s, 5"

Cowboy, 1947, 5" hard plastic marked "Hollywood Dolls" in circle on back, sleep eyes, molded hair, all fingers molded together, black painted on shoes. Wrist tag says "Cowboy" white box has blue stars, labeled "A Hollywood Doll", Western Series.

Little Friends, 1940s, 1950s, 5"

Little Snow Baby, 1940s, 1950s, 5"

Lucky Star Series, 1940s, 1950s, 5"

Lullaby Baby Series, 1940s, 1950s, 5"

Nun, 1940s, 1950s, 5"

Nursery Rhymes, 1940s, 1950s, 5"

Old Mother Witch, 1940s, 1950s, 5"

Peter Rabbit, 1940s, 1950s, 5"

Playmates, 1940s, 1950s, 5"

Princess Series, 1940s, 1950s, 5"

Queen for a Day, 1947, 6" , marked Star "Hollywood Dolls" on back, painted eyes, molded hair under wig, fat tummy, white satin and lace dress, red velvet robe, gold crown, made for radio program.

Rock-A-Bye Baby, 1949-51, 5", hard plastic, white taffeta dress, bonnet, marked "Hollywood Doll" in circle on back, "Hollywood Doll" armtag, box marked "Rock-a-bye Baby" and "Hollywood Doll" with stars.

E. I. Horsman & Co.

1865-1980+, New York City, founded by Edward Imeson Horsman, distributed, assembled and made dolls. Merged with Aetna Doll & Toy Co., in 1909. Obtained first copyright for a complete doll with composition Billiken, later made hard plastic and vinyl dolls.

📖 1, 2, 14, 44, 46, 47-51

Angie Dickinson, Police Woman, 1976, 9" vinyl, marked "HORSMAN DOLLS INC. //U//L CPT// 19©76". Dickinson played Sergeant Suzanne 'Pepper' Martin on the TV show Police Woman.

Babs, 1931, 11 1/2" all composition Patsy-type, with tin blue eyes, dimple in chin, molded painted brown hair.

Baby Bumps, 1910-1917, 11" composition head, cloth cork stuffed body, blue and white cloth label on romper, copy of K*R # 100 baby mold, Black version also.

Baby Butterfly, 1913, 13", oriental baby, composition head, hands, painted features, label on sleeve.

Baby Dimples, circa 1927, 22", 25" and other sizes, composition flange head and arms and lower legs,, cloth body , molded painted blonde hair, gray tin sleep eyes, open mouth , two upper teeth. Marked E.I.H. Co. Inc.

Baby Horsman, 1923, 14", 20", 24", marked "E.I.© H. Co." on back of neck, composition head, hands, cloth body, limbs, disk joints at shoulders, painted and molded hair, painted blue eyes.

Baby Precious, 1970s, 14" vinyl one-piece body, blue sleep eyes, closed mouth, marked "21 Horsman" on head , hangtag, "Horsman's Precious Baby"

Billiken, circa 1908, 11 1/2", 15", 25" composition character, slit eyes, smiling closed mouth, molded painted hair, velvet jointed body, tagged" Copyright 1908//The Billikin// Company".

Bright Star, 1940s, 13"- 19", perhaps other sizes,

Above: 11 1/2" composition Horsman character, "Billikin" slit eyes, smiling closed mouth, molded painted hair, with velvet jointed body, label sewn on chest reads, "copyright 1908// The Billikin//Company", courtesy Connie Lee Martin.

Above: 13 1/2" composition Horsman "Baby Butterfly" with unmarked dome head, molded painted hair, molded ears, single stroke eyebrow, wearing kimono labeled, "Baby Butterfly//Horsman Co. New York//Produced Dec. 12, 1913" courtesy Nelda Shelton.

Above: 11" Horsman composition HEbee-SHEbee, circa 1926, jointed molded painted shirts and pink or blue slippers. Hair not painted or molded, blue painted eyes, closed mouth. HEbee-SHEbees were comic stip characters by Charles Twelvetrees.

Above: 12" composition Campbell Kid, siede glancing painted eyes, molded hair, painted socks and shoes, original clothing, no marks on body, courtesy McMasters Doll Auctions.

all composition, mohair wig, sleep eyes, open mouth, four upper teeth, no marks on body, paper tag, "Horsman//Bright Star//Quality Doll."

Circa 1950s, 17", hard plastic, synthetic wig, blue sleep eyes, open closed mouth with four teeth, hangtag.

Campbell Kid Mascot Boy, 1912, 11" composition with side glancing eyes, molded painted hair, in tagged gold and black striped shirt and tan pants, disk jointed sawdust stuffed body, label on sleeve: "The Campbell Kids//Trade Mark//Copyright Campbell Company//Mfg. By E. Horsman Co."

Cotton Joe, 1914, 14", composition flange head, cloth body, and limbs, black painted hair, brown eyes, open/closed mouth, no marks on body, label sewn in body seam: "Copyright 1910//By E. I. Horsman//Cotton Joe"

Ella Cinders, 1925, composition flange head, arms, legs, cloth body, painted black hair, middle part, painted blue eyes, open/closed mouth, white line for teeth, freckles, original polka dot blouse, patched skirt with apron, marked, "©//1925//M.N.S." Dress tagged, " Ella Cinders//Trade Mark Reg. U.S. Pat. Offr.//Copyright 1925//Metropolitan Newspaper Service." Ella Cinders was a comic strip character by Bill Conselman and Charlie Plumb.

Gene Carr Kids, 1915, 14" composition characters from Gene Carr comic strip, "Lady Bountiful" designed by Bernard Lipfert. Painted molded hair, cloth body and limbs, disk jointed.

> **Blink,** eyes shut
> **Jane**
> **Mike**
> **Skinny,** eyes shut
> **Snowball,** Black boy

HEbee-SHEbee, circa 1926, 10", all composition, jointed molded painted shirts and pink or blue slippers. Hair not painted or molded, blue painted eyes closed mouth. HEbee-SHEbees were comic strip characters by Charles Twelvetrees.

Jackie Coogan Kid, 1914, 14", composition, cloth body, legs, bent composition arms, molded painted hair with bangs and brown eyes, closed mouth, marked "E.I. H.//19©21", cloth label on pants: "Jackie Coogan Kid//Licensed by Jackie Coogan//

Patent Pending", wears checked pants, turtleneck, checked cap. Jackie Coogan was a child movie star.

Jap Rose Kid, 1911, 14" composition, cloth body, upper arms, legs disk joints, molded painted black hair, brown eyes, open/closed mouth, label on sleeve reads: The Jap Rose Kid//Trade Mark//Process Pat. Nov. 1911//Lic'd by Jas. S. Kirk & Company// Copyright by E. I. Horsman Co. advertising to Kirk Soap Company.

Jeannie, circa 1937, 15", composition head, arms, legs, cloth body, crier, molded painted brown hair, with slight top knot, small closed mouth, tin sleep eyes, marked " 'C' Jeanie//Horsman".

Jo-Jo, 1937, 12" all composition, molded hair or mohair wig, tin sleep eyes, closed mouth, marked"JOJO//©1937 Horsman".

Little Debbie, 1972, 11" doll made for Little Debbie Snack Cakes 25th anniversary. Marked "HORSMAN DOLLS, INC. //19©72" on head, wears blue checked dress, white hat, white apron marked Little Debbie.

Little Mary Mix-Up, 1920, 15" composition head, upper arms and legs, after a comic strip character by R. M. Brinkerhoff, shoulderhead, cloth body, molded painted hair, pinhole for ribbon, painted blue eyes, closed mouth, yellow and white dress.

Mary Poppins, 1965-69, 11 1/2", vinyl, rooted hair, wears, blue coat, blue hat, has umbrella, carpet bag, marked "H" on head, other costumes available.

Patty Duke, 1965, 11" vinyl, marked "H" on head, wears red top, gray pants, comes with telephone, Patty Duke Show was on T.V. .

Peggy, 1930, 12", 14", 20", 10" cloth body, others all composition, some with jointed waist, these were all Patsy-types with molded painted hair, painted eyes, 20" unmarked, 12" marked "IT", 14" marked "Amberg//Pat. Pend.//L.A. & SD. Amberg was bought by Horsman and Horsman used the dolls with the old mold mark.

Peggy name used for vinyl dolls 1950-1970 and on.

Peggy Pen Pal, 1970, 18" vinyl with rooted blonde hair in ponytails, red dress, blue ribbon, twist waist, came with writing desk, Sears Christmas catalog.

Peterkin, 1915, 11", Tommy Peterkin, glass eyes, wigged, molded hair version has painted eyes,

Above: 25" Dimples, tin sleep eyes, molded painted hair, open mouth, courtesy Barb Hilliker.

E. I. H. Co.
©E.I. HORSMAN
Various hangtags

Above: 13" Peterkin, closed slightly smiling mouth, painted eyes, molded hair, courtesy McMasters Doll Auctions.

Above: 27" unmarked composition Horsman "Sweetheart", wigged, original blue dress, white collar and belt, hantag,"Horsman's Sweetheart", courtesy Margie Welker.

Above: 17 1/2" composition "Rosebud", cloth body, sleep eyes, original human hair wig, original print dress, courtesy Chantal Jeschien.

composition head, arms, legs, and lower torso, cloth body, design by Grace Drayton.

1929, 13", all composition, painted molded hair and painted eyes, cloth body, closed smiling mouth.

Pippi Longstocking, 1972, 11" vinyl, orange braids, freckles, lime green shirt, orange and red apron reads, "Pippi" marked on head, "12// HORSMAN DOLLS INC.//19©62"; 1973, 17 1/2" vinyl, freckles, orange hair in braids, has lime dress, orange and red apron that reads: Pippi Longstocking" and is marked HORSMAN DOLLS INC//1972" on head.

Polly Prue, circa 1911, 13" composition head, cloth body, limbs, molded painted blonde hair, painted blue eyes, closed mouth, marked "E.I.H. ©1911" also known as "Fairy" used as premium for Fairy Soap, N.K. Fairbank Co. Chicago.

Poor Pitiful Pearl, 1963, 10 1/2", 13", marked "1963//Wmn. Steig//Horsman". Pearl was first made by Brookglad in 1957, then Horsman, then Tristar.

Rosebud, 1930s, 1940s, 20" composition head, shoulderplate, limbs, cloth body, mohair wig, tin sleep eyes, real upper lashes, multi-stroke brows. Open mouth, four upper teeth, dimples in cheeks. Some with gold paper hangtag that reads: A// Genuine//Horsman//Rosebud//Doll"

Ruthie, 14", 16", 17", 19" and various other sizes, some marked "HORSMAN//T.21" on vinyl head, closed mouth, sleep eyes.

Sweetheart, 1938, 24", 28", composition, hard rubber arms, brown mohair wig, green sleep eyes, open mouth, six upper teeth, wears original dress with white collar. Tagged "Horsman's// Sweetheart/ /A Horsman Art Doll".

Tynie Baby, 1924, 17", 21", composition flange head and arms, cloth body, legs, molded painted blonde hair, tin sleep eyes, closed mouth, marked "© 1924//E.I.H. Co. Inc." some unmarked.

Uncle Sam's Kids, 1917, 15 1/2", marks "T. T. Co., " cloth label: "Uncle Sam's Kids//Trade Mark// Design Patent Applied For//E. I. Horsman Co., New York"- composition shoulderhead, short arms, cloth body, molded painted hair, painted blue eyes, , wearing red striped coverall, blue jacket trimmed in red stripes, matching hat.

Mary Hoyer

1937 on, Reading, PA, made dolls of composition and hard plastic, some vinyl. Today, granddaughter Mary Lynne Saunders carries on the family tradition with the Mary Hoyer play dolls.

   📖   **26, 44, 46, 47-51**

Cathy, 1961, 10" vinyl infant, by Unique Doll Co.
Gigi, 1950, 18" hard plastic, circle Mary Hoyer mark, only 2,000 made by Frisch Doll Co.
Janie, 1962, 8" vinyl baby
Margi, 1958, 10", vinyl toddler rooted hair, made by Unique Doll Co. for Hoyer
Mary Hoyer, 14", composition, 14" hard plastic (circle mark), 14" vinyl play doll
Vicky, 1957, 10 1/2", 12", 14" vinyl high heel bendable waist, rooted Saran hair, larger sizes discontinued

THE
MARY HOYER
DOLL

ORIGINAL
Mary Hoyer
DOLL

Adolf Hulss

1915-1930, Germany, made bisque babies and children, with jointed composition bodies and some all bisque.

   📖   **12, 14, 46**

Molds: 156, 1926, 14"-20", character by Simon & Halbig
      176, ca. 1927-29, 15"-22"

SIMON HALBIG

Made in Germany
156

Huret, Maison

1812-1930, 9-19", France, may have pressed, poured bisque or China head, painted or glass eyes, closed mouth, cloth, composition kid, gutta percha, wood fashion type or child body, some with metal hands.

Body can be marked

Ideal Novelty & Toy Co.

1906-80s, Brooklyn, NY, produced cloth and composition, later hard plastic and vinyl dolls.

   📖   **1, 2, 27, 30-31, 44, 46, 47-51**

Baby Coos, 1948-1952, 14"- 27" hard plastic head, Magic Skin body, jointed arms, sleep eyes, real lashes, molded painted hair. Magic Skin, an early plastic, usually turned black and split. Marked on head: "IDEAL DOLL//MADE IN USA".
Baby Crissy ®, 1973-1976, 24" vinyl, foam filled arms and legs, rooted red grow hair, two painted teeth, brown sleep eyes, marked, "©1972//IDEAL

IDEAL NOVELTY & TOY Co.

Above: 12" composition Ideal Flexie Fanny Bryce as "Baby Snooks", painted molded hair with loop, original costume, wood torso and feet, flexy wire arms and legs, designed by Joseph Kallus, circa 1939, courtesy Odis Gregg.

TOY CORP.//2 M-5511//B" also Black version.

Bamm-Bamm, 1964, 12", 16", all vinyl, with felt loincloth, bone, cap and club, marked: "©HANNA-BARBERA PRODS., INC.//IDEAL TOY COPR.// BB-12" on head and body.

Belly Button Babies, 1971-72, 9 1/2", all vinyl, rooted hair, painted eyes, bent legs, button in belly makes arms, legs, head move. Marked, "©1970// IDEAL TOY CORP.//E-9-H165 (or H169) on head; "IDEAL TOY CORP. //HONG KONG" on back.

Betsy McCall, 1952-54, 14" vinyl head, hard plastic Toni body, glued on dark wig, sleep eyes, closed mouth, marked: "McCall CORP.®" on head, "IDEAL DOLL//P-90" on back.

Betsy Wetsy, 1937-38, 11"-19", hard rubber head, soft rubber body, molded hair, sleep eyes, lashes, marked "IDEAL" on head and back.

1946, 12-16", hard plastic head, rubber body, sleep eyes, marked "MADE IN USA//PAT. NO. 2252077" on head.

1954-56, 11 1/2", 13 1/2", 16", 20" hard plastic head, vinyl body, marked, "MADE IN USA// PAT. NO. 225207" or "IDEAL DOLL//MADE IN USA"

1959-1962, 11 1/2", 13 1/2", 16", 23" sizes, new face design, all vinyl, rooted Saran hair, marked "IDEAL TOY CORP//PW-20".

Bizzie Lizzie, 1971-72, 18" vinyl, rooted blonde hair, sleep eyes, battery operated, she irons, vacuums, dusts, also Black.

Bonnie Braids, 1951-53, 11 1/2", 14", vinyl, Magic Skin rubber one-piece body (may have turned black) open mouth, one tooth, painted yellow hair, with Saran pigtails, painted blue eyes, crier, marked: "©1951//Chi. Tribune//IDEAL DOLL//USA" on neck, comic strip daughter of Dick Tracy.

Buster Brown, 1929, 16", composition head, hands, legs, cloth body, tin eyes, marked: "IDEAL" in a diamond, a cartoon character by Richard Felton Outcault.

Charlie McCarthy, 1938-39, 8", composition head, hand puppet, felt hands, molded hat, molded features, wire monocle, cloth body, painted tuxedo, marked: "Edgar Bergen's//©CHARLIE MCCARTHY//MADE IN U.S.A."

Chelsea, 1967, 24", vinyl head, Jet Set Doll, posable body, rooted long straight hair, mod fashions, earrings, strap shoes.

Cinderella, 1938-1939, 13", 16", 18", 20" 22", 25", 27", all composition, human hair wig, flirty glass sleep eyes, open mouth, six teeth, dimple in chin, formal evening gowns, rhinestone tiara, silver snap shoes, 13" doll in ski outfit, six costume changes. 13" marked: "SHIRLEY TEMPLE//13" on body.

Cinnamon, 1972-1974, 13½", originally called "Velvet's Little Sister", vinyl head, painted eyes, rooted growing hair, orange polka dotted outfit, also came in Black version. Marked: "©1971// IDEAL TOY CORP.//G-H-12-H18//HONG KONG//IDEAL 1069-4" on head, "©1972//IDEAL TOY CORP./7.S. PAT-3-162-976//OTHER PAT.PEND.//HONG KONG", on back.

Clarabelle, 1947, 27", soft cloth cotton-stuffed girl, mask face, wig with braids, printed percale slacks outfit.

Cracker Jack Boy, 1917, 14", composition head, gauntlet hands, cloth body, molded boots, molded hair, sailor suit, cap, carries package of Cracker Jacks by special arrangement with Rueckheim Bros. and Eckstein, manufacturers of Cracker Jacks.

Cricket, 1971-1972, 15", Sears exclusive, vinyl, member of the Crissy® family, growing hair doll, painted teeth, swivel waist. Marked: "©1970// IDEAL TOY CORP.//CR-H-177//HONG KONG P" on shoulder, "©1970//IDEAL TOY CORP.// MO15//HONG KONG".

Crissy®, 1969-1974, 17½", all vinyl, dark brown eyes, long hair, turn knob in back to make hair grow, some with swivel waist (1971), reissued 1982-1983. First year, hair grew to floor length, also in Black version. Marked "©1968//IDEAL TOY CORP.//GH 17-H129" on head, "©1972// IDEAL TOY CO. MO 18//U.S.PAT. 3,182,76// OTHER PAT. PENDING" on back.

Daddy's Girl, 1961, 38", 42", vinyl head, arms, plastic body, swivel waist, jointed ankles, rooted Saran hair, sleep eyes, closed smiling mouth, preteen girl. Marked: "IDEAL TOY CORP.//G-42-

Above: 12" composition Ideal Liberty Boy with molded painted blonde hair, painted blue eyes, jointed body with World War I Army uniform, black ties, buttons, brown molded boots, marked Ideal in a diamond on back, circa 1918, courtesy Marilyn Ramsey.

Above: 14" composition Ideal Tickletoes, flange neck, flirty eyes, open mouth, cloth body, rubber arms with squeeker, original costume, tag, circa 1928-39, private collection.

1" on head, "IDEAL TOY CORP./G-42" on body.

Davy Crockett, 1955-1956, 4½", all plastic, painted features, sits astride white stallion, dressed in simulated buckskin, coonskin cap, can be removed from horse.

Dennis the Menace, 1976, 7", 14", all cloth, printed doll, comic strip character by Hank Ketcham, blond hair, freckles, wearing overalls, striped shirt.

Diana Ross, 1969, 17½", all vinyl, rooted black bouffant hairdo, two versions: "On-stage" gold fabric sheath with feathers and gold shoes, "Off-stage" was a chartreuse knit mini dress, print scarf and black shoes. From the "Supremes" (singing group).

Dorothy Hamill, 1977, 11½", vinyl head, plastic posable body, rooted hair, painted eyes, ice rink with skates, five separate outfits, Olympic skating star. Marked: "©1977 D.H.//IDEAL//H-282//HONG KONG P" on head.

Evel Knievel, 1972, 7", all vinyl, fully jointed wired for posing, painted hair and features, stunt figure, stunt cycle, helmet. Unmarked.

Flexies: 1938, 13", composition head, gauntlet hands, flexible wire tubing for arms and legs, wooden torso and feet, molded painted hair, painted eyes.

> **Baby Snooks,** 1938, 13", based on a character by Fannie Brice, designed by Joseph Kallus, open/closed mouth with painted teeth, marked "IDEAL DOLL// Made in U.S.A." on head.
>
> **Clown,** 1938, 13", looks like Mortimer Snerd, painted white as a clown, clown outfit, marked: "IDEAL DOLL//MADE IN USA" on head.
>
> **Mortimer Snerd,** 1938, 13", Edgar Bergen's radio show dummy, molded painted blond hair, smiling closed mouth showing two teeth, marked: "IDEAL DOLL//MADE IN U.S.A." on neck.
>
> **Soldier,** 1938, 13", closed smiling mouth, dressed in khaki uniform, marked: "IDEAL DOLL" on head.
>
> **Sunny Sam and Sunny Sue,** 1938, 13", Sunny Sue has painted molded bob style hair, pouty mouth, Sunny Sam has closed

Above and below: 19" composition Ideal "Flossie Flirt" original cotton dress, hang tag reads "Flossie Flirt", IDEAL//Sleeping/ Talking Walking Dolls, mohair wig, flirty tin eyes, cloth torso with crier, circa 1924-1931, courtesy Stephanie Prince.

smiling mouth, both marked: "IDEAL DOLL" on head.

Flossie Flirt, 1924-1931, 14", 16", 18", 20", 22", composition head, limbs, cloth body, crier, tin flirty eyes, open mouth, upper teeth. Marked: "IDEAL" in diamond with "U.S.of A."

Harriet Hubbard Ayer, 1953, 7½", 14", 16", 19", 21", vinyl head, hard plastic (Toni) body, wigged or rooted hair, came with eight-piece H.H. Ayer cosmetic kit. Marked: "MK 16//IDEAL DOLL" on head, "IDEAL DOLL//P-91" on body.

Hopalong Cassidy, 1949-1950, 18", 21", 23", 25", 27", vinyl stuffed head, vinyl hands, molded painted gray hair, one piece cloth body, dressed in a cowboy outfit, leatherette boots, guns, holster, black felt hat, marked "Hopalong Cassidy" on buckle. Unmarked.

Howdy Doody, 1950-1953, 20", 24", hard plastic head, television personality ventriloquist doll, mouth operated by pull string, painted freckles, molded painted red hair, cloth body and limbs, dressed in cowboy outfit, scarf reads: "HOWDY DOODY", marked: "IDEAL" on head.

1954, 18", 20", 25", with vinyl hands, marked "IDEAL DOLL".

Jiminy Cricket, 1940, 8½", composition head, wood segmented body, yellow painted suit with black coat, blue felt trim on hat, ribbon necktie, wooden umbrella, marked "JIMINY CRICKET// DES & BY WALT DISNEY//MADE BY IDEAL NOVELTY & TOY CO." on foot.

Joan Palooka, 1953, 14", vinyl head, magic skin body, jointed arms, legs, yellow molded hair, Saran topknot, painted eyes, open/closed mouth, came with Johnson's Baby Powder, daughter of comic strip character Joe Palooka. Marked "©1952// HAM FISHER//IDEAL DOLL" on head.

Judy Garland, As Dorothy from *The Wizard of Oz*, 1939-1940, 13", 15 ½", 18", all composition, jointed wig with braids, brown sleep eyes, open

mouth, six teeth, checked rayon jumper, white blouse. Marked "IDEAL" on head with size number and "USA" on body.

Teen, 1940-1942, 15", 21", all composi-

Above: 24" all composition Ideal "Deanna Durbin" marked on head "Ideal Doll//Deanna Durbin" and Ideal Doll/ 25" on back, brown human hair wig, open mouth, six upper teeth, sleep eyes, circa 1938-1941, courtesy Cornelia Ford.

Above: 18" composition Ideal Judy Garland as "Dorothy" from the Wizard of Oz movie, brown sleep eyes, open mouth, tongue, six teeth, dark brown human hair wig in braids, blue checked rayon jumper dress, circa 1939-1940. 17" cloth Ideal "Strawman" with hangtag reading "The Strawman//by Ray Bolger of//THE WIZ-ARD//OF OZ" yellow yarn hair, navy blue jacket and hat, tan pants, all original, circa 1939, courtesy Martha Sweeney.

tion, wig, sleep eyes, open mouth, four teeth, Original pin reads "JUDY GARLANDS METRO GOLDWYN MAYER STAR", Marked: "IDEAL Dolls", with a backwards "21" on body.

Judy Splinters, 1949-1950, 18", 22", 36", Vinylite head, ventriloquist doll, cloth body, jointed arms, legs, turns head, open/closed mouth, painted eyes, yarn-like pigtails, from TV show created by Shirley Dinsdale. Marked: "IDEAL DOLL" on head.

Kissy, 1961-1964, 22 ½", vinyl head, rigid vinyl toddler body, rooted Saran hair, sleep eyes, jointed wrists, press hands together and mouth puckers, makes kissing sound, came in eight different outfits. Marked: "©IDEAL CORP.//K-21-L" on head, "IDEAL TOY CORP.//K22//PAT.PEND." on body.

Liberty Boy, 1918, 12" all composition, molded on brown uniform, boots, jointed neck, shoulder, hips, molded painted hair, felt hat, gold cord, marks, "IDEAL" in a diamond on back. Arm raises in a salute.

Little Miss Revlon, 1958-1960, 10 ½", vinyl head, strung body, jointed head, arms, legs, swivel waist, high-heeled feet, rooted hair, sleep eyes, pierced ears, many extra boxed outfits available. Marked: "IDEAL TOY CORP//VT-10 ½" on head.

Lori Martin, 1961, 30", 36", 38", 42", all-vinyl, character from *National Velvet* show, swivel waist, jointed body, jointed ankles, sleep eyes, rooted dark hair, individual fingers. Marked: "Metro Goldwyn Mayer Inc.//Mfg. By//IDEAL TOY CORP.//38" on head, "©IDEAL TOY CORP.//G-38" on back.

Magic Skin Baby, 1941, 1946-1949, 13", 15", 17", 20", hard plastic head, one-piece molded latex body and legs, jointed arms, sleep eyes, molded painted hair. Patent applied for by Abraham M. Katz of the Ideal Toy Co.

Mary Hartline, 1952, 7 ½", 16", 23", hard plastic, fully jointed, blond nylon wig, sleep eyes, lashes, black eyeshadow over and under eye, drum majorette costume, baton, TV personality from *Super Circus* show. Marked: "P-91//IDEAL DOLL//MADE IN U.S.A." on head, "IDEAL DOLL//P-91" or "IDEAL//16" on body.

Miss Clairol, Glamour Misty, 1965-1966, 12", vinyl head, arms, rigid plastic body and legs, rooted

Saran hair, sideglancing eyes, teen doll with cosmetics to change her hair, high-heeled feet. Marked: "©1965//IDEAL TOY CORP//W-12-3" on neck, "©1965 IDEAL" in oval on back.

Miss Curity, 1953, 14 ½", hard plastic, Saran wig, sleep eyes, black eyeshadow, nurse's outfit, cape, Bauer & Black first aid kit and book, uses Toni body. Marked: "P-90 IDEAL DOLL, MADE IN U.S.A." on head.

Miss Ideal, 1961, 25", 30", all vinyl, rooted nylon hair, jointed ankles, wrists, waist, arms, legs, closed smiling mouth, sleep eyes, came with beauty kit and comb. Marked: "©IDEAL TOY CORP.//SP-30-S" on head, "©IDEAL TOY CORP.//G-30-S" on back.

Miss Revlon, 1956-1959, 15", 18", 20", 22 1/2", and 26" (1957), vinyl, hard plastic teenage body, jointed shoulders, waist, hips, knees, high-heeled feet, rooted Saran hair, sleep eyes, lashes, pierced ears, hang tag. Marked: "VT 20//IDEAL DOLL", "VT-22//IDEAL DOLL", IDEAL//15//n" on head, IDEAL DOLL//VT-18 on neck.

Mysterious Yokum, (Li'l Honest Abe), 1953, Son of comic strip character, Li'l Abner, hard plastic head, body, "Magic Skin" arms and legs, painted eyes, molded hair, forelock, wears overalls, one suspender, knit cap.

Patite, 1960, 18", all vinyl, rooted Saran hair, sleep eyes, check dress, white pinafore with name, looks like Patti Playpal. Marked: "IDEAL TOY CORP//G-18". Made 18" Walking Patite in 1961.

Patti Playpal, 1959-1962, 35", all vinyl, jointed wrists, sleep eyes, curly or straight Saran hair, bangs, closed mouth, checked dress with pinafore, three-year-old size, reissued in 1981 and 1982. Also came in Black version. Marked "IDEAL TOY CORP.//G 35 OR B-19-1" on head.

Peanuts Gang, 1976-1978, 7", 14", all cloth, stuffed printed dolls from Peanuts cartoon strip by Charles Schultz, Charlie Brown, Lucy, Linus, Peppermint Patty, and Snoopy.

Pebbles, 1963-1964, 16", Tiny Pebbles, 12", **Baby Pebbles,** 1963-64, 14", 1963-64 12", 16", 8 1/4" 1966, vinyl head, arms, legs, vinyl or soft body, sideglancing painted eyes, rooted hair with topknot and bone, character from Flintstone cartoons by

Above: 16" all original hard plastic Ideal "Mary Hartline" , a T.V. celebrity, with eyeshadow over eyes, marked "P-91" dark blue music note original costume also comes in green or red dress, circa 1952, courtesy Stephanie Prince.

Above: 21" vinyl Ideal "Harriet Hubbard Ayer" cosmetic doll, marked "MK 21//Ideal Doll" on head, "Ideal Doll//P-93" on back, courtesy McMasters Doll Auctions.

Above: 13 1/2" vinyl Ideal "Cinnamon" originally called Velvet's Little Sister, painted eyes, rooted auburn growing hair, orange polka dot outfit, also had other wardrobe available, 1972-74, courtesy Penny Pittsley.

Hanna-Barbera.

Penny Play Pal, 1959, vinyl, jointed body, rooted curly Saran hair, sleep eyes, individual fingers, Patti's two-year-old sister, made only one year. Marked "IDEAL DOLL//32-E-L" or "B-32-B PAT. PEND." on head, "IDEAL" on back.

Peter Play Pal, 1960-1961, 38", vinyl, gold sleep eyes, freckles, pug nose, rooted hair, size of a four-year-old. Marked: "©IDEAL TOY CORP.//W-38// PAT. PEND" on body.

Pinocchio, 1939, 8", 11", 20", composition head, wood segmented body, painted features and clothes, yellow felt cap. Marked: "PINOCCHIO//Des.© by Walt Disney//Made by Ideal Novelty & Toy Co." on front, "W.D.P.//Ideal Doll//Made in USA" on back.

Plassie, 1942, 17", 19", 22", 24", hard plastic head, composition shoulderplate, composition limbs, stuffed pink oilcloth body, sleep eyes, molded painted hair. Marked: "IDEAL DOLL/;/MADE IN USA//PAT.NO. 225 2077" on head.

Princess Beatrix, 1938-1943, 14" (sleep eyes), 16", 22", 26", composition head, limbs, cloth body, flirty sleep eyes, fingers molded into fists, rosebud mouth. Represents Princess Beatrix of the Netherlands.

Samantha and Tabitha, 1965 (Samantha), 15", 1966 (Samantha), 12", vinyl head, body, rooted hair, witch's costume with broom, painted sideglancing eyes, from TV show *Bewitched,* marked "IDEAL DOLL//M-12-E-2" on head.

Tabitha, 1966, 14", vinyl head, body, rooted hair, painted blue sideglancing eyes, closed mouth, came in pajamas, baby from TV show *Bewitched.* Marked: ©1965//Screen Gems, Inc.//Ideal Toy Corp.//T.A. 18-6//H-25" on head.

Saucy Walker, 1951-1955, 14", 16", 22", 25", 26", all hard plastic, walks, turns head from side to side, flirty eyes, crier, open/closed mouth, teeth, Saran wig, plastic curlers, came as toddler (1953), boy (1952), and 25" "Big Sister" (1954). Marked "IDEAL DOLL" on head and back. Also came in Black.

1960-1961, 28", 32", all vinyl, rooted Saran hair, sleep eyes, closed smiling mouth, walker.

Marked "©IDEAL TOY CORP.//T28X-60" or "IDEAL TOY CO.//BYE S 285 B" on head,

"IDEAL TOY CORP.//T-28 Pat. Pend." on body.

Seven Dwarfs, 1938, 12", composition head and cloth body, or all cloth, painted mask face, heads turn, removable clothes, each dwarf has name on cap, pick and lantern. Marked: "Snow White//and the Seven Dwarfs//©1937/W.D.Ent." on tag.

Shirley Temple - Listed under Shirley Temple

Smokey the Bear, 1953, 18", 25", Bakelite vinyl face, paws, rayon plush body, vinyl ranger hat, badge, shovel, symbol of US National Forest Service, Smokey marked belt, twill trousers, came with Junior Forest Ranger kit. Issued on the 50th anniversary of Ideal's original "Teddy Bear".

Snoozie, 1933, 14", 16", 18", 20", composition head, painted hair, rubber hands and feet, cloth body, open yawning mouth, molded tongue, sleep eyes. Marked: "©B. Lipfert//Made for Ideal Doll & Toy Corp. 1933" or "©by B. Lipfert" or "IDEAL SNOOZIE//B. LIPFERT" on head.

1949, 11", 16", 20", 1933 doll reissued in vinyl, cloth body with Swiss music box.

1958-1965, 14", all vinyl, rooted Saran hair, sleep eyes, open/closed mouth, cry voice, knob makes doll wiggle, closes eyes, flannel pajamas.

1964-1965, 20", vinyl head, arms, legs, soft body, rooted Saran hair, sleep eyes, turn knob for action. Marked: "©1965//IDEAL TOY CORP//YTT-14-e" on head, "IDEAL TOY CORP//U.S. PAT.NO.3,029,522" on knob on back.

Snow White, 1938, 11 ½", 13", 14", 18", 22", 27", all composition, jointed body, mohair wig, flirty glass eyes, open mouth, four teeth, dimple in chin, red bodice, rayon taffeta skirt pictures seven Dwarfs, cape, some marked: "Shirley Temple//18" or other size number on back. Black version is rare with molded painted hair.

Soozie Smiles, 1923, 16", 17", two headed composition doll with smiling face, sleep or painted eyes, and crying face with tears, painted molded hair, cloth body and legs, composition arms.

Sparkle Plenty, 1947-1950, 14", 16", 18", 20", hard plastic head, "Magic Skin" body (may turn dark), yarn hair, sleep eyes, cries or coos when squeezed, character from Dick Tracy comic strip, daughter of B.O. Plenty and Gravel Gertie. Marked: "Made in

Above: 25" all vinyl Ideal "Miss Ideal" brown rooted hair, marked "© Ideal Toy Copr-SP-S" on head, "© Ideal Toy Corp. P-25" on body, sleep eyes, closed smiling mouth, came with beauty playwave kit and hat box, circa 1961, courtesy Cornelia Ford.

Above: 10 1/2" vinyl Ideal "Little Miss Revlon" swivel waist, high heeled feet, rooted, sleep eyes, pierced ears, all original, circa 1958-60, courtesy Chantal Jeschien.

Above: 35" vinyl Ideal "Patti Play Pal" marked "Ideal Doll//G-35" on head, hard to find orange-red rooted Saran hair with bangs, walker, wears original orange print and green school dress, circa 1960-1961, courtesy Cornelia Ford.

USA, Pat. # 2232077".

Strawman, 1939, 17", 21", all cloth scarecrow character portrayed by Ray Bolger in *The Wizard of Oz,* yarn hair, dark jacket and hat, pants, round paper hangtag.

Tammy and family, 1962-1965, 12", White, Black, Pos'n, Dad, Mom, Ted, 9" Pepper, vinyl head, arms, plastic legs and torso, head joined at neck base. Marked "©IDEAL TOY CORP.//BS12" on head, "©IDEAL TOY CORP.//BS-12//1" on back.

Tara, 1976, 15 ½", all vinyl Black doll, authentic Black features, long rooted grow hair, sleep eyes, marked: "©1975//IDEAL TOY CORP//H-250// HONG KONG" on head, ©1970//IDEAL TOY CORP//GH-15//M5169-01//MADE IN HONG KONG" on body.

Thumbelina, 1961-1962, 16", 20", vinyl head, limbs, cloth body, painted eyes, rooted Saran hair, open/closed mouth, wind knob on back moves body, crier in 1962.

1982-1983, 7", all vinyl, one-piece body, rooted hair, quilted carrier, also Black version. Marked: "1974//IDEAL (in oval) //B-6-H361" on head, "IDEAL (in oval)//1974/B.B.-8-52" on back.

1983-1985, 18", 24", reissue from 1960s mold, vinyl head, arms, legs, cloth body, painted eyes, crier, open mouth, molded or rooted hair.

Tiny Thumbelina, 1962-1968, vinyl head, rooted hair, wind key in back makes body and head move. Marked: "IDEAL TOY CORP.//OTT 14" on head, "U.S.Pat.#3029552" on body.

Tickletoes, 1928-1939, 15", 17", 20", 24", composition head, rubber arms, legs, cloth body, squeaker in each leg, flirty sleep eyes, open mouth, two painted teeth. Marked: "IDEAL" in diamond with "U.S. of A." on head.

Tiffany Taylor, 1974-1976, 19", all vinyl, rooted hair, top of head turns to change color, painted eyes, teenage body, high-heeled, also in Black. Marked: "IDEAL" (in oval) //Hollis NY 11429/2M-5854-01// 1" on back.

Toni, 1949-1953, 14", 16", 19", 21", 22 ½", Walkers 1954-1956, 14 ½", 16 ½", 19 ½", 21 ½", all hard plastic, jointed body, Dupont nylon wig, sleep eyes, rosy cheeks, closed mouth, came with Toni wave set and curlers. Marked: "IDEAL DOLL// MADE IN U.S.A." on head, "IDEAL DOLL" and P-series number on body.

Tuesday Taylor, 1976-1977, 11 ½", vinyl, posable body, painted eyes, rooted hair, turn head to change color of hair, clothing tagged "IDEAL Tuesday Taylor".

Uneeda Kid, 1914, 14", 24", composition head, gauntlet arms, legs, bent right arm holds miniature box of Uneeda Biscuits, molded painted hair, sleep or painted eyes, closed mouth, cloth body, black painted molded pants and boots, wears yellow satin fisherman's coat and hat. Marked, "IDEAL" n a diamond on back of head, label on coat, "Uneeda Biscuit, pat'd Dec. 1, 1914 MFD. by IDEAL NOVELTY & TOY CO."

Velvet, 1971-1973, 15", Crissy's younger cousin, vinyl head, body, grow hair, pull-string talker, marked: "©1969//IDEAL TOY CORP.//GH-15-H-157" on head, "©1971//IDEAL TOY CORP.//TV 15//US PAT 3162973//OTHER PATENTS PEND." on back.

1974, 15", non-talker, grow hair, other accessories.

Whoopsie, 1978-1981, 13", 1984-1985, 14", vinyl, rooted hair, watermelon mouth, painted eyes, one piece soft foam filled body, push tummy and braids go up and she makes "whoopsie" sound. Also in Black version. Marked: "22//©IDEAL TOY CORP// HONG KONG//1978//H298".

Wizard of Oz Series, 1984-1985, 9", all-vinyl, six-piece posable bodies, Tin Man, Lion, Scarecrow, Dorothy and Toto.

Wonder Woman, Mera, Queen of Atlantis, Bat Girl, and Super Girl, 1967-1968, 11 ½", all vinyl, posable bodies, rooted hair, painted sideglancing eyes, comic strip character from National Periodical Publishers.

ZuZu Kid, 1916-1917, composition head, molded hair, composition hands, feet, cloth body jointed at hip and shoulders, clown costume, hat, holds small box ZuZu gingersnaps, licensed by National Biscuit Co.

Above: 28" vinyl Ideal "Saucy Walker" rooted blonde Saran hair, blue sleep eyes, closed smiling mouth, original red dress with marked pinafore, marked, head "Ideal Toy Corp.// T28X-60" "© Ideal Toy Crop, 1-28 Pat. Pend." circa 1960-1961, courtesy Cornelia Ford.

Above: 12" vinyl Ideal "Tammy" painted features, side glancing eyes, rooted wig, wearing original black and white sheath dress, boxed, excellent color, circa 1962, $55.00, courtesy Andrea Kavanagh.

JULLIEN

1827-1904, Size 4 - 15", Size 5 - 17", Size 6 - 19", Size 7 - 21", Size 8 - 23", Size 9 - 25", some marked: "Jullien" with size number. Paris, made bisque and composition children, marottes and novelties, open and closed mouth. Joined S.F.B.J.
  📖 **14, 20, 46**

Jumeau
1842-1899, Paris, in 1900 joined S.F.B.J. Early bisque dolls have pressed head, after 1886, heads were poured, metal coil spring used 1881+ for attaching head, various sizes
  📖 **14, 46, 74, 76**
Molds: 203, 208, 221, 230, 306, 1907
Poupee, Fashion-type, with slim waist, 1850s-80s, 11"- 27", mostly pressed bisque, black, green or blue body stamp, "JUMEAU Medaille d'Or", some E.J. marks 1885-1886. Red, brown or black checks on back of head, circa 1883+. Paperweight eyes, after 1879. Bodies pre-1860 were hand sewn.
Bébé Incassable (Premier evolved from poupee) 1876-77, 16-18", size marks, standard face, pressed bisque, socket head, closed mouth, pierced ears
Bébé Jumeau Portrait 1877-78, evolved from deluxe poupee, size marks only, pressed bisque, socket head, closed mouth, pierced ears
Bébé Jumeau Triste, 1879-1886, marked with number only 9 to16, long face, pressed bisque, pierced applied ears, closed mouth, pointy nose, dimple in chin, eyelid shelf covers 1/8th of eye, paperwieght eyes, straight wrists marked Jumeau body
E. J. A. Bébé, 1879-1882+ in two sizes, 10 or 12, pressed bisque, marked "E.J. A." or "A" or only "10" or "12", closed mouth, long face, full cheeks, narrow almond shape eye, applied ears, dimple in chin, high forehead, paperweight eyes, mohair wig, cork pate, head attached with wooden button, body has eight wooden balls, fat limbs, oversized hands, separate fingers, defined toes.
E. J. Bébé, 1881-86, marked with size number over initials E.J., sizes 1-16, pressed bisque socket head, paperweight eyes, pierced ears, closed mouth, straight wrists.

JUMEAU

Above: rare early mark from Incassable or Premier.

E J
A
10

E.J. Bébé , mid era, size number (1-16) between initials

E.J. Depose Bébé 1885-1886, size number (1 -16) between initials preceded by DEPOSE, may also have artist check marks, pressed bisque, paperweight eyes, closed mouth, pierced ears

Depose Jumeau, 1886-1889, marked "Depose// Jumeau" and size number (1-20), may have artist check marks, poured bisque, pierced ears, closed mouth, paperweight eyes, mohair wig, straight wrist body may be marked "Medaille d'Or Paris"

Tete Jumeau, 1885-1898, poured bisque head, red stamp on head, stamp or sticker on body, wigged, paperweight or sleep eyes, eyeshadow, pierced ears, closed or open mouth with teeth, mohair or human hair wig, jointed composition body with straight wrists or wooden limbs.

1892-1899, Tete face, may be marked E.D.

Paris Bébé, (like mold 223) closed mouth, paperweight eyes, pierced ears, marked in red "PARIS-BÉBE//TÉTE DEPOSÉE" with size mark incised.

Bébé Francais, 1891- (like mold 225) long face, pointy chin, small mouth, marked "B.F."

1907 marked Jumeau, circa 1900s, some with Tete stamp, poured bisque sleep or set eyes, open mouth, jointed French body.

Bébé Louvre, 1892, marked B.L.for Louvre department store, Tete socket head, wig, pierced ears, paperweight eyes, closed mouth, jointed composition body.

Bébé Naduad, 1892 made for Jeanne Laumonerie for Nadaud store

D, M, P, R. R. or X marked Bébé , 1892+, commissioner unknown, Tete face, glass eyes, closed mouth, straight wrist composition jointed body.

Bébé Reclame, 1890s, various sizes, overstock like Tete but with removed red stamp, may have untinted white square on back of neck, may only have size number.

Bébé Phonographe, 1893-99, size 11, Tete Bébé with cylinder type mechanism in torso to play tunes.

Characters:

Mold 203, 1890s, sizes 4-13, smiling child
Mold 205, 1890s, sizes 9-13, whistling boy
Mold 206, 1890s, sizes 9-13, frowning child

1881-1886:
EJ   EJ
8   A

8
E J

E. 11 J.

DEPOSE
E. 9 J.

DEPOSE
JUMEAU
8

DEPOSE
E 8 J
1886-1889
Depose Jumeau
1885+Tete:
red stamp on head

PARIS-BÉBE
TÉTE DEPOSÉE
1
12

117

Above: 19" poured bisque Jumeau sockethead, paperweight eyes, pierced ears mohair wig, closed mouth, marked Tete Jumeau Paris on head, marked Jumeau jointed composition body with straight wrists, nicely dressed, circa 1885+, courtesy Elizabeth Surber.

K ✡ R
Germany
1 126-21

Mold 208, 1890s, sizes 9-13, wildly laughing child
Mold 209, 1890s, sizes 9-13, hole in mouth
Mold 210, 1890s, sizes 9-13, fretful child
Mold 211, 1890s, sizes 4-13, wailing child
Mold 213, 1890s, sizes 9-13, smiling child with clenched teeth
Mold 217, 1890s, sizes 9-13, child sticking out tongue
Mold 218, 1890s, sizes 9-12, child with startled expression
Mold 221, 1890s, sizes unknown, adult woman
Mold 223, various sizes, closed mouth, same as Paris Bébé
Mold 225, 1890s, various sizes, oval face, pointed chin, closed small mouth, same as Bébé Francasi.
Princess Elizabeth, circa 1938, various sizes, bisque socket head, high color, closed mouth, flirty eyes, jointed composition body, made after Jumeau joined S.F.B.J. and adopted Unis label, mark will be "71 Unis//France 149//306//Jumeau//1938//Paris"

Kämmer & Reinhardt

1886-1930s, Waltershaausen, Germany, many heads were made by Simon & Halbig for them, made in various sizes, mark may include size in centimeters.
📖 **8, 12, 14, 46**
Molds:
100 series refers to characters
200 series refers to bisque or celluloid shoulderheads
400 series refers to walkers in celluloid and bisque marked S & H and K&R
700 series refers to celluloid
800 series refers to rubber (mid 1920s)
900 series refers to composition circa 1920+
Mold 100, 1909, 12", 15", 20", bisque socket head, once called "Kaiser Baby", character baby, dome head, jointed bent-leg body, intaglio eyes, open/closed mouth. Also Black version.
Note: The following dolls were made in these and various other sizes.
Mold 101, Peter or Marie, 1909, 7-8", 12", 15", 18", 19", bisque socket head, painted eyes, closed mouth. Also Black version.
Mold 102, Elsa or Walter, 1900, 14", bisque

socket head, painted eyes, molded hair, closed mouth, very rare.

Mold 103, 1909, 19", bisque socket head, painted eyes, closed mouth.

Mold 104, 1909, 18", bisque socket head, painted eyes, laughing closed mouth, very rare.

Mold 105, 1909, 21", bisque socket head, painted eyes, open/closed mouth, very rare.

Mold 106, 1909, 22", bisque socket head, painted intaglio eyes to side, closed mouth, very rare.

Mold 107, Carl, 1909, 21", bisque socket head, painted intaglio eyes, closed mouth.

Mold 109, Elise, 1909, 14", 24", painted eyes, closed mouth.

Mold 112, 1909, 13", bisque socket head, painted eyes, open/closed mouth. 10 ½", glass eyes.

Mold 114, Hans or Gretchen, 1909, 9", 13", 18", 24", bisque socket head, painted eyes, closed mouth. Also Black version.

Mold 115, 1911, 15", bisque solid dome socket head, painted hair, sleeping eyes, closed mouth.

Mold 115A, 1911, 12", 19", bisque socket head, sleep eyes, closed mouth, wig, bent leg baby body. 15-16", 18", jointed composition toddler body.

Mold 116, 1911, 17", bisque dome socket head, sleep eyes, open/closed mouth, bent-leg baby body. Also Black version.

Mold 116A, 1911, 15", 16", bisque socket head, sleep eyes, open/closed mouth or open mouth, wigged, bent-leg baby body or toddler body. Also Black version.

Mold 117, Mein Leibling (My Darling), 1911, 15", 18", 23", bisque socket head, glass eyes, closed mouth.

Mold 117A, 1911, 18", 24", 28", flapper body 8", bisque socket head, glass eyes, closed mouth.

Mold 117N, Mein Neuer Liebling, 1916, 17", 20", 28", bisque socket head, flirty eyes, open mouth.

Mold 117X, 1911, 42", bisque socket head, sleep eyes, open mouth.

Mold 118, 118A, 15", 18", bisque socket head, sleep eyes, open mouth, baby body.

Mold 119, 1913, 25", bisque socket head, sleep eyes, open/closed mouth, five piece baby body. Marked "Baby".

Above: 18 1/2" bisque Kammer & Reinhardt mold 115A character toddler, marked "115A// K(star)R" on head, blue sleep eyes, closed mouth, chin dimple, auburn human hair wig, composition toddler body, one piece checked outfit, circa 1911, courtesy Elizabeth Surber.

Above: 23 1/2" bisque Kammer & Reinhardt mold 117N character "My New Darling" (Mein neur Liebling), blue flirty eyes, open mouth, rosy cheeks, red human hair wig, wood and composition body, circa 1916, courtesy Elizabeth Surber.

Above: 18" bisque Kammer & Reinhardt Mold 114, Hans, with painted intaglio eyes, closed mouth, mohair wig, wood and composition jointed body, circa 1909, courtesy McMasters Doll Auctions.

Mold 121, 1912, baby body, 10", 16", 24", toddler body, 14", 18", bisque socket head, sleep eyes, open mouth.

Mold 122, 1912, 11", 16", 20", bisque socket head, sleep eyes, bent-leg baby body. Also Black version.

Mold 123 (Max), Mold 124 (Moritz), 1913, 16", bisque socket heads, flirty sleep eyes, laughing/closed mouth.

Mold 126, Mein Liebling Baby, 1914-1930s, 14", 18", 22", bisque socket head, sleep or flirty eyes, bent-leg baby. Marked: "K*R//126". Also Black version.

Toddler body, 6", 8", 17", 22", 24".

Child body, 22", 32".

Mold 127, 127N, 1914, 14", 18", bisque domed head-like mold 126, bent-leg baby body, some with flirty eyes. Toddler body, 20", 26".

Mold 128, 1914, 10", 13", bisque head, sleep eyes, open mouth, baby body.

Mold 131, 8 ½", 13", 15", bisque head, Googly eyes, closed mouth. Marked: "S&H//K*R".

Mold 171, Klein Mammi (Little Mammy), 1925+, 18", bisque dome socket head, open mouth.

Mold 191, 1900, 17", 30", bisque socket head, open mouth sleep eyes, jointed child's body.

Mold 192, 1900, 9", 18", 22", bisque head, open mouth, sleep eyes, jointed child's body.

Mold 214, 1909, 12", bisque shoulder head, painted eyes, closed mouth, similar to mold 114, muslin body.

Mold 402, 402, 403, 12", 19", 25", bisque socket head, glass eyes, lashes, open mouth. Marked: "K*R". 14", closed mouth, flapper body.

Louise R. Kampes

Circa 1920s, Atlantic City, NJ, made cloth dolls

📖 **2, 13, 14, 29, 46**

Kamkins, 1920s, 19", all cloth, molded mask face, painted eyes, swivel head, jointed shoulders, hips, mohair wig.

KAMKINS
A DOLLY MADE TO LOVE
PATENTED BY L.R.KAMPES
ATLANTIC CITY, N.J.

Kenner

Circa 1970s-80s, at one time was a subsidiary of General Mills, made cloth, plastic and vinyl dolls and action figures

📖 **1, 2, 7, 46, 47-51, 61**

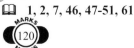

Baby Alive, 1973, 16", vinyl, soft body, rooted hair, painted eyes, open mouth, diaper shirt and disposable diapers, spoon activates mouth to "chew", fills her diaper, battery operated.

Baby Bundles, 1970s, 16" vinyl, also Black

Baby Yawnie, 1974, vinyl, 16" vinyl, sleep eyes, rooted hair, cloth body, squeeze hand, yawns goes to sleep, activated by bellows

Blythe, 1972, 11 1/2" hard plastic with oversize head, pull string changes eye colors, mod clothes, small body marked "Blythe ©//KENNER PRODUCTS// CINCINNATI, OHIO//©1972 GENERAL MILLS// FUN GROUP INC.//PATENT PENDING//MADE IN HONG KONG".

Bob Scout, 1974, 9" all vinyl, molded painted features, replicas of Boy Scouts of America uniforms and Scout comic book, also Black version.

Butch Cassidy, 1979, 4" all vinyl, fully jointed, painted features, clothing as portrayed by Tom Berenger in *Butch and Sundance: The Early Days,* #53010.

Charlie Chaplin, 1973, 14", all cloth, Lithographed features, special walking mechanism lets him perform waddle when walked, as the tramp in *City Lights..*

Crumpet, 1971, 18" vinyl, jointed waist, wrists, battery operated and pull string, comes with plastic table, teapot, cups, saucers, cookie plate, pours tea, holds plate, marked "1970//KENNER//PRODUCTS CO//CINCINNATI, OHIO//PATENT PENDING// MADE IN HONG KONG"on back.

Darci, 1978 Cover Girl, 12 1/2" vinyl, rooted blonde hair, posable elbows, knees, jointed hands, marked "115//HONG KONG//©1978//KENNER:CIN'TI., O/ /#47000:MADE IN HONG KONG". Had lots of fashions for her and friends, red head **Erica**, Black **Dana**.

Dusty, 1975, 11 1/2" vinyl athletic action figure teenage doll, rooted shag hair, painted eyes, open/ closed mouth, dimples, spring loaded arms, body, to hit balls, advertised in 1975 Wards catalog, swivel waist, marked "185//©G.M.F.G.I." on head, "©1974 G.M.F.G.I. KENNER PROD.//CINCINNATI, OHIO 45202//'DUSTY'//MADE IN HONG KONG" on back.

Above: 12 1/2" vinyl Kenner "Darci" with red rooted hair, painted blue eyes, with eyeshadow above eyes, open/closed mouth with white teeth, fashion type body, marked "74//HongKong/ /© GMFGI 1978" wears red striped top/ blue cotton skirt, original pak clothes, circa 1978, courtesy Jaci Jueden.

Gabbigale, 1972, 18" vinyl, blonde rooted hair, open/closed mouth with teeth, pull string, repeats conversation, marked "©1972//KENNER PRODUCTS CO.//16" on head, "GABBIGALE//1972 KENNER PRODUCTS//GENERAL MILLS//FUN GROUP INC.//PATENTS PENDING" on her back.

Garden Gals, 1972, 6 1/2" all vinyl, jointed, rooted hair, painted features, three different faces, different costumes, holds watering can.

Hardy Boys, 12" all vinyl, painted hair and eyes, Shaun Cassidy as Joe and Parker Stevenson as Frank Hardy, from TV show. Head marked "©1978 U.C.S.I." back, "© G.M.F.I.G.I. 1978 KENNER PROD.//CINCINNATI, OHIO 45202//MADE IN HONG KONG."

Indiana Jones, 1981, 12" all vinyl character from *Raiders of the Lost Ark* movie, played by Harrison Ford with hat, jacket, whip and gun.

1982, 4 3/4" all vinyl, molded clothing.

International Velvet, 1976, 11 1/2" vinyl, jointed waist, rooted blonde hair, blue eyes, movie character Sarah Velvet Brown played by Tatum O/Neil, head marked "HONG KONG//©1976 U.C.S.I." back. "© 1978 G.M.F.G.I. KENNER PROD//CINCINNATI, OHIO//45202//MADE IN HONG KONG".

Jenny Jones, 1973, 9" all vinyl, jointed, bendable, rooted hair, painted features, marked: "1973//GM. F.G. INC.//KENNER PRODUCTS DIV.//CINTI,O 45202//MADE IN HONG KONG" with 2 1/2" vinyl drink/wet baby, John.

Madcap Molly, 1971, 12", pink plastic windup doll, with hot pink dress, red hair, has shopping cart, groceries, scooter, skis.

Rose Petal, 1984, 7" vinyl scented

Six Million Dollar Man: T.V. show, with Lee Majors as Steve Austin; Lindsay Wagner as the Bionic Woman.

Bionic Man , 13" vinyl, marked, "©1975 GENERAL MILLS FUN// GROUP, INC. BY ITS DIVISION// KENNER PRODUCTS, CINCINNATI// OHIO 45202 CAT. NO.65000//MADE IN HONG KONG."

Bionic Woman, 1976, 12 1/2" vinyl, marked, "©GENERAL

Above: 13" vinyl Kenner "Jaime Sommers" Bionic Woman, played by Lindsay Wagner in the T.V. show, all original in box, blonde rooted hair, painted features, open mouth with teeth, circa 1976, private collection.

MILLS FUN GROUP INC. 1976 BY ITS DIV. KENNER PRODUCTS// CINCINNATI OHIO 45202//NO. 65900//MADE IN HONG KONG/ CHARACTER © Universal City Studios,/Inc.1974//ALL RIGHTS RESERVED."

Oscar Goldman, 1976, 13" vinyl with exploding suitcase, marked "B" on head and "©1976 G.M.F.G.I. KENNER PROD.//CINCINNATI OHIO 45202//CAT. NO. 65600// MADE IN HONG KONG//CHAR ACTER//©UNIVERSAL CITY STUDIOS, INC. 1973//ALL RIGHTS RESERVED."

Mark on Oscar Goldman, Six Million Dollar Man Figure:

©1977 GENERAL MILLS FUN GROUP INC. BY ITS DIVISION KENNER PRODUCTS CINCINNATI OHIO 456202 CAT. NO. 65100 MADE IN HONG KONG

Star Wars figures, 1974-78, vinyl figures of Ben-Obi-Wan Kenobi, Boba Fett, C-3PO, Peter Mayhew as 15" Chewbacca, David Prowse as 15" Darth Vader, Han Solo, IG-88, Jawa, Carrie Fisher as 11 1/4" Leia Organa, Mark Hamill as 11 3/4" Luke Skywalker, R2-D2, Stormtrooper, all from Star Wars movie.

Mark on 12" Han Solo from Star Wars:
©G.M.F.G.I. 1979
(On head)
©G.M.F.G.I 1978 KENNER PROD. CINCINNATI, OHIO 45212 MADE IN HONG KONG
(On back)

Steve Scout, 1974, 9" all vinyl, molded painted features, replica Boy Scouts of America uniform, and Scout comic book.

Strawberry Shortcake, circa 1980-86+, 5"-18", vinyl, synthetic hair, freckles, painted features, green striped tights, pink and red strawberry outfit , matching bonnet..

Sweet Cookie, 1972, 18" vinyl

Terminator - Arnold Schwartznegger, 1991, 13 1/2" vinyl talker, movie character.

J. D. Kestner

1805-1930, Waltershausen, Germany, made wooden, papier mâché, wax-over-composition, china, and bisque dolls, all dolls with plaster pate reportedly made by Kestner.

📖 1, 2, 8, 12, 14, 21, 46

Molds: XL, 103, 128, 129, 130, 142, 143, 144, 145, 146, 147, 149, 154, 155, 160, 161, 162, 164, 166, 167, 168, 169, 171, 172, 173, 174, 175, 176, 177, 177, 178, 179, 180, 181, 182, 184, 185, 187, 188, 189, 190, 196, 206, 208, 210, 211, 214, 220, 226,

F made in Germany 10 243

234, 235, 237, 239, 241, 243, 245, 247, 249, 255, 257, 260, 262, 263, 1070 made in many various sizes

JDK, 1910+, 14", 17", open mouth, 15", 20", closed mouth, solid dome bisque socket head, sleep eyes, molded painted hair, composition bent-leg baby body. Marked: "JDK" on head.

Daisy, 1911, 18" size only, bisque socket head, sleep eyes, open mouth, four teeth, tongue, composition jointed body, jointed wrists. Marked: "Germany// 171" on head. Only this size of Mold 171 was advertised in Ladies Home Journal as Daisy, a premium doll, obtained by selling subscriptions.

Gibson Girl, Mold 172, 1900, 10", 18", 20", bisque shoulder head, glass eyes, closed mouth, kid body, bisque forearms, rivet joints at elbows, hips and knees.

Wunderkind, 11", 15", set includes doll body with four interchangeable heads, some with extra apparel, one set includes heads with mold numbers 174, 178, 184, and 185.

Kewpie

Ca. 1912, designed by Rose O'Neill, manufactured and distributed by various companies, like George W. Borgfeldt & Co. of New York, Joseph L. Kallus of Cameo Doll Co., Jesco and others. They were made in a very broad range of bisque, celluloid, composition, cloth, hard plastic and vinyl.

    📖 **1, 2, 8, 12, 14, 44, 45,46, 47-51**
Molds: 4843-4883, various sizes from 1"-27"

Kimport Dolls

Circa, 1933-1985, Independence, MO, Arthur E. McKim and Ruby Short McKim who founded McKim Studios and Kimport Doll Company, Imported and sold many ethnic and artist dolls. The broad range of their imported dolls has not been documented.

    📖 **1, 2, 8, 29-35**

All in various sizes
State dolls,
Nationality (Ethnic)
Portrait dolls:
    Abraham Lincoln

Anne Boleyn
Catherine of Aragon
General Chiang Kai-Shek
George Washington
Gremlin
Ichabod Crane
Madame Chiang
Martha Washington
Sequoyah
Uncle Sam

Kley & Hahn

1902-1930, Thüringia, Germany, made bisque, composition and celluloid dolls in various sizes

📖 **8, 12, 14, 46, 65**

Molds: 133, 135, 138, 154, 158, 160, 161, 162, 166, 167, 169, 178, 180, 250, 266, 282, 292, 325, 520, 525, 526, 531, 546, 549, 554, 567, 568, 680 all in various sizes

Mold 680, 1920, bisque head (made by Kestner), character, sleep eyes, open mouth. Marked: "K & CO K&H" with "266 K&H".

Molds 154, 166, 169, 1912, 17", 19", 27", 12", bisque solid dome head (made by Hertel Schwab & Co.), glass eyes, closed mouth.

Mold 162, 1912, 17", bisque head (made by Hertel Schwab & Co.), open mouth, voice cut out.

Mold 180, 1915, 17", bisque head (made by Hertel Schwab & Co.), Googly eyes, open/closed mouth.

Mold 292, 1930, bisque head (made by J.D. Kestner), character face.

Mold 520, 1910, bisque head (made by Bahr & Proschild), painted eyes, closed mouth.

Mold 525, 1912, bisque dome head (made by Bahr & Proschild), sleep eyes, open/closed mouth, lightly molded and brush stroked hair, jointed wood and composition child body. Marked:; "Germany//K&H (in banner)//9//525" on head.

Mold 526, 1912, bisque head (made by Bahr & Proschild), painted eyes, closed mouth.

Mold 531, 1912, 9 ½" (bent-leg baby body), 14", 17", 21" (child), bisque solid dome head (made by Bahr & Proschild), painted eyes, open/closed mouth.

Mold 546, 1912, 16", 18", bisque solid dome head (made by Bahr & Proschild), glass eyes, closed

525
6
Germany
⟩K & H⟨

Above: 27 1/2" bisque Kley & Hahn "Walkure" (mold 282 made by J.D. Kestner, Jr.), marked "Walkure// Germany" on back of head, socket head, brown sleep eyes, open mouth with four upper teeth, pierced ears, human hair wig, jointed wood and composition French Jumeau-type body, circa 1920, courtesy McMasters Doll Auctions.

Germany
Kling mark

Cardboard sewn-on tags, some Klumpes imported by Effanbee have a gold paper heart tag.

mouth, child body. Marked: "K & H (in banner)// 546//8//Germany" on head.

Mold 549, 1912, 16", 18", bisque solid dome head (made by Bahr & Proschild), painted eyes, closed mouth, also in celluloid.

Mold 554, 1912, bisque head (made by Bahr & Proschild), character face, open/closed mouth.

Mold 568, 1912, 21", bisque socket head (made by Bahr & Proschild), sleep eyes, smiling mouth.

Mold 680, 1920, bisque head (made by Kestner), character, sleep eyes, open mouth. Marked: "K & CO K&H" with "266 K&H".

Dollar Princess, Mold 325, 1909, bisque socket head, sleep eyes, painted lashes, molded painted brows, open mouth, four teeth, mohair wig, composition jointed body. Marked: "THE DOLLAR PRINCESS//62//SPECIAL//Made in Germany" on head.

Walkure, Mold 250, 282, 1920, 21", 24", 28", 33", bisque head (made by J.D. Kestner, Jr.), dolly face sleep eyes, open mouth, four teeth, jointed composition body. Marked: "250//K.H.//Walkure//2 ¾".

C.F. Kling & Co.
1830-1930+, Thüringia, Germany, made chinas, bisque dolls and Snow Babies in many different sizes.
    📖 8, 10, 12, 14, 35, 46
Molds: 123, 124, 131, 135, 167, 178, 182, 189, 202, 370, 372, 372, 377

Klumpe
Circa 1950s-70s, 10 ½", 11", cloth, felt over wire armature with painted mask face, tagged. Spain, made felt cloth caricature figures of professionals
    📖 46, 47-51
Doctor
Musician
Smoker
Spanish Dancer and others

Knickerbocker
1927 on, New York City, made cloth, composition, hard plastic and vinyl dolls
    📖 1, 2, 46, 47-51
Daddy Warbucks, 1982, 7", all vinyl, bald head,

painted features, character from Annie movie played by Albert Finney.

Daisy, 1990s, 16" vinyl Black fashion doll with mod-type costumes.

Donald Duck, circa 1930s, 9" composition with felt clothes; 12" all cloth with felt clothing.

Holly Hobby, 1974- cloth, various sizes

Jiminy Cricket, 1939, 10" composition Disney cartoon character, with top hat, orange felt vest, big eyes, molded shoes, hangtag reads "Walt Disney's Pinocchio Jiminy Cricket" with profile drawing of Pinocchio, marked "Jiminy Cricket//Pat Sullivan"

Katzenjammer Kid, circa 1920s

(Little Orphan) Annie, 1982, 6"all vinyl, jointed, rooted red hair, red dress, painted freckles played by Aileen Quinn in Annie movie. Other costumes available.

6" all cloth with tote bag 16", 29" all cloth, red yarn hair, jointed arms, legs, red dress.

Mickey Mouse, circa 1930s, 12" all cloth, mitt glove hands, felt shoes, swivel head.

14", cloth with composition red molded shoes, three fingers stitched together. Also made composition and wood version.

Pinocchio, circa 1939, 10"-14", 17" composition, jointed arms and legs, felt costume. Disney cartoon character. Mark on head, "PINOCCHIO//KNICKERBOCKER TOY CO.//MADE IN USA//WALT DISNEY TOY PRODUCT". Paper hangtag has profile drawing of head and reads "Walt Disney's Pinocchio".

Snow White and Seven Dwarfs, 1937+, 13", 15", 20" composition Snow White, molded blue hair ribbon, marked "©WALT DISNEY//1937//KNICKERBOCKER"; Dwarfs, 1937+, 9" composition, marked, "© WALT DISNEY//KNICKERBOCKER TOY CO. round paper hangtag reads, "WALT DISNEY'S SNOW WHITE and the SEVEN DWARFS"; some all cloth.

Soupy Sales, 1966, 13" vinyl head, cloth body, head marked, "©1966KNICK//JAPAN"

Willow, 1990s, 16" vinyl fashion doll, blonde hair.

Knickerbocker Toy Co.
New York
Used labels and paper hangtags.

Above: 10" composition Knickerbocker Pinocchio and 10" Jiminy Cricket, courtesy McMasters Doll Auctions.

Above: 6" hard plastic brown Knickerbocker Indian girl rattle, floss wig, painted side-glancing eyes, molded painted centerstrap shoes, socks, marked Knickerbocker Plastic Co. on back, ca. 1950s courtesy Elizabeth Surber.

G K
N

Made in Germany
201. 6/0
DEP.

K & W
HARTGUMMI555 0
GERMANY

Gebrüder Knoch

1887-1918, Thüringia, Germany made dolls in various sizes

📖 1, 2, 3, 8, 10, 12, 14, 46, 65

Molds: 179, 181, 190, 192, 193, 201, 203, 204, 205, 206, 216, 223, 230, 232

Mold 203, 1910, 12", 14", bisque shoulder head, character face, painted eyes, closed mouth, stuffed cloth body.

Mold 205, 1910, 12", 14", bisque shoulder head, character face, painted eyes, open/closed mouth, molded tongue, marked "GKN".

Mold 223, 1912, solid dome or shoulder head, character face, painted eyes, molded tears, closed mouth, marked "GKN GES. NO. GESCH".

Mold 179, 181, 190, 192, 193, 201, 1900, 13", 17", bisque socket head, dolly face, glass eyes, open mouth. Mold 201 also came in Black version.

Mold 204, 205, 1910, 15", bisque socket head, character face.

Mold 206, 1910, 11", solid dome socket head, intaglio eyes, open/closed mouth, marked "DRGM".

Mold 216, 1912, 12", solid dome socket head, intaglio eyes, laughing open/closed mouth, marked "GKN".

Mold 230, Mold 232, 1912, 13", 15", bisque shoulder head, molded bonnet, character face, painted eyes, open/closed laughing mouth.

König & Wernicke

1912-1930, Waltershausen, Germany, made bisque, celluloid and hard rubber dolls in various sizes

📖 8, 12, 14, 46

Molds: 98, 99, 1070

Mold 98, Mold 99, 1912, 18", 22", 27", bisque socket head (made by Hertel Schwab & Co.), character face, sleep eyes, open mouth, teeth, tremble tongue, wigged, composition bent-leg baby body. Marked: "made in Germany".

Mold 1070, 1915, 12", 16", 17", 19", bisque socket head, open mouth, bent-leg baby body or toddler body.

Richard Krueger

Circa 1917+, New York made cloth dolls, including Babies, Children, Cuddle Kewpies and Walt Disney characters, like Snow White and Dwarfs and Pinocchio in various sizes,

📖 **1,2, 18, 46**

Käthe Kruse

1910-1980 +, Bavaria, cloth, Magnesit, celluloid and hard plastic dolls.

📖 **1,2,14, 18, 46**

Doll I Series, 1919-29, 17", all cloth, jointed shoulders, wide hips, painted eyes and hair, three vertical seams in back of head, marked on left foot.

    1911, 17"Ball-jointed knees, variant
    1929+, 17" slim hips
Doll I H Series, 1929, wigged
Bambino, 1915-25, 8" all cloth

Doll II Series, "Schlenkerchen" ca. 1922-36, 13", smiling baby, open/closed mouth, stockinette covered body and limbs, one seam head

Doll V, VI, Sandbabies Series, 1920+, 19 5/8", cloth "Traumerchen" (closed eyes) and "Du Mein" (open eyes) , painted hair, some sand weighted, some with belly buttons, one or three seam heads, or cloth covered cardboard.

    1930s, 20"-40", used heavy magnesit
    composition

Doll VII Series, 1927-1930, 14" Du Mein open eye baby, painted hair, or wigged, three seam head, wide hips, sewn on thumbs

    14" smaller Doll I version, wide hips, sewn on thumbs

    1930-52, 14", slimmer hips, thumbs part of hand

Doll VIII, Deutsche Kind, (the Litte German Child) 1929+, 20", cloth hollow swivel head, one seam back of head, wigged, disk jointed legs, later plastic

Doll IX Series, The Little German Child, 1929+, 14", wigged, one seam head, smaller version of Doll VIII.

Doll X Series, 1935+, 14", smaller Doll I swivel head, one seam.

Doll XII Series, 1930s 14", cloth Hampelchen, loose legs, three seams back of head, painted hair, button and band on back to help stand.

16" cloth Hempelschatz, (Doll 1) also known as Doll XIIB

Above: 16" cloth Series I Kathe Kruse boy, painted brown eyes, rosy cheeks, painted brown hair, early wide hips, applied thumb, rub on nose, damage to hand, original clothing, brown jacket and matching boots, knitted cap, circa 1910-1930, courtesy Allan Zimberoff.

XIIH, 18" wigged version of Hempelschatz
XII/I, 1951+, 18" legs have disk joints
U. S. Zone, post WWII, 1946+, 14" cloth, 14"-40" magnesit (composition)
Hard Plastic, 1952-1975, (Celluloid or synthetics, some turtle marked dolls, 1955-1961 with synthetic bodies) 14", 16", 18", glued on wigs, 18", 21", sleep or painted eyes, pink muslin body
1975 on, 14"-16" and others, marked with size in centimeters, B for Baby, H for hair, G for painted hair.

Kuhnlenz, Gebrüder

1884-1930, Bavaria, made bisque dolls, swimmers, movable children in various sizes.
    📖   **12, 14, 29, 32, 46**
Molds 32, 34, 38, 41, 44, 165
Mold 32, 1890, 19", 23", bisque socket head, closed mouth, glass eyes, pierced ears, wig, wood and composition jointed body.
Mold 34, 12 ½", bisque head, Bru type, paperweight eyes, closed mouth, pierced ears, composition jointed body.
Mold 38, bisque solid dome turned shoulder head, closed mouth, pierced ears, kid body.
Mold 41, 16", bisque solid dome socket head, open mouth.
Mold 44, 7", 9", bisque socket head, glass eyes, open mouth, five-piece composition body, molded painted socks and shoes. Marked: Gbr. K in sunburst.
Mold 165, 1900, 22", 33", bisque socket head, dolly face, sleep eyes, open mouth, teeth. Marked: "31// Gbr 165 K//12//Germany" on back of head, "Gernamy//6" on right lower back.

Leopold Lambert

L. B.

1888-1923, Paris, made automatons (mechanical dolls) in various sizes used dolls from different companies.
    📖   **12, 14, 46**

Lanternier

1915-1924, Limoges, France, made bisque dolls
📖 **14, 46**

Lanternier mark

Caprice, 1915, 12 ½" (painted eyes), 17", 22", bisque socket head, open/closed mouth, teeth, composition adult body.

Cherie, 1915, 12 ½" (painted eyes), 17", 22", bisque socket head, open/closed mouth, teeth, composition adult body.

Favorite, 1915, 12 ½" (painted eyes), 17", 22", bisque socket head, open/closed mouth, teeth, composition adult body.

La Georgienne, 1915, 12 ½" (painted eyes), 17", 22", bisque socket head, open/closed mouth, teeth, composition adult body.

Lorraine, 1915, 12 ½" (painted eyes), 17", 22", bisque socket head, open/closed mouth, teeth, composition adult body.

Toto, 1915, 12 ½" (painted eyes), 17", 22", bisque socket head, open/closed mouth, teeth, composition adult body.

Lenci

1918-1980+, Turin, Italy, made felt dolls, some have ink Lenci mark on foot, oil painted swivel heads, many with side glancing eyes, third/fourth fingers sewn together, sewn on double felt ears, may have scalloped socks. 1920s-1930s dolls more elaborate with accessories, eyeshadow, dots in corner of eyes, two-tone lips, lower lip highlighted
📖 **1, 2, 14, 18, 29, 46**

Aladdin, 1920+, 14",
Bach, 1920+, 17",
Bellhop, 11", winking with love letter,
Facist Boy, 1920+, 14", 17", pressed felt head, painted features, all cloth, swivel head, jointed felt body.
Fadette, circa 1923+, 25", smoker, boudoir-type doll with long limbs
Golfer, 1930, 23"
Jack Dempsey, 1920+, 18"
Madame Butterfly, 1926, 17", 25"
Mozart, 1920+, 14",
Pan, 1920+, 8", all cloth, swivel head, painted

Above: Lenci ID clues: mark on foot, fingers stitched together.

Above: Lenci ID clue, scalloped socks.

Rita
3/0

Made in Germany
Armand Marseille
560a
A 4/0 M
D.R.M.R. 232

Made in
Germany Florodora
A 4 M

Armand Marseille
Germany
390.
A 12/0X M.

1894
A.M.
0 D.E. P.
Made in Germany

sideglancing eyes, molded smiling mouth with teeth, hooved feet.

Salome, 1920, 17", brown felt, ball at waist allows doll to swivel, jointed shoulders and hips.

Surprise Eye, 16-21" with glass eyes, "O" shaped mouth

Tom Mix, 1920+, 18"

Limbach, AG.

1772-1927, Thüringia, Germany, made bisque, china, bathing and all-bisque dolls.

   📖   **3, 8, 10, 12, 14, 20, 46, 65**

Molds: 8661, 8682

Mold 8661, 1893-1899, 6", 8", all bisque, molded hair or wigged, painted eyes (some 6" had glass eyes), molded painted shoes and socks, may have mark "8661" and cloverleaf.

Mold 8662, 1893-1899, 8 ½", bisque socket head, glass eyes, bent-leg baby body, wig, open/closed mouth, clover mark.

Norma, after 1919, 17"-19", 23"-24", Marked: "Rita//3/0//(clover leaf and crown mark)//Limbach"

Rita, after 1919, 17"-19", 23"-24", Marked: "Rita//3/0//(clover leaf and crown mark)//Limbach".

Maiden Toy Co.

1915-1919, New York City, made composition dolls

   📖   **3, 8, 10, 12, 14, 46, 65**

The National Doll, 1915-1917, 8", all composition, jointed at arms only, legs molded together, painted sideglancing eyes, painted molded hair pulled off face into topknot, red, white and blue ribbon tied into big bow in back. Unmarked.

Armand Marseille

1885-1930s+, Thüringia, Germany, one of the largest suppliers of bisque doll heads made in many various sizes.

   📖   **3, 8, 12, 14, 46**

Molds:

225, 1920, AM character, sleep eyes, open mouth

230, 1912, AM character, solid dome, sleep eyes, closed mouth

231, 1912, "AM 248 Fany" character sleep eyes, closed mouth

240, 1914, AM character, solid dome, painted googly eyes

242, 244, 246, 1930, character, painted bisque

250, 251, 1912, , character, solid dome, painted eyes, open mouth for Borgfeldt

253, 1925, "AM Nobbikid Reg U. S. Pat. 066 Germany", character, googly eyes, closed mouth

256, 1920, "AM" with and without "Maar" character baby for E. Maar & Sohn

257, 1913, "AM" character, googly, closed mouth

259, 1920, "AM GB" character baby for Geo. Borgfeldt

300, 1925, "AM/HH" flapper, glass eyes, closed mouth

310, 1929, "AM Just Me" character, googly eyes, closed mouth for Geo. Borgfeldt.

326, 1913, "AM 259" character, solid dome, glass eyes, open mouth

327, 328, 329, character baby for Borgfeldt

333, 1925, solid dome character, Black or Oriental

340, 341, 1926, "My Dream Baby" infant, solid dome flange neck; **341,** socket head

345, 1926, Kiddiejoy, character

350, 1926, character, sleep eyes, closed mouth

351, 1926, infant "My Dream Baby"

352, 1926, infant, solid dome, sleep eyes, open mouth

353, 1926, Oriental infant, sleep eyes, closed mouth

360, 1913, "AM 252" character, sleep eyes, open mouth

370, 1900, shoulderhead, dolly face

371, character infant, solid dome, glass eyes, open mouth for Amberg

372, 1925, Kiddiejoy character shoulderhead, molded hair, painted eyes, open/closed mouth, two upper teeth

390, 1900-38, socket head, dolly face

400, 401, 1926, character, sleep eyes, closed mouth

414, 1925, composition

449, 1930, composition

450, 1938, sleep eyes, closed mouth, composition

451, 1936, sleep eyes, open mouth, Native American

500, 520, 1910, solid dome character, closed mouth

550, 1926, solid dome character, closed mouth

560, 1910, solid dome character, open/closed mouth

570, 1910, character

Above: 11 1/2" bisque Armand Marseille mold 390N "Baby Betty", dolly face, blue sleep eyes, open mouth/four teeth, crude papier mache body, original blue dress/white apron, white stockings, in marked Baby Betty box, circa 1912, courtesy Debbie Hamilton.

Above: 16" bisque Armand Marseille mold 341 "My Dream Baby", glass sleep eyes, closed mouth, flange neck, solid dome, newborn, cloth body, celluloid hands, old baby dress, circa 1926, courtesy Barbara DeBiddle.

Above: 14" bisque Armand Marseille mold 600 character boy, marked "600//A(dot)M// Germany//DRGM" on head, painted eyes, closed mouth, molded painted hair, green sweater, brown pants and hat, circa 1910, , courtesy Elizabeth Surber.

Above: 9" bisque Armand Marseille Mold 310, "Just Me", flirty glass eyes, mohair wig, closed mouth, composition body, courtesy McMasters Doll Auctions.

590, 1926, character, open/closed mouth
600, 1910, character, shoulderhead, closed mouth
620, 1910, character
630, 1910, solid dome character shoulderhead, painted eyes, open/closed mouth
700, 1910, character, sleep eyes, closed mouth
701, 1920, character, closed mouth
710, 1920, Native American
711, 1920, shoulderhead, closed mouth
750, 1913 character
760, 790 , 1920, character
800, 1910, character, open or open/closed mouth
810, 1915, shoulderhead, open/closed mouth
900, 1920, character
927, 951, 1920, character baby
970, 1922, character
971, 1913, character, open mouth, sleep eyes
972, 973, 1926, character for Amberg
975, 1922, character baby for Otto Gans
980, 985, 1920, character baby, open mouth
990, 1925, character baby, also Black
991, 1930, character, open mouth, sleep eyes
995, 1930, character, Black and painted bisque
1890, 1890, shoulderhead, dolly face
1892, 1892, shoulderhead, dolly face
1893, 1892, shoulderhead dolly face for Dressel
1894, 1894, shoulder or socket head, dolly face
1897, 1897, shoulder or socket head, dolly face
1898, 1898, shoulderhead dolly face for Dressel
1899, 1899, shoulderhead, dolly face
1900, 1900, dolly face
1901, 1901, shoulderhead, dolly face
1902, 1902, shoulderhead, dolly face
1903, 1903, shoulderhead, dolly face
1909, 1909, shoulderhead, dolly face
3200, 1896, shoulderhead, dolly face
Alma, 1900, shoulderhead for Geo.Borgfeldt
Baby Betty, 1912, character for Butler Brothers
Baby Gloria, 1910, character
Baby Phyllis, 1925, baby for Baby Phyllis Doll Co.
Beauty, 1898, shoulderhead for W.A. Cissna & Co.
Columbia, shoulderhead for C.M. Bergman and Louis Wolf & Co.
Duchess, for Geo. Borgfeldt
Ellar

Fany, 1912, character head
Florodora, 1903-1925, shoulder and socket head for Geo. Borgfeldt
Just Me, 1929, googly for Geo. Borgfeldt
Kiddiejoy, 1920, character shoulderhead for Hitz, Jacobs & Cassler.
Lilly, shoulderhead
Mabel, shoulderhead
Majestic, 1902, shoulderhead for E. U. Steiner
My Dream Baby, 1925, baby for Arranbee
My Playmate, for Geo. Borgfeldt
Nobbi Kid, for George Borgfeldt
Our Pet, baby for Gebr. Eckardt
Princess, shoulderhead
Queen Louise, sockethead for Louis Wolf & Co.
Rosebud, socket and shoulderhead for B. Illfelder & Co.

Louis Marx & Co.

Circa 1921- 1980, New York City, London, made mechanical metal toys, later hard plastic and vinyl dolls and toys.

📖 **1, 2, 24, 36, 46, 47-51, 61**

Archie comic strip characters, 1975, 9" vinyl head, Archie, Jughead, Betty, and Veronica comic characters, Jughead and Archie have molded hair, Betty and Veronica are wigged, painted features.

Freddy Krueger, 1989, 18", vinyl, pull string talker, from the horror movie *Nightmare on Elm Street* character played by Robert England.

Gepetto, 1950s, 6", vinyl head, painted eyes, molded painted glasses, molded painted hair and mustache, large hands, rigid plastic body, green pants, black suspenders, maroon vest, big feet with brown shoes. Marked "Made in Hong Kong//Walt Disney Productions".

Johnny West Action Figures, 1965-1975, 11 ½" Johnny West, Jane West, Sam Cobra, Princess Wildflower, Bill Buck, Captain Tom Maddox, Chief Cherokee, Daniel Boone, Fighting Eagle, General Custer, Geronimo, Jeb Gibson, Sheriff Pat Garrett, Zeb Zachary, 9" Jay West, Jamie West, Janice West, Josie West, rigid vinyl, articulated figures, accessories, removable clothing.

Knights, 1960s, 11 ½", rigid vinyl articulated

figures, Gordon the Gold Knight, Sir Stuart the Silver Knight, molded clothing, hair, beard and mustache.

Miss Marlene, 1960s, 7", hard plastic, Barbie-type, blonde rooted wig, high heeled.

Miss Seventeen, 1962, 15", molded painted hair, painted eyes, closed mouth, fully jointed hard plastic body. Marked: "MADE IN HONG KONG//© 1961// LOUIS MARX & CO. INC.".

Miss Toddler, 21", rigid vinyl, molded painted hair, dress, blue decal eyes, battery operated walker. Marked: "LOUIS MARX AND CO. INC.// MCMLXV//Patent Pending".

PeeWee Herman, 1987, 18", 26", vinyl head, cloth body, ventriloquist doll in gray suit, red bow tie. 18" PeeWee Herman is a pull string talker.

Sindy, 1970s, 11", vinyl, fashion-type doll, rooted hair, painted eyes, wires in limbs allow her to pose.

Soldier, 1960s, 11 ½", rigid vinyl articulated action figures with accessories, Buddy Charlie, molded on military uniform, Stony "Stonewall" Smith, molded on Army fatigues.

Viking Series, 1967, 11 ½", Brave Erik, Odin, vinyl articulated action figures, molded blond hair, molded clothing.

Mattel

Circa 1948, Hawthorne, CA, made hard plastic and vinyl dolls

 📖 **1, 2, 4, 7, 9, 17, 18, 24, 29, 36, 37, 38, 42, 46, 47-51, 61, 72**

Celebrity Dolls:

Cheryl Ladd, 1978, 11 ½", all vinyl, fully jointed, rooted blond hair, painted eyes. She played Kris Monroe on TV show *Charlie's Angels.* Marked: "©MATTEL INC.//1966//15 KOREA" on back.

Debbie Boone, 1978, 11 ½", all vinyl, fully jointed, twist waist, rooted hair, painted eyes, famous for singing "You Light Up My Life". Marked: "©RESI, INC. 1978//TAIWAN" on head, "©MATTEL, INC. 1966//TAIWAN" on back.

Donnie & Marie Osmond, 1976, 11 ¾", all vinyl, fully jointed, painted features, Donnie has painted hair, Marie has rooted hair, smiling open/closed mouth, microphones attached to hands. Marked:

"1088-0500 4//©MATTEL//INC.//1968//HONG KONG" on back.

1976, 30", Marie, all vinyl, fully jointed, rooted hair, painted eyes, smiling mouth, a "Modeling Doll". Marked: "©OSBRO PROD.//1976..U.S.A." on neck.

Jimmy Osmond, 1978, 10", all vinyl, fully, jointed, painted hair and eyes, freckles, open smiling mouth, microphone. Marked: "2200-2109 2//©MATTEL INC.//1969//TAIWAN" on back.

Grizzly Adams, 1978, 9 ½", all vinyl, fully jointed, painted hair, beard and eyes, as portrayed by Dan Haggerty in TV series *The Life and Times of Grizzly Adams.* Marked: "©1971 MATTEL, INC.//HONG KONG US &//FOREIGN PATENTED" on back.

Julia (Diahann Carroll), 1969, 12", all vinyl, fully jointed, rooted hair, painted eyes, some with pull string talker, from TV show *Julia.* Marked: "©1966//MATTEL INC.//U.S. PATENTED//U.S. PAT. PEND.//MADE IN//JAPAN" on hip.

Kate Jackson, 1978, 11 ½", all vinyl, fully jointed, rooted hair, painted eyes. She played Sabrina Duncan on TV's *Charlie's Angels.*

Mork & Mindy, 1979, 4", 9", all vinyl, fully jointed, from TV's *Mork and Mindy* series. Marked: "©1979 PPC TAIWAN" on head.

Twiggy, 1967-1968, 10 ¾", vinyl head, arms and legs, hard plastic body, fully jointed, twist waist, painted eyes, rooted hair, long lashes. Marked: "©1966//MATTEL, INC.//U.S.PATENTED//U.S. PAT. PEND.//MADE IN//JAPAN" on hip.

Welcome Back Kotter Series – 1976, all vinyl, fully jointed, painted hair and eyes,

> **Barbarino,** 1976, 9", Vinnie Barbarino as portrayed by John Travolta.
>
> **Epstein,** 1976, 9 ¼", Juan Epstein as portrayed by Robert Hegyes.
>
> **Horshack,** 1976, 9 ¼", Arnold Horshack as portrayed by Ron Palillo.
>
> **Mr. Kotter,** 1976, 9 ¼", as portrayed by Gabe Kaplan.
>
> **Washington,** 1976, 9 ¼", Freddie "Boom-Boom" Washington as portrayed by

Above: 10 1/2" vinyl Mattel Talking "Buffy & Mrs. Beasley", as portrayed by Anissa Jones from TV sitcom "Family Affair", painted blue eyes, rooted blonde hair, pull string in plastic torso, vinyl arms and legs, ca. 1969, courtesy McMasters Doll

Above: 24" vinyl Mattel "Charmin' Chatty" hard vinyl body, long rooted hair, five records placed in left side slot play, "Charmin' Chatty//© 1961 Mattel Inc.// Hawthorne, Calif. USA// U.S. Pat.//Pat'd. In Canada//Other U.S. and Foreign//Patents Pending" circa 1963-64, courtesy Connie Lara.

Above: 18" vinyl Mattel Dancerella, ca. 1972, marked "U.S.A. // ©1972 MATTEL, INC."on head, "©MATTEL, INC 1968 1978//U.S.A." on back, courtesy Angie Gonzales.

Above: 2" vinyl Mattel "Funny Bunny Kiddle", #3523, orange hair under blue bunny suit, blue painted side-glancing eyes, in package, circa 1967, courtesy Adrienne Hagey.

Lawrence-Hilton Jacobs.

Talking and Other Dolls:

Baby Cheryl, 1965-1966, 16", vinyl, rooted hair, sleep eyes, says nursery rhymes in baby talk, lace trimmed print dress.

Baby Colleen, 1965, vinyl, talking Drowsy-type, carrot-red hair, flannel nightgown, says 11 bedtime things.

Baby First Step, 1965-1967, 18", vinyl, rooted hair, sleep eyes, hard plastic body, pink dress, white plastic baby shoes, battery operated walking doll. Marked: "©1964 MATTEL, INC.//HAWTHORNE, CALIFORNIA//MADE IN U.S.A.//U.S. PATENTS PENDING".

1968-1970, 19", new doll, restyled hair, red and gold bodice, gold skirt.

Baby Fun, 1969-1970, 8", vinyl, rooted hair, painted eyes, blows up balloons, bubbles, toots horn when squeezed.

Baby's Hungry, 1967-1968, 17", vinyl, battery operated, eyes move and lips chew when magic bottle or spoon is put to mouth, wets, plastic bib.

Baby Pattaburp, 1964-1966, 16", vinyl, drinks milk, burps when patted, pink jacket, lace trim.

Baby Say 'n See, 1967-1968, 17", vinyl, eyes and lips move when talking, rooted hair.

Baby Secret, 1966-1967, 17", vinyl face and hands, name on bib, blue eyes, rooted hair, stuffed body, whispers 11 phrases, moves lips.

Baby Sing Along, 1969-1970, 16 ½", vinyl, sings first line of ten songs.

Baby Walk n' See, 1967, 18", vinyl, battery operated, doll walks, moves eyes, skates.

Baby Whisper, 1968-1969, 17 ½", striped blouse with Bermuda shorts, whispers 11 phrases.

Beany and Cecil, 1962-1963, 15" (non-talking Beany), 17 1/2" Beany, vinyl head and hands, molded painted hair, painted eyes, open/closed smiling mouth, cloth stuffed clothes for body, talking ring, from *Beanie and Cecil* cartoon, marked "MATTEL INC. TOYMAKERS" on shoe; 14 ½" (non-talking Cecil), 18" Cecil the Seasick Sea Serpent, plush body, 22" slim Cecil, twistable plush body.

Bouncy Baby, 1969-1970, 11", vinyl, rooted hair with topknot curl, blue eyes, jiggles when picked up; also Black version.

Bozo the Clown, 1964-1973, 18", cloth TV character.

Buffy, 1967, 1974, 6 ½", vinyl, rooted hair, painted features, holds small Mrs. Beasley, vinyl head on cloth body, characters from TV sitcom, *Family Affair.*
Talking Buffy, vinyl, 1969-1971, holds tiny 6" rag Mrs. Beasley.

Bugs Bunny, 1962-1974, 26 ½", molded face, plush body, talking doll.
      1962-1963, 19", plush, non-talking.

Captain Kangaroo, 1967, 19", talking character, host for TV kids program.

Casper, the Friendly Ghost, 1964, 16", talking doll, says 11 phrases, terrycloth body.
      1971, 5", talking Casper the Friendly Ghost.

Charmin' Chatty, 1963-1964, 25", vinyl, rooted Saran hair, sideglancing sleep eyes, closed mouth, glasses, five records fit in slot in side of doll, pull ring for voice. Marked: "CHARMIN' CHATTY//©1961 MATTEL INC.//HAWTHORNE, CALIF. USA//U.S. PAT.//PAT'D. IN CANADA//OTHER U.S. AND FOREIGN//PATENTS PENDING.

Chatty Baby, 1962-1964, 18", red pinafore over rompers.

Chatty Cathy, 1960-1963, 20", vinyl head, hard plastic body, pull string activates voice,
      1963-1965, says 18 new phrases.
Marked: "Chatty Cathy™//Patents Pending//©MCMLX//By Mattel, Inc.//Hawthorne, Calif." on back.

Above: 9" all-vinyl Mattel "Mork" from the planet Ork, portrayed by Robin Williams from the TV series "Mork and Mindy", marked "© 1979 PPC TAIWAN", painted hair and features, fully jointed, space pack has talking mechanism that says eight phrases, mint in package; package with damage, circa 1979, courtesy Betty Strong.

Above: 23" vinyl Mattel "Scooba Doo" rooted blonde hair, heavy eyeshadow, closed mouth, pale lips, cloth body with pull string talker, says 11 phrases, gold necklace, advertised in 1964 Sears catalog, , courtesy Oleta Woodside.

Above: 16" cloth Mattel "Shrinkin' Violette", long thick yellow yarn hair, pull-string-talker mouth moves, eyelids flutter, says 11 phrases, marked "Copyright 1963 by The Funny Company", ca. 1964, courtesy Sue Amidon.

Cheerful – Tearful, 1966-1967, vinyl, blond hair, face changes from smile to pout as arm is lowered, feed her bottle, wets and cries real tears.

Cinderella, 1969-1970, 10 ½", vinyl, hard plastic body, Storybook talking doll, says eight phrases, infant voice.

Dancerina, 1969-1971, 24", battery operated, posable arms, legs, turns, dances with crown on head, pink ballet outfit.

1972, 18", Dancerella, turn-knob on head, white ballet outfit, battery operated crown, dances like Dancerina.

Dee-Dee, 1965-1966, 15", doll comes with costumes to make, Mattel's "cut 'n button" method.

Dr. Doolittle, 1968, 24", vinyl, character patterned after Rex Harrison in movie version, talker, cloth body. All vinyl 6" version.

Drowsy, 1965-1974, 15 ½", vinyl head, stuffed body, sleepers, pull-string talker.

Goldilocks, 1969-1970, 10 ½", vinyl, hard plastic body, Storybook talking doll, says eight phrases, infant voice.

Little Bo Peep, 1969-1970, 10 ½", vinyl, hard plastic body, Storybook talking doll, says eight phrases, infant voice.

Little Kiddles, 1966+, 2", 2 ¾", 3", 3 ½", 4", vinyl over wire frame, posable, painted features, rooted hair, bright costumes and accessories. Marked: "1965//Mattel Inc.// Japan" on back.

Little Sister Look 'n Say, 1967, 17" vinyl, cloth body, rolls eyes, moves lips.

Matty Mattel, 1961-1963, 17", vinyl head, cloth stuffed body, yarn wig, TV character, says 11 phrases, pull string talker. Marked: "©Mattel, Inc.//Hawthorne//Calif." on head.

Mr. Potts, talking Dick Van Dyke rag doll based on movie character in *Chitty, Chitty, Bang, Bang.*

Mrs. Beasley, 1967-1974, 22", vinyl head, cloth body, square glasses, blue polka-dot dress, pull-string talker. 1973, 15 ½" non-talker.

Patootie, 1966-1967, 16", vinyl clown with happy face and sad-faced mask, talker.

Porky Pig, 1965-1967, 17", cloth, talking cartoon character.

Randi Reader, 1968, 1970, 20", vinyl, battery operated, recites 15 nursery rhymes, holds 15 different conversations, eyes move from side to side, comes with nursery rhyme book.

Scooba-Doo, 1964, 23", vinyl head, rooted hair, cloth body, talks in Beatnik phrases.

Shrinkin' Violette, 1964-1965, 16", cloth, yarn hair, pull-string talker, eyes close, eyelids flutter, mouth moves, long thick yellow yarn hair, says 11 phrases. Marked: "Copyright 1963 by The Funny Company".

Sister Belle, 1961-1963, 16", vinyl, pull string talker, cloth body.

Snow White, 1970, 10 ½", vinyl, hard plastic body, Storybook talking doll, says eight phrases, infant voice.

Tatters, 1965-1967, 19", cloth, wears rag clothes, talker.

Teachy Keen, 1966-1970, 16", vinyl head, cloth body, ponytail, talker, tells child to use accessories included, buttons, zippers, comb.

Tippee-Toes, 1968-1970, battery operated, legs move, rides accessory horse, tricycle, knit sweater, pants.

Woody Woodpecker, 1965, 1971, 18", corduroy body, cartoon character, talker.

Above: 16" vinyl Mattel Talking "Sister Belle", cloth body, yarn hair, TV character, pull string talker, says 11 different phrases, #0730, circa 1961-1963, courtesy Marie Emmerson.

Mego

Circa 1970s-1983, made vinyl action
    figures and celebrity dolls.
    📖   **2, 7, 14, 24, 46, 47-51, 61**

Action Jackson

Batman, 1973, 7 ¾", all vinyl, fully jointed, who resembles Adam West who played Batman, but the production did not coincide with the TV series. It is actually a comic character doll.

Captain Daryl Dragon and Tennille, 1977, 12 ½",

Kiss doll marks, head:
©1978 AUCON
Back marked:
MGMT. INC.
© MEGO CORP.
1977
MADE IN HONG
KONG

Above: 12 1/4" all-vinyl Mego "Cher", rooted eyelashes, pink lips, long black rooted hair, fully jointed poseable body, wearing long pink nylon dress, pink shoes, in orange box, NRFB, circa 1976, courtesy McMasters Doll Auctions.

all vinyl, fully jointed, twist waist, rooted hair, painted hair on Captain, painted eyes, long lashes. Marked: "©MOONLIGHT 7//MAGNOLIAS INC." on head. No marks on Captain Daryl Dragon.

Cher, 1976, 12 ¼", all vinyl, fully jointed, waist and wrists jointed, rooted hair, painted eyes, long lashes. Also growing hair Cher. Marked: "MEGO CORP// 19©75" on head.

1981, 12", vinyl head, five-piece hard plastic body, rooted long hair. Marked: "3906//AF// MEGO CORP//19©76" on head.

ChiPs, 1981, 3 ¾", 8", all vinyl, fully jointed, painted hair, Ponch from *ChiPs* as portrayed by Erik Estrada, Sarge as portrayed by Robert Pine, and Jon as portrayed by Larry Wilcox.

Diana Ross, 1977, 12 ¼", all vinyl, fully jointed, rooted black hair, painted eyes, long lashes. Marked: "©MOTOWN//RECORD CORPORATION" on head.

Farah Fawcett, 1977, 12 ¼", all vinyl, fully jointed, wrists and waist jointed, rooted blond hair, painted eyes, long lashes.

1981, 12", vinyl head, rooted blonde hair, painted eyes, long lashes, five piece hard plastic body. Marked: "©FARRAH" on head, "HONG KONG" on back.

Flash Gorden Series, 1976, 9 ½", all vinyl, fully jointed, painted hair, eyes. Flash Gordon, Ming the Merciless, Dr. Zarkov, and Dale Arden based on comic strip. Marked: "©KING FEATURES//SYN INC.//1976" on head, "©1976 MEGO CORP.//MADE IN HONG KONG" on back.

Happy Days Series, 1976, 8", all vinyl, fully jointed, painted hair, eyes. Ron Howard as Richie, Anson Williams as Potsie, Henry Winkler as Fonzie and Donny Most as Ralph Malph. Marked: "©1976 PARAMOUNT//PICTURES CORP" on head, "MEGO CORP. 1974//REG U.S. PAT OFF//PAT PENDING//HONG KONG" on back.

Joe Namath, 1970, 12", all vinyl, fully jointed, painted hair and features. Marked: "BROADWAY JOE™//©MEGO CORP. MCMLXX//MADE IN HONG KONG" on back.

KISS, 1978, 12 ½", all vinyl, fully jointed, rooted hair, painted features and makeup, Gene Simmons, Ace (Paul) Frehley, Peter Criscoula and Paul Stanley

from the rock group. Marked: "1978 AUCION//
MGMT. INC." on head, "©MEGO CORP. 1977//
MADE IN HONG KONG" on back.

Kristy McNichol, 1978, 9 ½", all vinyl, rooted hair,
painted eyes, as "Buddy" on *Family.* Marked:
"©MEGO CORP.//MADE IN HONG KONG" on
head.

Laverne and Shirley, 1977, 11 ½", all vinyl, fully
jointed, rooted hair, painted eyes from TV show
Laverne and Shirley portrayed by Cindy Williams as
"Shirley" and Penny Marshall as "Laverne".
Marked: "©PARAMOUNT//PICT. CORP" on head,
"©MEGO OF HONG KONG//1977//MADE IN
HONG KONG" on back.

Our Gang, 1975, 6", all vinyl, fully jointed, painted
hair and features, Alfalfa Switzer, Spanky
McFarland, Buckwheat Thomas, Darla Hood,
Mickey Gubitosi, Porky Lee from *Our Gang.*

Planet of the Apes Series, 1975, 7 ¾", all vinyl,
fully jointed, painted features, Ron Harper as Alan
Verdon, Mark Lenard as Urko, Roddy McDowall as
Galen, James Naughton as Peter Burke. Marked:
"©1974 MEGO CORP." on head.

Star Trek Series, 1979, 3 ¾", 12", Leonard Nimoy
as Mr. Spock, William Shatner as Captain Kirk,
Stephen Collins as Decker, James Doohan as Scotty,
DeForest Kelley as Dr. McCoy (Bones), Persis
Khambatta as Ilia, Mark Lenard as Klingon Captain,
Nichelle Nichols as Lt. Uhura, all vinyl, fully jointed,
painted features. Marked: "©PPCo." On head, "1977/
/MADE IN HONG KONG" on back.

Starsky and Hutch, 1976, 7 ½", all vinyl, fully
jointed, painted features, Paul Michael Glaser as
Starsky, David Soul as Hutch from TV series *Starsky
and Hutch.*

Suzanne Somers, 1978, 12 ¼", all vinyl, fully
jointed, rooted hair, painted eyes, long lashes, as
Chrissy of TV's *Three's Company.* Marked:
"©THREE'S//COMPANY" on head.

Waltons, 1975, 7 ½", all vinyl, fully jointed, Richard
Thomas as John Boy, Judy Norton-Taylor as Mary
Ellen, Michael Learned and Ralph Waite as Mom and
Pop Walton, Ellen Corby and Will Greer as Grandma
and Grandpa Walton. Marked: "©1974//LORIMAR
INC." on head.

Above: 12 1/4" all-vinyl
Mego "Sonny", painted
eyes, molded painted
brown hair and mus-
tache, fully jointed
posable body, wearing
denim jeans, white and
black shirt, black shoes,
in orange box, NRFB,
circa 1976, courtesy
McMasters Doll Auc-
tions.

©Mego Corp.

Wonder Woman, 1976, 12 ½", all vinyl, fully jointed, rooted hair, painted eyes, long lashes, as portrayed by Lynda Carter. Marked: ©D.C. COMICS//INC. 1976" on head.

Molly'es
on several different
hangtags

Molly'es

Circa 1929-1930+, Mollye Goldman of International Doll Co., Philadelphia, PA, dressed dolls, made cloth and composition, hard plastic and vinyl dolls, 13"-27", Also see Raggedy Ann. Identification clue, Molly'es cloth dolls had finer painted eyelashes, painted pouty smaller mouth, machine sewn back body seams, used yarn and mohair wigs on her cloth dolls.

📖 **1, 2, 5, 18, 23, 29, 46, 47-51**

Babies
Children
Ladies
Internationals, 1920s-30s, 13 1/2", 15", 24", 27"
    Illeana the Roumanian Girl, 1938
    Marassa of Russia, 1938
    Margot of Tyrol, 1937-43
    Rosita of Mexico, 1937-43

Montanari Manufacturer
251 Regent St.
and 180 Soho Bazaar

Montanari

Circa 1850s-70s, London, England, made wax dolls, many unmarked, various sizes.
📖 **14, 46**
Babies and Children

Morimura Brothers

1915-26+, Japan, made dolls when German exports were cut off in WWI, various sizes
📖 **14, 46**
Babies and Children

B.M.

Alexandre Mothereau

1880-95, Paris, made bisque dolls in various sizes,
📖 **14, 46**
Bébé Mothereau

Nancy Ann Storybook Dolls, Inc.

1936+ , San Francisco, CA, made painted bisque, hard plastic and vinyl dolls, made many in Series with special theme.

📖 **1, 2, 33, 34, 46, 47-51**

Nancy Ann Storybook, painted bisque

1936 only, Baby, 3 1/2"-4 1/2", mottled or sunburst box, gold foil sticker, marked "Nancy Ann Dressed Dolls" and "87" "88" or "93" and "Made in Japan", no brochure

1937, Baby 3 1/2-4 1/2" or Child 5", Child marked "Made in Japan" "1146", "1148" or "Japan", sunburst box, gold label, gold foil sticker on clothes reads "Nancy Ann Dressed Dolls", no brochure.

1938, Baby 3 1/2-4 1/2" or Child 5", marked "America" (baby marked "87, "88" or "93 "Made in Japan", colored box, sunburst pattern, gold label, gold foil sticker on clothes, "Judy Ann", no brochure.

Marked "Judy Ann USA" and "Story Book USA", baby marked "Made in USA" and "88", "89" or "93" "Made in Japan" colored box, sunburst pattern with gold or silver label, gold foil sticker on clothes reads, "Storybook Dolls," no brochure.

1939, Baby 3 1/2-4 1/2" or Child 5", baby has star shaped hands, child has molded socks and molded bangs, colored box with silver dots, silver label, gold foil sticker on clothes reads, "Storybook Dolls", no brochure.

1940, Baby 3 1/2-4 1/2" or Child 5", baby has star-shaped hands, child has molded socks only, colored box with white polka dots, silver label, gold foil sticker on clothes reads, "Storybook Dolls, has brochure.

1941-42, Baby 3 1/2-4 1/2" or Child 5", baby has star-shaped hands or fist, child has pudgy tummy or slim tummy; white box with colored polka dots, silver label, gold foil bracelet with name of doll and brochure.

1943-47, Baby 3 1/2-4 1/2" or Child 5", baby has fist hands, child has one-piece head, body and legs, white box, colored polka dots, silver label, ribbon tie or pin fastener, gold foil bracelet with name of doll and brochure.

1947-49, Baby 3 1/2-4 1/2" or Child 5", child now has hard plastic body, painted eyes, baby has bisque body,

Made in Japan
Judy Ann
USA
Storybook

USA
StoryBook
Dolls

Above: 5" painted bisque Nancy Ann Storybook "Little Boy Blue" with mohair wig, original costume, gold foil wrist tage, brochure and white box with blue dots, circa 1940s, courtesy Faye Newberry.

plastic arms and legs, white box, colored polka dots, with "Nancy Ann Storybook Dolls" between dots, silver label, brass snap, gold foil bracelet with name of doll and brochure.

1949, Baby 3 1/2-4 1/2" or Child 5", hard plastic, both baby and child have black sleep eyes, white box with colored polka dots and "Nancy Ann Storybook Dolls" between dots, silver label, brass or painted snaps, gold foil bracelet with name of doll and brochure.

Other Dolls

> **Audrey Ann,** 6", marked "Nancy Ann Storybook"
> **Baby Sue Sue,** 1960s, vinyl
> **Debbie,** 10", hard plastic, later vinyl
> **Little Miss Nancy Ann,** 1959, 8 1/2",
> **Lori Ann,** 7 1/2" vinyl
> **Mammy and Baby,** 5" painted bisque
> **Miss Nancy Ann,** 1959+, marked
> **Nancy Ann,** vinyl head, rooted hair, rigid vinyl body, high heel feet
> **Muffie,** 1953, 8", hard plastic, wig, sleep eyes, straight leg, painted lashes
> 1954 hard plastic, walker, molded eyelashes
> 1955-56, vinyl head, molded or painted upper lashes, rooted Saran wig, walker
> 1968, reissued in hard plastic
> **Nancy Ann Style Show,** 18", hard plastic, vinyl
> **Topsy,** 5", painted bisque

Above: 8" hard plastic Nancy Ann Storybook "Muffie", #500B, marked "Storybook Dolls//California//MUFFIE", brunette Saran wig with ponytails, sleep eyes, painted lashes, closed mouth, walker, hard plastic body, with marked Muffie box, circa 1956, courtesy Peggy Millhouse.

Old Cottage Dolls

1948+, England, Mrs. M.E. Fleischmann made composition and hard plastic dolls, stuffed felt bodies, 5"- 10"

Baby, 5"
Child, 8-1/2, 9"
Elizabethan Boy and Girl, 9-10"
London Policeman, 10"
Guardsman, 10"
Pearlie King & Queen, 7-1/2", 9", pearl buttons
Royalty, with molded fingers, 10"

Teahouse of August Moon, 10"
Tweedle Dee and Tweedle Dum, 1968, 10"
Victorian Girl, 9"

Gebrüder Ohlhaver
1913-1930, Sonneberg, Germany, made bisque and
composition dolls in various sizes. Trademark Revalo
is Ohlhaver spelled backwards omitting the two "h"'s

📖 **12, 14**
Babies, Toddlers and Children

REVALO
GERMANY

Parsons Jackson Co.
Circa 1910+, Cleveland, OH, made celluloid collars
and dolls, used stork trademark
📖 **14, 19, 46**
Babies and Children, 12-15"

The Parsons Jackson Co.
Cleveland, Ohio

Peck, Lucy
Circa 1891-1930, London, England, made dolls of
various sizes, 21-28" and repaired wax dolls.
📖 **14**
Babies and Children

Petitcollin
Circa 1914+, made celluloid dolls in various sizes
used profile of eagle for logo.
📖 **14, 19, 46**
Babies and Children

FRANCE

Ronnaug Peterssen
Circa 1901-1980, Norway, 8 1/2"-14 1/2", made
cloth dolls with pressed felt head, painted side-
glancing or glass eyes, intricate costumes, paper tags
📖 **29, 46**

Dora Petzold
Circa 1919-1930, Berlin, Germany, made composition character dolls in various sizes.
📖 **14, 46**

Pierotti
Circa 1770s-1935, England, made wax dolls in
various sizes, babies, children and portraits.
📖 **14**

Most unmarked
Pierotti

Pleasant Company

Circa 1986+, 18" Pleasant Rowland, Middleton, WI, made vinyl historical dolls; company later sold to Mattel., sleep eyes, cloth body

📖 46

Addy, 1864 era
Felicity, 1774 era
Josefina, 1824 era
Kirsten, 1854 era
Kit, 1934 era
Molly, 1944 era
Samantha, 1904 era

P.M

Porzellanfabrik Mengersgereuth

Circa 1908-1930, Mengersgereuth, Germany, made bisque and composition dolls in various sizes, also made dolls for other companies.

📖 **12, 14, 46** .

Molds: 255, 800, 828, 830, 904, 914, 916, 924, 926

R. 3 D.

Early mark:
Patented Sept. 7, 1915

Rabery & Delphieu

1856-1930+, Paris, later part of S.F.B.J. ,made bisque dolls

📖 **14, 46**

Bébés, 11"- 28"

Above: 18" cloth Georgene Novelties Raggedy Ann, redressed, tagged body, wear spot on face, circa 1950s, courtesy Debbie Crume.

Raggedy Ann and Andy

Created in 1915 by Johnny Gruelle, from children's book, cloth, made commercially:

📖 **1, 2, 18, 23, 29, 46, 47-51, 69-71**

P. J. Volland, 1918-1934, 14", 17", 36", hand painted face, crude hands early, cardboard heart inside torso, shoe button eyes, brown wool stringy hair, turned out feet, no elbow or knee joints,

Early 1920s, printed face in early 1920s with six eyelashes, may have stamp on torso

Late 1920s, triangle eyebrows, one eyelash, outlined nose, smile has red center, no patent stamp

1931-1934, four eyelashes, no painted eye white, brown or auburn hair, thick arched eyebrows

Exposition, 1935, 18", no heart, stripes to hip, removable felt shoes, pie cut eyes, no red center in smile, no eyebrows or lashes, magenta tint hair

Mollye Goldman, 1934-1937, 14", 18", 21",

printed red heart, marked on chest "Raggedy Ann and Raggedy Andy Dolls//Manufactured by Molly'es Doll Outfitters" seam jointed elbows, auburn wool wig, smile has red center, long outline nose, defined thumbs, seam jointed knees, multicolored stripes to hips, blue shoes point forward, printed sideglancing eyes

Georgene Novelties, 1938-1962, many sizes, shoe button eyes with red dots, long outline nose, red wool wig, net backed, seam jointed elbows and knees, new I love you printed heart, stripes to hips, four eyelashes, printed eye whites

      1944-46, sewn on cotton red wig, no outline on long nose

      1946-47, (Silsby design) short nose, real shoe button eyes, curved smile, with cheek-lines, label sewn in body seam

      1950s-62, bolder eyebrows, red wig glued on, flat tin eyes, wider nose, broader smile

Knickerbocker, 1963-1982, many sizes, new synthetic wig glue on, domed plastic eyes, eyebrows thicker at one end, bold eye dots, Symmetrical smile, printed heart, says "I Love You", Joy of a Toy label in body seam, white collar has two rows of red stitiching

Applause, 1981-83, , many sizes,

Hasbro (Playskool,) 1983+ also many sizes.

Other Characters

Beloved Belindy

Camel with Wrinkled Knees

Pirate Chieftain and other characters from Gruelle's books about Raggedy Ann.

Above top: 18" cloth P. F. Volland "Pirate Chieftain", button eyes, yarn hair and beard, pink felt coat, black belt, purple short pants, striped legs, gold boots and white felt gloves.

Above: Red lettering on white round paper hangtag on Volland Pirate Chieftain.

No marks reported
on
Raleigh doll

Jessie McCutcheon Raleigh

Circa 1917-1920, Chicago, IL, made composition and cloth dolls; three types of bodies, shoulderhead with composition arms, cloth torso and legs; shoulderhead with cloth body, upper arms and legs, compo lower limbs and an all composition five piece body. Some mohair, human hair, or molded hair, some with character faces.

     📖 14, 44, 46, 41-47

Babies and Children, 11"-24"

     Goldilocks, 1919, 11"

No marks on Ravca doll, some carried hangtags.

Circa 1924-1935 on, Paris and New York, made cloth and composition/papier mâché dolls, sizes 8"-36"

📖 **1, 2, 14, 18, 29, 46, 47-51**

Celebrities

     Benjamin Franklin, 9" cloth

     Abraham Lincoln, , 9" cloth

     George Washington, 8" cloth

     Martha Washington, 8" cloth

     Queen Elizabeth, 36"

Literary characters

     Scarlett O'Hara, 9" cloth

     Rhett Butler, 9" cloth

Military figures

     Mussolini, 9" composition

     Sam Houston, 9", cloth

     Robert E. Lee, 9" cloth

Peasants and old people, 7"- 23"

Recknagel Mark

1886-1930+ Thüringia, Germany, made bisque dolls in various sizes.

📖 **12, 14, 46**

Molds: 22, 28, 44, 1907, 1910, 1909, 1914

Kiddie Pal Dollie

Regal Doll MFG. Co. Inc.

Below: 1929 advertisement in Playthings Magazine for Kiddie Pal Dollies

Circa 1918-1930+, New York City and Trenton, NJ, made composition dolls.

📖 **14, 44**

Kiddie Pal Dolly, circa 1919, 19", 22" composition shoulderhead, arms and legs, cloth body molded painted hair, painted or sleep eyes, open or open/closed mouth.

Maisie, 1931, all composition, Patsy-type, no marks, tin sleep eyes, molded painted blonde hair, closed pouty mouth

Our Lindy, circa 1928, 27", celebrity Charles Lindsberg composition shoulderhead, molded painted hair, painted blue eyes, cloth body, aviator suit, gloves, paper tag reads: "Our Lindy//America's Pride//MFD by Regal Doll Mfg. Co//N.Y.C.// Copyright Reg. 83336"

Reliable Toy Co.

Circa 1920-90s, made composition, cloth, and hard plastic dolls; many were licensed copies or were similar to popular dolls made in the United States.

📖 **2, 19, 30, 33, 44, 46, 47-51, 68**

Air Force, 1943, 18", all composition, jointed body, sleep eyes, lashes, mohair wig, open mouth, teeth. Marked: "RELIABLE//MADE IN CANADA".

Army, 1942, 13", 18", composition head, composition forearms, cloth body, painted eyes, molded hair, closed mouth, khaki uniform and cap with maple leaf and Canada printed on, black fabric boots are part of leg. Marked: "RELIABLE DOLL//MADE IN CANADA" on shoulderplate.

Baby Bubbles, 1929, 18", composition head, arms, cloth body and legs, painted eyes, molded painted hair, open/closed mouth, two painted teeth, unmarked.

1957, 21", vinyl head, one-piece vinyl-flex body, coo voice, sleep eyes, deeply molded curly hair with bangs, closed mouth, unmarked.

Baby Bunting, 1935-1948, 14", composition head, arms, cloth body with softly stuffed bent legs, sleep eyes, molded hair, open mouth, two teeth. Marked: "RELIABLE DOLL//MADE IN CANADA".

Baby Fonda, 1933, 25", composition head, arms and legs, cloth body, tin sleep eyes, lashes, molded hair, open mouth, two teeth, tongue. Marked: "A RELIABLE DOLL//MADE IN CANADA" on head.

Baby Jean, 1947, 1948, 12", 14", all composition, jointed hips and shoulders, one piece head and body, painted eyes, molded painted curls, closed mouth. Marked: "RELIABLE//MADE IN//CANADA" on body.

Baby Lovums, 1942, 1945, 1947-1949, 13", 17", 23", 24", 26", composition head, hands and bent-limb legs, cloth body, sleep eyes, some with eyeshadow, molded painted hair or wigged, closed mouth. Marked: "RELIABLE" on head in 1947, "A//RELIABLE//DOLL" in 1948, "RELIABLE//MADE IN CANADA" in 1949.

1968-1975, 1985, 13", 15", 16", vinyl head, hard plastic jointed body, pierced ears, sleep eyes, rooted hair, open nurser mouth. Vinyl arms and legs in 1986. Marked: "RELIABLE TOY CO. LTD.//

Above: 15" composition Reliable celebrity skater, "Barbara Ann Scott", marked "Reliable//Made in Canada", blue sleep eyes, real lashes, eyeshadow, unusual eyebrows with short dashes, open mouth with teeth, reddish mohair wig, redressed, circa 1948-1953, courtesy Oleta Woodside.

Above: 15" composition Reliable "Bride", marked "Reliable//Made in Canada", blue sleep eyes, real lashes, painted lower lashes, closed mouth, auburn mohair wig, long veil, long white dress trimmed in lace, circa late 1940s, courtesy Taras Antonick.

19©68//MADE IN CANADA" on head in 1968, "Reliable" (in script) on head and body in 1985.

Baby Marilyn, 1936-1948, 14", 15", 20", all composition, jointed body, sleep eyes, molded hair or wigged, closed mouth, open mouth with teeth in 1939, sleep eyes. Marked: "RELIABLE//MADE IN CANADA" on head. Some unmarked.

Baby Skin, 1951, 12", composition head, stuffed latex body with coo voice, plastic sleep eyes, molded hair, closed mouth. Marked "RELIABLE//MADE IN CANADA" on head.

Barbara Ann, 1948-1954, 15", all composition, sleep eyes, lashes, mohair wig, open smiling mouth, teeth, jointed body, modeled after Canadian figure skating champion, Barbara Ann Scott. Marked: "RELIABLE//MADE IN CANADA" on head.

Betsy Wetsy, 1957, 14", all vinyl, jointed body, sleep eyes, lashes, molded painted hair or rooted curly hair, open nurser mouth. Marked: "RELIABLE (in script) //12" on back.

Bonnie Braids, 1950, 14", vinyl head, Magic Skin one-piece body, jointed shoulders, painted eyes, molded hair, two inset Saran braids, open/closed mouth, comic strip daughter of Dick Tracy. Marked: "RELIABLE (in script) //13BVE" on head.

Chubby, 1924, 15", composition head, arms and legs, cloth body, sleep eyes, caracul wig, open mouth, two teeth, unmarked.

1935, 17", marked: "RELIABLE//MADE IN CANADA" on head.

1967, 14" vinyl head, hard plastic jointed body, sleep eyes, rooted hair, open/closed mouth. Marked: "RELIABLE TOY CO. LTD.//19©67// MADE IN CANADA//2654 10 EYE 11" on head.

1984, 21", vinyl head, arms and legs, hard plastic body, open/closed mouth, two teeth. Marked: "RELIABLE//MADE IN CANADA" on head.

Chuckles, 1940, 14", 20", all composition, jointed body, sleep eyes, molded hair, open mouth, two teeth. Marked: "RELIABLE//MADE IN CANADA" on head.

1968, 17" vinyl head, hands, cloth body, legs, painted eyes, rooted hair, open/closed mouth, laughing with two top teeth. Marked: "©1967// RELIABLE//MADE IN CANADA" on head.

Cindy Lou, 1961, 14", vinyl head, arms, hard plastic body, sleep eyes, rooted Saran hair, closed mouth. Marked "RELIABLE" on head.

Cuddlekins, 1940, 19", all composition, jointed body, metal sleep eyes, molded hair, wig, open mouth, two teeth. Marked: "RELIABLE//MADE IN CANADA" on head.

1941, 15", composition head, arms and legs, cloth body, tin sleep eyes, painted molded hair, open mouth, two teeth. Marked: "RELIABLE DOLL//MADE IN CANADA" on shoulderplate.

Davy Crockett, 1956, 12", vinyl, one-piece Magic Skin body, coo voice, plastic inset eyes, molded hair, closed mouth. Marked: "MADE IN TORONTO, CANADA//BY RELIABLE TOY CO. LIMITED//WALT DISNEY'S OFFICIAL DAVY CROCKETT" on tag.

Dream Baby, 1952-1953, 19", 20", vinyl head, arms and legs, cloth body, sleep eyes, rooted Sarah hair, open/closed mouth. Marked "RELIABLE// 4CV28" or "RELIABLE (in script) //MADE IN CANADA//V18" on head.

Dress Me, 1953, 11", all hard plastic, jointed body, sleep eyes, wig, closed mouth. Marked: "RELIABLE//PAT. PEND. 1953" on back.

Drum Major, 1951, 16", composition head, cloth and fur body, arms and legs, painted sideglancing eyes, molded hair, closed mouth. Marked: "RELIABLE DOLL//MADE IN CANADA" on head.

Eskimo, 1939, 14", all composition, jointed body, almond shaped painted eyes, molded painted hair, closed mouth. Marked: "1//RELIABLE//MADE IN CANADA" on head.

Gigi, 1964, 14", vinyl head, hard plastic jointed body, sleep eyes, rooted hair, closed mouth. Marked: "RELIABLE//19©64//MADE IN CANADA" on head.

Ginger, 1967, 15", vinyl head, hard plastic jointed body, sleep eyes, open/closed or watermelon mouth. Marked: "RELIABLE TOY//MADE IN CANADA" or "RELIABLE" (in script) on head.

Glamour Girl, 1956-1959, 15", vinyl head, one-piece vinyl-flex body, sleep eyes, rooted hair, closed mouth. Marked: "RELIABLE" on head.

Gloria, 1940-1948, 18", composition head, arms

Above: 14" all composition Reliable Toy Co. "Her Highness Coronation", marked "Reliable Doll//Made in Canada" on head, blue sleep eyes, eyeshadow, open smiling mouth, four upper teeth, auburn saran wig, five piece body, white gown, gold trim, dark red velvet cape lined with white satin, gold paper crown, red sash reads "Her Highness Coronation Doll", unplayed with in original box, circa 1953, courtesy McMasters Doll Auctions.

Above: 14 1/2" composition Reliable Indian shoulderhead, painted brown eyes, closed mouth, yarn braided wig over molded hair, cloth body/legs, composition arms, felt clothing, circa 1940s, courtesy Oleta Woodside.

and legs, cloth body, tin or sleep eyes, mohair wig, open mouth, teeth. Marked: "A//RELIABLE//DOLL//MADE IN CANADA" on shoulderplate.

1974-1983, 16", vinyl head, hard plastic jointed body, stenciled eyes, rooted hair, closed. Marked: "RELIABLE TOY CO. LTD//MADE IN CANADA" on head.

Grenadier Guard, 1960, 16", vinyl head, hard plastic jointed body, sleep eyes, molded painted hair, closed mouth. Marked: "Reliable (in script) // CANADA" on back.

Hairbow Peggy, 1932-1953, 18", 1950, 16 ½", composition head, arms, cloth body, painted eyes, molded painted hair with hole for ribbon, closed mouth. Marked: "A//RELIABLE//DOLL//MADE IN CANADA" on shoulderplate.

Her Highness Coronation Doll, 1953, 14", all composition, jointed body, sleep eyes, wig, open smiling mouth, six teeth. Marked: A//RELIABLE DOLL" on head.

1953, 11 ½", 15", all hard plastic, marked: "RELIABLE" (in script) on body.

Hiawatha, 1948+, 12", all composition, jointed hips, shoulders, painted eyes, wig in braids, closed mouth. Marked: "RELIABLE//MADE IN CANADA" on back.

1955, 8", all hard plastic, jointed body, sidetracking eyes, molded hair, nurser mouth. Marked: original Reliable label.

Highland Lassie, 1951, 15", all composition, jointed body, sleep eyes, mohair wig, open mouth, teeth. Marked: "A//RELIABLE DOLL//MADE IN CANADA" on head.

Honey, 1953, 16", hard plastic head, cloth body, stuffed latex arms and legs, painted eyes, molded painted hair, closed mouth. Marked: "Reliable" (in script) on head.

Joan, 1940, 20", all composition, jointed body, sleep eyes, molded painted hair, open mouth, teeth, tongue. Marked: "RELIABLE//MADE IN CANADA" on head.

1948, 9 ½", composition, bent-limb baby body, painted eyes.

1955, 19", vinyl head, one-piece latex

stuffed body, sleep eyes, molded hair, open/closed mouth. Marked: "RELIABLE" on head.

Kenny Tok, 1940, 16", 24", composition head, moveable jaw, cloth body, mouth opens when string is pulled, painted teeth, painted sidetracking eyes, molded painted hair. Marked: "MFG. BY//RELIABLE TOY CO//CANADA" on head.

Kissy, 1963, 22", vinyl head, hard plastic jointed body, jointed wrists, sleep eyes, rooted hair, nurser mouth. Marked: "Ideal" on head and body. Original box marked "Reliable, under license from Ideal Toy Corp."

Laddie, 1939-1947, 12", all composition, jointed hips and shoulders, painted eyes, molded painted hair, closed mouth. Marked: "RELIABLE//MADE IN//CANADA" on back.

Little Mister Bad Boy, 1961, 18", vinyl head, hard plastic jointed body, sleep eyes, rooted Saran hair, closed mouth. Marked: "RELIABLE" on head.

Louisa, 1961, 1962, 30", vinyl head, hard plastic jointed body, waist, upper legs, wrist and ankles, sleep eyes, rooted Saran hair, closed mouth. Unmarked.

Maggie Muggins, 1947+, 15", all composition, jointed body, sleep eyes, freckles, mohair wig, open mouth, teeth. Created to represent the little girl from the Canadian TV show *Maggie Muggins*. Marked: "RELIABLE//MADE IN CANADA".

1956, 16", vinyl head, magic skin body, rooted Saran hair. Marked: "RELIABLE" on head.

Margaret Ann, 1955, 1956, 17", 20", vinyl head, one-piece vinyl-flex body, sleep eyes, rooted hair, closed mouth. Marked: "14" on head.

Mary Ann, 1957-1959, 14", 19", 21", 23", 26", vinyl head, one-piece vinyl-flex body, sleep eyes, rooted hair, closed mouth, early dolls were unmarked. Marked: "RELIABLE" on head in 1959.

Mary Had a Little Lamb, 1952, 5 ½", all hard plastic, one-piece body, painted sideglancing eyes, mohair wig, closed mouth. Taffeta and net dress with "Mary had a little Lamb" around the skirt.

Mary Poppins, 1965, 12 ½", vinyl head, arms, hard plastic jointed body, painted sideglancing eyes, rooted hair, closed mouth. Marked: "RELIABLE (in script) //CANADA" on body.

Above: 17" composition Reliable Royal Canadian Mountie, molded/painted hair, painted blue eyes, closed mouth, straw stuffed cloth body/legs, composition arms, marked "Reliable//Made in Canada" original Mountie uniform, replaced hat, circa 1936, courtesy Oleta Woodside.

Above: 8" all-composition Reliable "Nurse", marked "Reliable//Made in//Canada" on back, black painted side-glancing eyes, painted upper lashes, closed mouth, dark blonde mohair wig, jointed shoulders, molded socks and shoes, blue dress with white apron, nurse's hat with red circle with cross, circa 1942, courtesy Betty Strong.

Miss Canada, 1957, 1958, 1960, 10 ½", 18", 20", 25", vinyl head, arms, hard plastic jointed body, pierced ears, sleep eyes, molded lashes, rooted hair, closed mouth. Marked: "P" on head.

Miss Capri, 1962, 22", vinyl head, hard plastic jointed body, swivel waist, freckles, sleep eyes, rooted hair, closed smiling mouth. Marked: "RELIABLE TOY//MADE IN CANADA" on head.

Mitzi, 1961, 12", vinyl head, hard plastic teen body, painted eyes, black line around eye, rooted ponytail with bangs, closed mouth. Marked: "RELIABLE" in script on body.

1974, 18", vinyl head, plastic jointed teen body, sleep eyes, rooted hair, open/closed mouth. Marked: "RELIABLE" on head, "RELIABLE//CANADA" on body.

Mountie, 1936-1953, 17", composition head, arms, cloth body, legs, painted eyes, molded painted hair, closed mouth, on cloth covered horse (in 1936), wooden platform with metal wheels. Marked: "RELIABLE//MADE IN CANADA" on head.

Nell Get Well, 1962, 16", vinyl head, three faces, hard plastic jointed body, painted features, turn knob on head to change faces. Marked: "RELIABLE (in script) //CANADA".

Nurse, 1940-1944, 8", 18", 24", composition shoulderhead, arms, cloth body and legs, (some with composition legs), painted eyes, molded painted hair or wigged, closed mouth, nurse's uniform. Marked: "RELIABLE//MADE IN CANADA" on shoulderplate.

Old Fashioned Girl, 1941, 15 ½", all composition, jointed body, sleep eyes, mohair wig, open mouth, four teeth, long cotton gown, pantalettes, white pinafore, matching bonnet. Marked: "RELIABLE//MADE IN CANADA".

Patsy, 1959, 9", all hard plastic, jointed body, sleep eyes, molded lashes, molded painted hair, closed mouth. Marked: "RELIABLE" (in script) on back.

1962, 11", vinyl head, hard plastic jointed body, sleep eyes, rooted hair, closed mouth. Marked: "RELIABLE//MADE IN CANADA".

Patty, 1953-1960, 14", all hard plastic, jointed body, sleep eyes, mohair wig, closed mouth. Marked:

"RELIABLE" (in script) on back.

1960, 14", vinyl head, hard plastic walker, sleep eyes, rooted hair, closed mouth. Marked: "RELIABLE" on body.

Patty Sue Playmate, 1960, 35", vinyl head, hard plastic jointed body, sleep eyes, rooted Saran hair, closed mouth. Unmarked.

Peggy, 1930+, 1950 with sidetracking eyes, 13", composition shoulderhead, arms, cloth body, painted eyes, molded painted hair, closed mouth. Marked: "A//RELIABLE//DOLL//MADE IN CANADA" on shoulderplate.

Peter Playpal, 1961, 30", vinyl head, hard plastic walker body, sleep eyes, molded painted hair. Marked: "RELIABLE" on head.

Pigtails, 1939-1951, 15", 18", 18 ½", 19", 22", all composition, jointed body, sleep eyes, eyeshadow over eyes, mohair braided wig, open mouth, four teeth. Marked: "RELIABLE//MADE IN CANADA" on head.

Plassikins, 1948, 14", all hard plastic, jointed bent-limb baby body, jointed wrists, sleep eyes, molded painted hair, closed mouth. Marked: "RELIABLE//MADE IN CANADA".

Posie, 1955, 1957, 23", vinyl head, hard plastic jointed body, jointed knees, sleep eyes, rooted Saran hair, closed mouth. Marked: "RELIABLE" on head and body.

Revlon, 1957, 18", vinyl head, hard plastic jointed body, sleep eyes, rooted hair, closed mouth. Marked: "14RA" on head, "918" on body.

Rosalyn, 1958, 1959, 18", vinyl head, hard plastic jointed body, dimples, sleep eyes, rooted Saran hair, open/closed smiling mouth, painted teeth. Marked: "RELIABLE" on head.

1969, 18", closed mouth, no dimples. Marked: "22//Reliable" (in script) on head.

Ruthie, 1949, 17", composition head, cloth body, latex arms and legs, crier, sleep eyes, mohair wig, closed mouth. Marked: "RELIABLE DOLL//MADE IN CANADA" on head.

1956, 14", vinyl head, one-piece stuffed vinyl body. Marked: "RELIABLE" on head.

1965, 18", vinyl head, hard plastic jointed body. Marked: "RELIABLE" on head.

Sailor, 1942, 16", composition shoulderhead, arms, cloth body, painted eyes, molded painted hair, closed mouth, sailor suit. Marked: "RELIABLE// MADE IN CANADA" on shoulderplate.

Sally Ann, 1939+, 18", 20", composition head, arms, legs, cloth body, sleep eyes, mohair wig, open mouth, teeth. Marked: "A RELIABLE DOLL// MADE IN CANADA" on head.

1948, 16", 18", 22", all composition, jointed body, dimples, metal sleep eyes, mohair wig, open smiling mouth, six teeth. Marked: "RELI-ABLE//MADE IN CANADA" on head.

Saucy Walker, 1953, 22", all hard plastic, crier, jointed body, flirty eyes, saran wig, open mouth, two teeth. Marked: "RELIABLE//MADE in CANADA".

1955, 22", 1961, 35", vinyl head, hard plastic jointed body, rooted hair, closed mouth. Marked: "1391//RELIABLE (in script)".

Shirley Temple, 1934+, 13", 18", 19", 25", all composition, jointed body, dimples, sleep eyes, lashes, mohair wig. Marked: "SHIRLEY TEMPLE// Cop. IDEAL//N. & T. Co." on head, some marked: "A//RELIABLE//DOLL//MADE IN CANADA" on head.

Snow White, 1938, 15", composition shoulderhead, cloth body, legs, painted eyes, molded painted hair with molded bow, closed mouth. Marked: "A RELIABLE DOLL//MADE IN CANADA" on head.

Snoozie, 1950, 14", 21", vinyl head, hands and legs, cloth body and arms, painted eyes, painted molded hair, yawning or open/closed mouth. Marked: "RELIABLE" on head.

1953, 11", vinyl head, magic skin body, coo voice, plastic inset eyes, molded painted hair, open/closed yawning mouth. Marked "RELIABLE (in script) //121131" on head.

Star Bright, 1967, 16", vinyl head, hard plastic jointed body, painted eyes with star highlights, rooted hair, closed mouth. Marked: "RELIABLE TOY LTD.//MADE IN CANADA" on head.

Stoopy, 1950, 9", composition head, cloth body, felt hands, open/closed smiling mouth, hand puppet.

Unmarked.

Sunshine Suzie, 1951, 13", cloth head with rubberized face, painted features. Tagged.

1968, 20", all cloth, red and white striped cloth body, printed sidetracking eyes, yarn hair, watermelon mouth, removable apron. Tagged: "RELIABLE TOY CO. LTD."

Susie Stepps, 1949-1983, 15", 17", 20", 21", hard plastic, jointed body, sleep eyes, wig, open mouth, four teeth. Marked: "RELIABLE (in script) //MADE IN CANADA" on body.

1966, 21", vinyl head and arms, hard plastic body, legs, rooted hair, battery operated. Marked: "RELIABLE//MADE IN CANADA".

Tammy, 1964, 12", vinyl head, hard plastic jointed body, painted sidetracking eyes, rooted hair, closed mouth. Marked: "©Ideal Toy Company" on head, "RELIABLE//CANADA" on back.

Tickle Toes, 1953, 11", all hard plastic, jointed body, sleep eyes, wig, closed mouth. Marked: "RELIABLE//pat. Pend. 1953" on back.

Thumbelina, 1963, 20", vinyl head, arms and legs, cloth body, painted eyes, rooted hair, open/closed mouth, key-wind doll. Marked: "IDEAL TOY CORP.//OTT-10" on head.

Toddles, 1940-1943, 14", 20", all composition, jointed body, sleep eyes, mohair wig, open mouth, two teeth. Marked: "RELIABLE//MADE IN CANADA" on head.

Topsy, mid 1930s-48 (with braids), 1950+ (without braids), 17", all Black composition, jointed body, painted sidetracking eyes, molded hair with inset wool braids, open/closed mouth, two painted teeth. Marked: "RELIABLE//Made in Canada" on head.

1957, 14", vinyl head, one piece vinyl-flex body, sleep eyes, rooted Saran hair, closed mouth. Tagged: "TOPSY//RELIABLE//MADE IN CANADA".

1958, 12", all vinyl, jointed body, dimples, black painted eyes, hair molded in braids tied with ribbons, open/closed mouth. Marked: "RELIABLE" on head.

Toni, 1950+, 14", all hard plastic, jointed body, sleep

Above and back view opposite page:
13" composition Reliable Toy Co. "Shirley Temple" from "The Littlest Rebel", marked "SHIRLEY TEMPLE// Cop. Ideal N & T Co." on head, flirty sleep eyes, open mouth with teeth, curly mohair wig, original dress tag reads "A GENUINE// SHIRLEY TEMPLE// DOLL DRESS//RELIABLE TOY CO. LTD// MADE IN CANADA", pin reads "The World's Darling//Genuine Shirley Temple//A Reliable Doll", original cardboard store tag, mint-in-box, circa 1934+, courtesy Rachel Quigley.

eyes, nylon wig, closed mouth. Unmarked.

Touslehead, 1933, 17", composition head, arms and legs, cloth body, sleep eyes, caracul wig, open mouth, two teeth. Marked: "A RELIABLE DOLL//MADE IN CANADA" on head.

Trudy, 1950, 12", all hard plastic, jointed body, sleep eyes, molded hair, open/closed mouth. Marked: "RELIABLE (in script)" on head.

Wetums, 1939, 11", 17", all composition, jointed body, painted eyes, molded painted hair, open nurser mouth. Marked: RELIABLE TOY//MADE IN CANADA" on head.

1961-1964, 20", vinyl head and arms, hard plastic jointed body, sleep eyes, molded painted hair or rooted hair, open mouth nurser. Marked "Reliable (in script) //MADE IN CANADA".

Wriggles, 1962, 19", vinyl head, arms and legs, cloth body, has pull cord in back, wind up mechanism causes head and body to wriggle when string is pulled, sleep eyes, rooted hair, open/closed mouth. Marked: "RELIABLE" on head.

REMCO

Above: 4 1/2" vinyl Beatles, each has name on guitar, circa 1964, courtesy Sarah Munsey.

Above: 5 1/2" vinyl "Heidi" with Pocketbook, circa 1966, courtesy Angie Gonzales.

Remco

Circa. 1960s-70s made vinyl dolls

📖 **6, 46, 47-51**

Adams Family, 1964, characters from T.V. comedy, all vinyl, molded clothing

> **Lurch,** 5 3/4" Ted Cassidy
> **Uncle Fester**, 5", Jackie Coogan
> **Morticia,** 5" Carolyn Jones

Beatles, 1964, vinyl, English rock group, marked "The//Beatles//Inc." name on guitar

> **Paul McCartney,** 4 7/8"
> **Ringo Starr**, 4 1/2"
> **George Harrison**, 4 1/2"
> **John Lennon,** 4 1/2"

Dave Clark Five, 1965, vinyl, rooted hair, one piece body, marked "Dave//Clark//19©64//Remco Inc.", English rock group, included Dave Clark 5", Mike Smith, Lenny Davidson, Rick Huxley and Denis Payton, all 3"

Heidi, the Pocketbook Doll, 1966, vinyl, came in vinyl pocketbook, painted sidetracking eyes, press button, dolls wave, wink, marked "©1964//REMCO

IND. INC." had many accessories
>**Heidi,** 5 1/2", blonde hair, red dress
>**Herby,** 4 1/2", little brother, no button
>**Hildy,** 4 3/4" sister, blonde, no button
>**Jan,** 5 1/2", black hair, Oriental
>**Pip,** 4 3/4", friend, blonde, no button
>**Spunky,** 5 1/2", friend, wears glasses

I Dream of Jeannie, 1966, 6 1/2" all vinyl T.V. sitcom character played by Barbara Eden, marked "©REMCO TOYS INC//MADE IN HONG KONG" wears Genie costume

Lyndon B. Johnson, 1964, 5 34" all vinyl, molded hat, one piece body, clothing, 36th President of U.S.

Laurie Partridge, 1973, 19" vinyl character from T.V. sitcom, The Partridge Family, played by Susan Dey, rooted brown hair, painted eyes, marked "©1973//REMCO IND. INC.//HARRISON J.J.// ITEM NO. 3461"

Littlechap Family, 1963, vinyl, set of four dolls, had available wardrobe and accessories, marked with doll name and "REMCO INDUSTRIES//1963"
>**Dr. John Littlechap,** 14 1/2" father
>**Judy Littlechap,** 12" daughter
>**Libby Littlechap,** 10 1/2" daughter
>**Lisa Littlechap,** 13 1/2" mother

Mimi, 19", vinyl, battery operated recorder, plays "I's Like to Teach the World to Sing" from Coca Cola® commercial, sings in different languages

Monkees, 1975, characters from T.V. comedy, Davy Jones, Mike Nesmith, Peter Tork, Mickey Dolenz 5"

Munsters, 1964, T.V. comedy characters, vinyl
>**Herman Munster,** 6 1/2" Fred Gwynne
>**Lily Munster,** 4 3/4" Yvonne DeCarlo
>**Grandpa Munster,** 4 3/4" Al Lewis

Tippy Tumbles, 1968, 16", vinyl rooted red hair, battery operated, does somersaults.

Rheinische Gummi und Celluloid Fabrik Co.

Circa 1890s+, Bavaria, later known as Schlildkröte, made celluloid dolls also for other companies. Made dolls in wide range of sizes with turtle mark in a diamond.

 14, 19, 46, 47-51

Babies and Children

No marks on Richwood dolls, black silouette on box.

Richwood Toys
Circa 1940s-50s, Annapolis, MD, made hard plastic dolls, no marks, sleep eyes, Saran wig, some with high heeled feet, some hang tags.
📖 **33, 34, 46, 47-51**
Cindy Lou, 14"
Sandra Sue, 8"

RODDY

MADE IN ENGLAND

Roddy
Circa 1934 - 1974, Lancashire, England, made composition, hard plastic and vinyl dolls, became Bluebel in 1965, 5 1/2" - 16"
📖 **1, 33, 41, 46, 47-51**
Babies, 8"
Children , 6", 8"
English Guardsman, 8"
Welsh Girl, 8"

Green stamp on body:

Rohmer
1857-1880, Paris, made China and bisque dolls, cork pates, painted or glass eyes, leather body with green Rohmer stamp.
Children and Fashion types in various sizes.
📖 **14, 46**

Paper tag reads:
ROLDAN

Roldan
Circa 1960s-1970s, made felt over wire armature characters like Doctors, Spanish dancers and Bull fighters; wore sewn-on cardboard tags. Sizes, 9-12"
📖 **1, 29, 46, 47-51**

Stamped in red on body

Gertrude F. Rollinson
Circa 1916-1929, Holyoke, MA, made cloth dolls with molded faces, produced by Utley Co. until 1922, and others.
📖 **14, 28, 46**
Babies and Children in sizes from 14"-28".

Rosebud

MADE IN ENGLAND

Rosebud
Circa 1947+, England, made composition, hard plastic and vinyl dolls. Used rose logo 1960+, Merged with Mattel in 1967, made dolls in large range of sizes 5"-22", babies and children
📖 **1, 33, 41, 46**

Roullet & Decamps

Circa 1865+ Paris, made mechanical dolls as Acrobats, Tambourine players, Magicians and Swimming dolls (Ondine) used bisque heads from a variety of companies in various sizes. Keys may be marked R.D.

📖 **14, 46**

R .D.

Sasha

Ca. 1965-1986+, by Sasha Morganthaler, Switzerland, Germany, England, made cloth and vinyl children and babies.

📖 **1, 41, 46, 47-51**

1940s-74, Switzerland, 20", hand made by Morganthaler, signed on soles of feet, wrist tags or labeled clothing

Gotz, Germany 1964-70, 16", marked "Sasha Serie" in circle on neck, three circle logo on back. Several different boxes. Used wrist tag and/or booklet.

1995+ 16 1/2", marked Sasha Serie on back, also made 12" babies

Frido-Trendon Ltd. 1965-1986, 16" unmarked on body, wore wrist tags, packed with catalogs, produced a 12" sexed baby, 1970-78, as well as a regular baby.

Bruno Schmidt

Circa 1900-1930, Waltershausen, Germany, made bisque, celluloid, composition and wood dolls, in a variety of sizes.

📖 **12, 14, 46**

Molds: 500, 529, 537, 539, 2023, 2033, 2048, 2072, 2094, 2095, 2096, 2097

Franz Schmidt & Co.

1890-1930+, Georgenthal, Germany, made bisque, celluloid, composition, and wood dolls in a broad range of sizes

📖 **12, 14, 46**

Molds: 269, 293, 927, 1071, 1180,1250, 1253, 1259, 1262, 1263, 1266, 1267, 1270, 1271, 1272, 1274, 1293, 1295, 1296, 1297, 1298, 1310

S & C
1310

F.S. & C.
Franz Schmidt Marks

Schmitt & Fils

Circa 1854-1891, Paris, made bisque and wax-over-composition dolls in a broad range of sizes marked crossed swords within a shield.

📖 **12, 14, 46**

Children

Schoenau & Hoffmeister

1901-1953, Bavaria, porcelain factory, made bisque dolls in a variety of sizes. Marked S (PB in a star) H; may also be marked "Porzellanfabrik Burggrub" without star.

📖 **12, 14, 46**

Molds: 169, 170, 914, 1906, 1909, 4000, 4600, 4700, 4900, 5500, 5700, 5800
Hanna, 8" - 22",
Princess Elizabeth, 1932, 16", 22"

Schoenhut & Co.

Circa 1872-1930+, Philadelphia, PA, made spring jointed wooden 14", 16", 19" and 21" and composition dolls, 1911-1930+. Incised on back or may have paper decal label.

📖 **14, 16, 46**

Bye-Lo Baby, ca. 1923+, 13"
Circus Performers, 1902+, 8"
Maggie and Jiggs, ca. 1900s, 8 1/2", 7 1/2"
Max & Moritz, ca. 1910-12, 7 1/2", 14 1/2" comic characters
Miss Dolly, Model 316, 1915-25, 15-21", open mouth, teeth, painted or decal eyes.
Model 317, 1921-28, 15-21", sleep eyes
Nature Limb Baby, Model 107, 1913-26, 11"-13"; Model 108 15", 17"; Model 109, 1921-23, 13", 14"; Model 110W, 1921-23, 15", 17";
Schnickel-Fritz, 1911-12, 15" carved hair, toddler
Teddy Roosevelt, 1910-14, 8"
Tootsie Wootsie, 1911-12, 15" carved hair
Models: 100, 101, 102, 103, 107, 108, 109, 110, 200, 201, 202, 203, 204, 300, 301, 302, 303, 304, 305, 306, 307, 400, 401, 402, 403, 404

Schuetzmeister & Quendt
1889-1930+, Thüringia, Germany, made bathing, bisque and cloth dolls in various sizes.
📖 **12, 14, 46**
Molds: 101, 102, 201, 204, 252, 300, 301, 1376

Germany

Shirley Temple
Composition, 1934-1940s
Licensed by Ideal Novelty & Toy Corp. New York, composition head, jointed body, dimples in cheeks, hazel sleep eyes, open mouth, teeth, blonde mohair wig, tagged costumes, pinback button, many named after her movies, center-snap shoes, 11-27" sizes.
📖 **1, 2, 6, 8, 14, 27, 30, 44, 46-52, 56**
Baby Shirley, 16-25" sizes
"Marama" 14-18", used Shirley mold; Hawaiian character from movie Hurricane.
Shirley at the Organ, special display set with music from record player.
Celluloid, ca.1937, 13", 15"in Dutch costume marked "Shirley Temple" on head.
Japanese composition, 7 1/2" unlicensed with heavily molded curls, stamped "Japan".

Marked on head:
SHIRLEY TEMPLE
IDEAL
NOV. & TOY
Marked on back:
SHIRLEY TEMPLE
or just a size number

Vinyl, 1957+
12" all vinyl, sleep eyes, synthetic rooted wig, tagged costume, plastic script pin reads "Shirley Temple" marked "ST//2" on head.
1958-1961
15", 17", 19" some with flirty eyes, in 1961, Cinderella, Bo Peep, Heidi and Red Riding Hood.
1960   1960, 35-36" with jointed wrists marked "ST-35-38-2"
1972   17" Montgomery Wards reissue, red/white costume.
1973   16" red dot "Stand Up & Cheer" costume.
1982-1983
8", 12" in various costumes.
1984   36" by Hank Garfinkle, marked "Doll Dreams & Love"
1996   Danbury Mint, 16" various costumes
Porcelain, 1987
Danbury Mint, 16", various costumes
1990+   Danbury Mint, 20" designed by Elke Hutchens

Above: 18" composition Ideal Shirley Temple in pink party dress from 1934 "Curly Top" movie, all original with pinback button, courtesy Iva Mae Jones.

**1079
HALBIG
S & H**
Germany

**S & H 1249
DEP**
Germany
SANTA

Germany
SH 13 1010 DEP

MRS. S. S. SMITH

MANUFACTURER OF AND DEALER IN

THE ALABAMA INDESTRUCTIBLE DOLL

ROANOKE, ALA

PATENTED

Sept. 26, 1905

**S. F. B. J.
247
PARIS**

**S. F. B. J.
PARIS
10**

STEIFF
on button

Simon & Halbig

1869-1930+, Germany, porcelain factory made heads for other companies, also bathing dolls, small dolls with wigs in a wide range of sizes.

📖 12, 14, 22, 46

Molds: 150, 151, 153, 530, 540, 550, 570, 600, 719, 720, 729, 739, 740, 749, 758, 759, 769, 852, 886, 905, 919, 929, 939, 940, 949, 950, 969, 979, 1009, 1010, 1019, 1039, 1040, 1049, 1059, 1069, 1070, 1078, 1079, 1080, 1099, 1109, 1148, 1159, 1160, 1246, 1248, 1249, 1250, 1260, 1269, 1279, 1294, 1299, 1303, 1304, 1388, 1428, 1448, 1469, 1478, 1488, 1489, 1498, 1898

Erika, mold 1489 , 1925
Mary Pickford, portrait
Santa, mold 1249 , ca. 1898

Ella Gauntt Smith

1900-1925, Roanoke, Alabama, made all cloth dolls with molded and painted features, wooden stick in head and body to keep erect, shoes painted on feet, some with wigs, Black versions available.

📖 14, 18, 46

Alabama Indestructible Dolls, 8-36"

Société Francaise de Fabrication de Bébés et Jouets (S. F. B. J.)

1899-1950s, Paris, group formed to compete with German manufacturers

📖 14, 46

Molds: 226, 227, 230, 233, 234, 235, 236, 237, 238, 239, 242, 247, 248, 250, 252, 252, 301
Bleuette Molds: 60, 301, 71   10 5/8", 11 5/8" only

Steiff

1877-1930s, Giengen, Germany, made cloth animals and dolls such as adults and children, conductors, firemen, policeman, comics such as Mutt & Jeff and Happy Hooligan in various sizes, marked with paper tags and metal button.

📖 1, 2, 14, 18, 29, 46

Hermann Steiner

1909-1930, Germany, made cloth, bisque, composition and celluloid dolls in various sizes.

📖 **12, 14, 36**

Molds: 128, 133, 134, 223, 240, 242, 245, 246, 247, 395, 401, 1000

Made in Germany Herm Steiner

Made Germany Herm Steiner 18 0

Jules Steiner

1855-1891, Paris, made bisque dolls, used cardboard pate, some open mouth have many tiny teeth.

📖 **14, 43, 46**

Bébé, 9" - 28", including Bébé with series marks: A, C, E, G

Gigoteur (Kicker)

BÉBÉ
"LE PARISIEN"
Medaille d'OrPARIS

J. STEINER
S^{TE} S.G.D.G.
PARIS
FL^{RE} A 11

Swaine & Co.

1910-1927, Thüringia, Germany, made porcelain dolls. Some with the following marks, "Lori", "DI", "DV", "FP", "AP", "BP" or "DIP" in varying sizes.

📖 **12, 14, 46**

Mold: 232, 1912

A
GERMANY
S & C
with green round stamp
Geschutzt Germany
S & CO.

Terri Lee

Circa 1946-1962, Lincoln, NE, and Apple Valley, CA, made composition, hard plastic and vinyl dolls

📖 **1, 2, 11, 46, 47-51**

Benji, 1947-58, 16", painted brown hard plastic
Bonnie Lou, circa 1947, 16" Black hard plastic
Connie Lynn , 1955, 19" hard plastic baby
Gene Autry, 1949-1950, 16" hard plastic
Jerry Lee, 16" hard plastic, caracul wig
Linda Lee, 1950-51, 12" vinyl; 1952-58 10" vinyl baby
Patty Jo, 1947,16" Black hard plastic
Terri Lee, 1946-47, 16" composition
    1947-50, 16" painted hard plastic
    1951-62, 16" hard plastic
Tiny Terri Lee, 1955-58, 10" vinyl

TERRI LEE

A. 10 T.

Betsy McCall
by
Robert Tonner
©1996 Gruner & Jahr USA PUC

Ann Estelle:
©ME INC 1998

Kitty Collier:
© Robert Tonner 1999

Tyler:
ROBERT TONNER
DOLL CO. INC.

UNEEDA

A. Thuillier

1875-1893, Paris, made bisque dolls
📖 **14, 46**
Bébé, 12-29"

Robert Tonner Doll Company

Circa 1996, New York, made vinyl and porcelain dolls.
📖 **46, 47-51, 75**
Ann Estelle, 1999, hard plastic, blonde, glasses
Betsy McCall, 1996, 14" vinyl, 2000 8" vinyl
Esme, 16" vinyl Black fashion
Kitty Collier, 2000, 18" vinyl fashion
Kripplebush Kids, 1997, hard plastic, Marni, brunette, Eliza, red hair, and Hannah, blonde.
Tyler Wentworth, 1999, 16" vinyl fashion

Uneeda Doll Co.

1917+ , New York City, made composition, hard plastic and vinyl dolls
📖 **1, 2, 46. 47-51**
Baby Dollikins, 8" vinyl head, plastic body
Dollikin, 1961, 20", marked "UNEEDA//2S" multi joints, ankle, hand, elbow, knee.
        1970, 11 1/2" marked"©UNEEDA DOLL CO. INC.//MCMLXIX//MADE IN HONG KONG" on head.
Granny and Me, 1977, 16" and 7", vinyl granny marked "UNEEDA DOLL //CO. INC.//©1963" on head, dimple in chin, painted on glasses.
Petal People, ca. 1968, 2 1/2" vinyl doll with side glancing painted eyes, came inside 12 1/2" flower pot stand. Included Daffi Dill, Dizzy Daisy, Polly Poppy, Rosy Rose, Sunny Flower and Tiny Tulip, marked on back "HONG KONG".
Pollyanna, 30" vinyl, from movie starring Hayley Mills, marked "©WALT DISNEY//PRODS.//MFD. BY UNEEDA"
Rita Hayworth, ca. 1948, 14", composition, as Carmen in "The Loves of Carmen" movie, no marks on body, cardboard hangtag.

Unis France

1916-1930+, France, made bisque dolls in various sizes, mark used by S.F.B.J.

📖 **14, 46**

Bleuette, pre 1933, 10 5/8", after 1933, 11 5/8" only

Molds: 60, 247, 251, 301

J. Verlingue

Circa 1915-21, France, made bisque dolls, used anchor logo, names "Lutin" or "Liane" found on some marks, some bodies labeled "Diplôme d'Honeur".

📖 **14**

FRANCE

Virga

Circa 1949 - 1965+, a division of Beehler Arts Company, made hard plastic dolls.

📖 **1, 2, 33, 46, 47-51**

Hi Heel 'Teen, 1957-65, 8 1/2" hard plastic walker, sleep eyes, wig, high heeled feet, 2nd and 3rd fingers molded together, no marks on doll, box marked "Beautiful Virga Dolls//Hi-Heel 'Teen// manufactured by Beehler Arts Ltd.//H-H3"

Lucy, ca 1956, 7 1/2", hard plastic walker, molded shoe strap, tube like arm hook, 2nd and 3rd fingers molded together, no marks.

Playmate in Jodhpurs, ca. 1955, 8", hard plastic walker, no marks on doll, box marked "Virga//play mates//WALKING DOLL//Riding Habit 198"

Schiaparelli, 1956-67, 8" vinyl head, hard plastic body, walker, clothes designed by noted designer, marketed in shocking pink box, marked VIRGA on head.

None
or

VIRGA

Box marked "Virga"

Vogue Doll Co.

1930s on, Medford, MA, founded by Jennie Graves, first dressed "Just Me" dolls then made composition, hard plastic and vinyl dolls

📖 **14, 28, 33, 34, 46, 47-51**

Baby Dear, 1959-1964, 18" vinyl baby designed by Eloise Wilkin, vinyl limbs, cloth body, topknot or rooted hair, white tag on body, "Vogue Dolls, Inc.", left leg stamped "1960//E. Wilkins".

VOGUE DOLLS

Above: Silver Vogue hangtag with blue writing reads, "Created// by//Vogue//VOGUE DOLLS, INC." circa 1956, courtesy Rae Klenke.

Above: 7" composition Vogue "Toddles", marked "Vogue" on head and "Doll Co." on lower back, painted blue side-glancing eyes, closed mouth, blonde mohair wig, box marked "Double-Spray//Pink// Blonde//#405", pink dress, hat and shoes, gold foil sticker on front of dress, mint-in-box, circa 1937-1948, courtesy Lee Ann Beaumont.

Brikette , 1959-1961; 22" swivel waist, green eyes, freckles, rooted straight orange hair, marked on head "VOGUE INC. //19©60"

1960", 16", sleep eyes, platinum, brunette or orange hair.

1979, 16", curly blonde or straight blonde or brunette hair, no swivel waist.

1980, 16" curly pink, red, purple hair

Cynthia, 1940s, 13", composition sleep eyes, open mouth, mohair wig, no marks.

Dora Lee, 1940s, 11", composition, sleep eyes, closed mouth, mohair wig, no marks.

Ginny, 1948-50, 8" painted hard plastic, marked "VOGUE" on head, "VOGUE DOLL" on body, painted eyes, molded hair under mohair wig, or poodle cut wig, closed mouth.

1950-54, 8" hard plastic walker, sleep eyes, painted lashes, strung Dynel wigs, marked on Torso "GINNY//VOGUE DOLLS//INC. //PAT. PEND// MADE IN U.S.A."

1954-56, seven-piece body, molded lash walker, sleep eyes, Dynel or Saran wig, marked: "VOGUE" on head, "GINNY//VOGUE DOLLS// INC.//PAT. NO. 2687594//MADE IN U.S.A."

1957-62, 8" hard plastic bent-knee walker, molded lashes, sleep eyes, Dynel or Saran wig, marked "VOGUE" on head, "GINNY// VOGUE DOLLS// INC.// PAT. NO. 2687594//MADE IN U.S.A." on torso.

1963-65, 8" soft vinyl , hard plastic walker body, sleep eyes, molded lashes, rooted hair, marked, "GINNY" on head, same mark as above on torso.

1965-72, 8" all vinyl, straight leg, non-walker, rooted hair, molded lashes, head marked "Ginny", back, "Ginny//VOGUE DOLLS INC."

1972-77, 8" all vinyl, non-walker, molded lashes, some painted lashes, head marked, "GINNY", "VOGUE DOLLS©1972//MADE IN HONG KONG//3" on back (made by Tonka).

1977-82, 8" all vinyl, now made by Lesney, similar to above doll made by Tonka.

1981-82, 8" vinyl Sasson Ginny, slimmer body, painted eye in 1982, head marked "GINNY", back marked "1978 VOGUE DOLLS INC.// MOONACHIE N.J.//MADE IN HONG KONG."

1984-86, 8" vinyl made by Meritus® in Hong Kong, similar to Vogue 1963-71 Ginny, head marked, "GINNY®" back, "VOGUE DOLLS//(a star logo)//M.I.I. 1984//HONG KONG" on back. All porcelain dolls, head marked, "GW//SCD//5184" "GINNY//®VOGUE DOLLS//INC// (star logo)MII 1984//MADE IN TAIWAN."

1986-95, 8" vinyl, by Dakin, marked "VOGUE® DOLLS//©1984 R.. DAKIN INC.// MADE IN CHINA"

After, 1995, Ginny acquired by Vogue Doll Co., Inc. 8" hard plastic, molded lashes, sleep eyes, marked on body, "Ginny®//©1988//VOGUE DOLL COMPANY//MADE IN CHINA"

Ginnette, 1955-69, 1985-86, 8" vinyl baby, jointed, open mouth, painted eyes or sleep eyes. Marked "VOGUE DOLLS INC."

Jan, 1958-60, 1963-64, 10 1/2" Jill's friend, vinyl head, rigid six-piece body, swivel wait, rooted hair, marked, "VOGUE".

Jeff, 1958-60, 11" vinyl head, five piece rigid vinyl body, molded painted hair, marked "VOGUE DOLLS".

Jennie, 1940s, 13", composition, sleep eyes, open mouth, mohair wig, five piece body.

Jill, 1957-60, 1962-63, 1965, 10 1/2" seven piece hard plastic teenage body, bentknee walker, high heels, big sister to Ginny, (vinyl in 1965)

Jimmy, 1958, 8", all vinyl, Ginny's baby brother, open mouth, painted eye Ginnette, marked "VOGUE/ /DOLLS//INC."

Li'l Imp, 1959-60, 10-1/2", vinyl head, bent knee walker, green sleep eyes, orange hair, freckles, marked "R" and "B//44" on head and "R & B Doll Co. on back.

Little Miss Ginny, 1965-71, 12" all vinyl preteen, one piece hard plastic body and legs, soft vinyl head, arms, sleep eyes, marked "VOGUE DOLL//19©67" on neck and "VOGUE DOLL" on back..

Littlest Angel, 1961-63, 10 1/2" vinyl head, hard plastic bent knee walker, sleep eyes, same as Arranbee Littlest Angel rooted hair, marked "R & B".

Above: 8" hard plastic Vogue molded lash Ginny walker in #345 Funtime pink ballarina outfit, in pink and white children box circa 1956, courtesy Sally DeSmet.

Above: 22" vinyl Vogue "Brikette" with rooted orange hair with bangs, green sleep eyes, freckles on face, sharp pointed eyebrows, closed smiling mouth, rigid vinyl, jointed waist body, original pink tutu, unmarked,circa 1959, courtesy Cornelia Ford.

1967-80, 11", 15" ,all vinyl, jointed limbs, rooted red, blonde or brunette hair

Love Me Linda, 1965, 15", vinyl, painted eyes, rooted long hair, came with portrait, advertised as "Pretty as a Picture" in Sears, Wards, catalogs, marked, "VOGUE DOLLS//©1965"

Miss Ginny, 1962-65, 1967-80, 15-16" vinyl, head, arms, two piece hard plastic body with swivel waist, flat feet, later no swivel waist.

Wee Imp, 1960, 8", hard plastic, sleep eyes, molded lashes, bent knee walker, orange Saran wig, head marked "VOGUE", back, "GINNY//VOGUE DOLLS//INC.//PAT. NO. 2687594//MADE IN U.S.A."

Welcome Home Baby, 1978-80, 18", vinyl head and arms, newborn, painted eyes, molded hair, cloth body, crier, marked "Lesney"

1980, 22" vinyl "Welcome Home Baby Turns 2" toddler, 42260 Lesney Prod. Corp.// VOGUE DOLL"

W. u. Z
Y
Germany

Wagner & Zetsche

1875-1930+, Thüringia, Germany, pre-1916 heads made by G. Heubach; in 1916 trademarked composition dolls "Harald" and "Inge". Made range of size as well as bodies and accessories.

📖 12, 14, 46

Eve:
© 2000 SWDC INC
Susan Wakeen

Susan Wakeen Doll Co.

Circa 1990s, Litchfield, CT, made vinyl dolls including 8" Days of the Week and Portrait Dolls.

📖 46

Eve, 16" vinyl fashion doll with painted eyes, closed mouth.

Patented Nov. 4th 1873

Izannah F. Walker

Circa 1870s, Central Falls, RI, , made cloth stockinette dolls, babies and children, in sizes, 15", 17", 18 1/2", 20", 21", 24" and 27"

📖 14, 18, 46

Walther & Sohn

Circa 1908-20s, Oslau, Germany, made bisque dolls in various sizes.

📖 12, 14, 46

Mold: 6789, 1922, character

Norah Wellings
Circa 1926- 1960, 71/2"-36", made cloth dolls with felt or velvet faces, side glancing eyes, produced Scots boys, Mounties, Islanders, and others, specializing in sailor souvenir dolls for cruise lines, all with embroidered label on sole of foot.

📖 1, 2, 14, 18, 46, 47-51

Harry, the Hawk, 7 1/2" cloth aviator, paper tag,

Adolf Wislizenus

1850-1930+, Thüringia, Germany, made bisque dolls in various sizes.

📖 12, 14, 46

Molds: 110, 1910, character, solid dome, painted eyes, open/closed mouth

A. W.
AW, AW

Louis Wolf & Co.
1870-1930+, Germany, Boston and New York, made and distributed dolls in various sizes.

📖 12, 14, 46

Mold 152, 1912, bisque character, sleep eyes, by Hertel Schwab & Co. marked L.W. & Co.

L. W. & Co.

Chapter 6

Solve the Mysteries

There is nothing so much of a challenge for most doll collectors as not knowing what a doll is. It intrigues us, piques our curosity and teases our mental data banks. So much more exciting than a crossword puzzle - perhaps because it is a real-life mystery. Here are some of the mysteries I worked on - why don't you try them?

File 1. The Case of Two Sisters

It was a cool rainy March Friday at the Southern Oregon Antique and Collectibles show in Medford, Oregon. I am a private investigator, a Doll Detective, and was doing investigative work at the show that opened at noon. The rainy weather brought a deluge of clients to my table all afternoon. There was a quiet spell during the dinner hour, luckily for me, and then the pace picked up again about 7 P.M. I spotted a tall blonde with an expectant smile on her face holding a large clear plastic Rubbermaid storage container with a blue plastic lid. She introduced herself as a client, PH, and placed the container on my table. On the top was a framed print of a lone wolf in a winter scene.

"Do you need my help?" I asked. She replied, "Yes, I hope you can. These things belonged to my mother and her sister. My mother is 80 years old and her sister was older. There are some of their childhood dolls in this container. Mother thinks they are French, but her memory is not like it used to be. Curiously, I can remember seeing my mother's doll since I was a little girl – it was always sitting out at our house. It is still bright and fresh looking. I think her sister's doll was kept stored away and is somewhat dingy in appearance. What can you tell me about them?"

What should you do first? If you determine to examine the doll, measure it and touch the face to be sure of the material, you would have taken the correct actions. If you check the head first and then the back of the torso for marks, that would be correct. Then you should scrutinize the rest of the body and the clothing for marks - your next step.

With no further ado, I lifted the lid from the container and placed

Above left and right: 15" felt cloth doll with mohair wig, oil painted features including side-glancing brown eyes, two tow-tone painted lips with highlights on lower lip, accent dots at nose, wearing crisp yellow organdy original dress, scalloped socks and felt shoes, marked on bottom of left foot, circa 1930s, courtesy Patricia Hunker.

the dolls before me on a towel to catch any thing that might drop from the doll. I measured the doll. Even without touching the dolls, I immediately recognized that they were both made of felt cloth. They had oil-painted side-glancing eyes with eye shadow and a painted closed mouth with highlighting on the lower lip. They had mohair wigs with the hair sewn in strips and then attached to the crown. There were no marks on the back of the swivel head – one of the first places to check for clues. The body was also felt and was jointed at the arms and hips. I paid close attention to the hands, noting that the middle two fingers of each hand

were sewn together. P. H.'s mother's doll measured 15 inches tall and was dressed in a crisp yellow organdy dress trimmed with felt. The crispness assured me that it had never been washed. She wore matching yellow felt shoes with a felt strip to tie at the ankle.

Her cotton socks were scalloped at the top. I quickly untied the left shoe and removed the sock, noting that there was some soil on the arms and legs that were not covered with the dress or socks. On the bottom of the left foot written in black script was a mark.

I examined the other 15-inch cloth doll, which seemed like a match in construction to the other.

It also was felt with painted side-glancing eyes, stiff molded face, mohair wig, side-glancing oil-painted eyes and painted lips. Her two middle fingers were also sewn together and she wore a somewhat dingy ecru organdy dress with pink felt flower trim. She also had matching felt shoes with a felt tie and scalloped cotton socks. I removed the scalloped sock and felt shoe and again found printed in black script – the mark.

You can find the answers in this book. Can you solve this mystery and tell who is the manufacturer of these dolls?   You can do two things. You can look for the name in the Indexes that start on page 188, or you can look for the mark listed alphabetically in the Maker's Marks section starting on page 66. The answer can be found on page 132.

File 2. The Case of the Skull Cap
It is always fun to look at interesting dolls and I could not help but be intrigued by a lady who pulled her childhood doll from a tote bag recently while I was identifying dolls at a club show. "I got this doll for Christmas during the 1950s. I loved her and still have her original clothes. What can you tell about my doll?" the lady shyly asked.

It was a hard plastic doll with a closed mouth, synthetic hair that was inset on a softer plastic vinyl base in the doll's head forming a skullcap. First you will measure the doll - and find that it is 15-inches tall.   Now this is a hard one. The unique clues are that the doll is hard plastic, 15-inches tall, made in the 1950s and has a skull cap. You can skim through the Maker's Marks section and see which doll companies made dolls during the 1950s, then look for any mention of a skull cap. You will be lucky, because this company is in the beginning of the alphabet. You will find the answer on page 73. If you want to find out more about this type of doll, check the suggested reading material number listed next to the book icon, 📖. Then refer to the Bibliography to find the titles associated with those numbers.

File 3. The Case of the Naked Shirley
With every doll, there is a story - there was one in the following letter.
Dear Doll Detective,
"I was born in 1936 and my Mother purchased a Shirley Temple doll for me. My doll is 22" long, has Shirley Temple printed on her back with the word Ideal printed in a triangle. There is

printed in a triangle. There is something printed on the back of her head (just above the neck) but I cannot make out what it says.

The doll is in exceptionally good shape for its age, however, I am missing her clothing. Do you have any idea as to where I could obtain a complete costume for my Shirley Temple doll? I attempted to try to ascertain the year of my doll and its value from your book but I think in my old age I am just too unsure. Any help would be appreciated."

How do you know what material a doll is made of without looking at it? This case can be solved using the information in this book. Can you solve the mystery? The essential clues are that the doll has been identified as a Shirley Temple and she received it in the 1930s. You would check the Indexes for Shirley Temple and look in the Index for Shirley Temple Then turn to page 166 of the Makers Marks to find out about Shirley Temple and what material she was made from in the thirties.

File 4. The Case of the Black Spot

A Black Spot in doll collecting is not all that bad - it just depends on where it is. A lady who had come across several dolls when clearing an estate asked me to look at one in particular. She wanted to know how old a certain doll was. I unwrapped the doll and looked at it laying in front of me on a towel.

Using just my eyes, I could tell that this doll was porcelain because of the shiny finish. I noticed the face had delicately painted blue eyes with black brows and pink accents and knew she was old. Many people today make reproduction china dolls, but usually the painting is not delicate. She wore a silk dress that was melting and a matching bonnet that covered up a wig. I asked did she mind of I undressed the doll - this is the courteous way to see if you can examine a doll. I could see she was a shoulderhead - you can look up this term and others in the Glossary in the back of this book. She was attached to a kid body and had china forearms and lower legs and feet with molded boots. I was careful not to let the feet bump against each other. (This book will tell you why.) I removed the bonnet and the wig, that I could tell from touching that the wig was mohair. You can check how to tell the difference in the Questioning the Suspect chapter in the front of the book. When the wig was removed I could see the head was a solid dome and on the top almost where a pate would be, was a round black spot. What was the significance of the black spot? How old was this doll? Did you read the Questioning the suspect chapter carefully? The answer is on page 14. Would you like to be able to know how much it is worth? You can consult my companion book,

Doll Values or other price guides.

File 5. The Case of Madeline who?

Another collector presented a smaller bisque doll at a doll identification clinic with the following story. "This doll belonged in my husband's family and I think her name is Madeline. I can just faintly see some marks on the back of her neck, but it looks like it is "Madeline" Do you know a Madeline doll and can you tell me anything about her?"

I got out my trusty magnifying glass and examined the marks. The doll was not Madeline at all - a common error made by the novice collector. What were the real marks incised on the back of her head? If you paid attention in this book you will know. Can you solve the mystery? Look on pages 17-18. You may need a magnifying glass to be able to see those marks. I like to use a lighted one. While you are checking out a bisque doll, you may want to look inside the head with a black light - to see if there are any visible cracks. Many people do not mind a small hairline that may have been with the doll for a long time. But, if you need to know if the doll has been repaired or has a major fault, you do need to look at it carefully.

File 6. The Case of Mysterious Pate

A lady brought in a doll wrapped in a cotton towel. She carefully placed the doll in front of me at a doll show. " This doll belongs to my mother who is in a nursing home. Mother cannot remember much about the doll, but she thinks it came from her grandparents who lived in France. Do you know who made her?"

I unwrapped the bisque shoulder head doll. She had glass eyes and a kid body with bique arms. The leather was worn and cracked and the doll smelled musty. She had the remnants of an old mohair wig and was dressed in fabric that smelled, looked and felt old and showed small moth holes. She had very nicely made cotton undergarments that were yellowed with age. I lifted up her wig and looked at the back of her head for marks. There were letters and numbers, but not a recognizable mold number or initials of a firm that would tell me who made her. I gently lifted the mohair wig up and noticed that she had a plaster pate covering the open crown. I needed to know no more - I instantly could identify this doll.

You, too, can find the answers in to the this mystery. Your one main clue is plaster pate. Only one company has been reported who made pates with this type of material; the answer is on page 12. You can then look in the Maker's Marks for the manufacturer's category and be able to find out more about this type of doll. Sometimes the clues are simple like this and sometimes not, but when you have no idea where to begin to find the answers, this book will clue you in on your road to discovery.

File 7. The Case of the White-washed Wooden.

Sometimes dolls can be in such a state when we see them, you can hardly recognize what they are. When our local doll club advertised their show, they received a call from a lady who wanted to find out about her doll. The lady was entering an assisted care home and did not want to part with an item - a wooden doll that was hers as a child. I told her I would have to look at it to be sure. She said the paint had faded and she had redone it - but she still wanted to know what it was. When she came, I was somewhat startled to see a completely wooden nude doll that looked like it had been white-washed. I touched the surface to verify it was indeed made of wood and measured it. The doll was 14-inches tall and had spring joints so that it could pose in many positions. It had a carved wooden head with a coiled braid. I knew immediately what this ghostly doll was. Can you solve this mystery? First measure the doll, touch the doll so that you know what the material is. Look at the photographs in the Gallery section of the books and see if you can find a similar doll made of wood. (You can find a

photo of a wooden doll on page 51 with spring joints. Check the manufacturers name in Makers Marks and egads, Watson, you have the answer!

Unsoved Mysteries

Not every mystery can be solved. There have been millions of dolls made - look at Mattel's Barbie. Many other lesser known companies have existed and made dolls. Only those dolls that have meant enough to someone have been researched enough for us to find the answer. Those that have a long term appeal to collectors have had articles written about them, been shown in competition or have such noteriety that they have been recorded. Today's collectors are busy researching the dolls of their childhood and some will record them. The investigation continues as new clues surface and new information is brought to light. For those cases that can be solved, this book will save you time, effort and direct you to other reading resources. Grab your detective tools, (magnifying glass, measuring tape, black light) this book and go for the hunt. Happy Detecting!

Chapter 7

Glossary

Adult - an adult doll has a torso with a smaller waist.

All Bisque - some smaller dolls have head, limbs and torso all made of bisque.

Applied Ears - Ears molded separately and then applied to the head.

Appropriate or Authentic Clothing - if not original to the doll, contemporary with the era the doll was made and which employ fabrics and trims also consistant with that time period. For example antique dolls should be dressed in all natural fabrics and trims.

Artist Doll - doll or figurine made to represent a doll made for sale to the public. These are usually made in limited numbers as opposed to mass production.

Automaton - a doll with a mechanical movement, usually a complex human like action. More desired are dolls with more than one movement or action.

Baby - a doll body with bent-legs represents a baby. When some dolls are dressed in a baby costume, they become a baby. The original costume decides what the doll will be.

Ball jointed - wooden ball joints are used in some doll bodies to make the movement smooth.

Bébé - refers to a French child doll.

Belton-type - refers to a solid dome head with two or three holes that were originally used for attaching wig.

Biscaloid - a ceramic-type heavy composition material used for making dolls.

Biskoline - celluloid-type composition used for making dolls.

Bisque - older dolls made of unglazed porcelain are often called bisque, while the newer dolls are described as porcelain. However, bisque is porcelain; it has a matte finish. When porcelain is glazed to have a shiny surface, it is called "China".

Bonnet-head - a doll with molded-on hat.

Boudoir or Bed Doll - doll with long skinny limbs that were popular 1920s-1940s. the heads can be composition or cloth, many had fancy long dresses and sat on the bed as a decoration.

Breather - doll with pierced nostrils.

Brevete (or Bte) - a mark on French dolls to show the patent is registered.

Caracul - Lambskin material used for making wigs.

Celebrity Doll - modeled after a living person who has reached some degree of notoriety - a well-known person, living or dead.

Celluloid - an early plastic type material invented in 1869 was used for dolls until after World War II.

Character-face - about 1910, dolls with more realistic looking faces were made.

Child - has chubby tummy or does not have a smaller waist.

China - glazed porcelain - the finish has a shiny look.

Collectible Dolls - Dolls made in the last 25-30 years. Note: United Federation of Doll Clubs defines collectible as those made 25-75 years ago.(See Modern Dolls).

Composition - material used in doll making that consists of glue, wood pulp or sawdust or paper products. Each company had their own recipe, but the main ingredient with cold pressed composition dolls was glue. Later when molds used heat in the process the recipe changed using less glue.

Cracking - in composition where the body is strung too tightly and the molds give way at the seams or where because of exposure to heat, cold or moisture the big pieces of the outer composition skin finish open up. Crazing may eventually lead to cracking.

Crazing - fine lines that occur in composition dolls when the surface glue/paint finish starts to disintegrate - usually caused when the relative humidity goes over 85% forming an ideal setting for bacteria to grow and cause a deterioration of the finish.

DEP - letters refer to the registration on French and German dolls.

DRGM - letters on German dolls refer to registration.

Dolly-face - face has open mouth, not much expression - a bland look.

Embossed - this type of mark is raised above the surface.

Ethnic - dolls in regional dress representing a nationality or ethnic classification. Native American dolls would belong in this category.

Fashion-type - a doll with narrow waist and can be used as a mannequin to display wardrobe.

Felt Doll - a doll with head made of felt, some may have whole body of felt.

Feathered Brows - eyebrows are painted with one to several to many fine brush strokes.

Five-piece-body - doll body with torso, two arms and two legs.

Flange neck - finished neck opening on a doll head with a ridge and perhaps holes so that it can be sewn or attached to a body.

Flirty eyes - eyes that move from side to side or eyes painted to the side.

Fortune Telling Doll - Dolls with fortunes written on parts of their skirts or holding a pointer to indicate a fortune.

Frozen Charlotte - China doll all molded in one piece with no joints.

Fur Eyebrows - some bisque dolls have openings in the head for fur to be inserted to make more realistic "eyebrows" for the doll.

GES. (Gesh) this mark on German dolls refers to the registration of the patent.

Googly - oversize large round eyes that also may flirt (move from side to side).

Gutta Percha - a rubbery type substance from sap similar but not the same as rubber. It will not float and is pinkish and very brittle when hard. When used in doll making was combined with other substances.

Half Doll - also known as pincushion doll; this doll was made with no lower torso or legs and used to make pin-cushions, pillows, lampshades, powder puffs and other accessories.

Hard Plastic - a more rigid material developed during World War II that was used for dolls after the war.

Ichimatsu - a child's play doll in Japan.

Incised - mark impressed or carved into the surface usually on the back of the head or shoulderplate of the doll.

Intaglio - eyes that curve inward giving an appearance of depth and texture to the eye.

Kid body - doll body made of leather.

Lifting - where composition outer skin finish has lifted from the composition molded part. Usually this is the result of extremes of heat or cold or exposure to moisture and bacteria.

Magic Skin - an early plastic material used in some dolls like Ideal's Baby Coos and Bonnie Braids. With time and exposure to the air, the material discolored and turned dark and deteriorated with age.

MaMa Doll - a composition doll with cloth body, swing legs and a voice box in the cloth body, designed by Georgene Averill in the 1920s, it remains a favorite body style today.

Mannequin - artist and store clothing models used in displays are sometimes recycled as dolls.

Marks - Logos, icons, letter and/or numbers incised, stamped on a doll head or body that may be used for identification.

Marotte - doll head and upper torso attached to a stick that can be twirled or manipulated. Usually has a musical mechanism of some kind.

Mask Face - face made of material pressed over a mold and when stiffened attached to the head.

Mechanical Doll - Doll with some type of movement, sound or action made by a special addition to the doll usually in the torso.

Metal Head -shoulderhead doll made of tin or brass were thought to be indestructible play toys for children circa 1850-1930s.

Milliners' Model -early molded hair papier mache dolls with molded heads, kid torsos and wooden limbs, circa Germany, 1810-1860, that early researchers thought to be used as clothing models. Unusual feature is their often elaborate molded hair.

Mint Doll - doll in original condition just as when it was new, including the clothing, accessories. Any flaw will cause it not to be mint.

Modern Dolls - Dolls made in the last 75 - 100 years. Note: United Federation of Doll Clubs defines Modern Dolls as made 25 - 75 years ago. (See also Collectible).

Mohair - wig material made from goat's hair.

Molded hair - where locks, curls, parts and waves are sculpted on the head and may additionally be painted.

Mold Number - many early bisque dolls retain a mold number on the back of the head that allowed early manufacturers to tell which model head it was. These may reflect only the size or some other characteristic.

Motschmann - was a type of doll body with a cloth middle section and upper limbs.

Multi-face/multi-head dolls - a multi-face doll has more than one face on one head. A multi-head doll has more than one head that can be exchanged with the body.

Nodders - also called Knotters, small dolls whose heads are attached with elastic so that the heads wobble. the Knotter name derived from knotting of elastic.

One-of-a-kind - a doll made with no copies or duplicates.

Open mouth - is a cut out space between the lips usually filled with a felt tongue and teeth and opens on into the dolls head.

Open/closed mouth - the space between the lips does not open into the dolls head, but the opening is molded shut.

Original Costume - the costume the doll wore when it was first made and sold. Coleman's defines original costume as made of the fabric and in the style of the era the doll originated.

Painted Bisque - when the porcelain is painted with a complexion just like a composition doll would be. Nancy Ann Storybook Dolls can be painted bisque.

Paperweight Eyes - are blown glass eyes with added crystal to give more depth to the eyes.

Papier Mache - is a material made of paper products used in doll making.

Parian-type - refers to bisque dolls, often with molded hair, with delicate white complexion and no tint. Parian is the color of a very white marble.

Pate -is a curved covering of plaster, cork or cardboard to cover the cut out opening in the crown of a doll's head. The German J. D. Kestner firm is the only one known to have a plaster pate on antique bisque dolls.

Peg Wooden Dolls - dolls made of wood with mortise and tonon peg joints. The dolls may have part carving and part turned on a lathe and have painted features. Many were made in the Grodner Tal, Austria area from the late 1790s to 1910s. Some early dolls are varnished and have a carved yellow comb on the head.

Piano Baby - figurine, often a reclining baby, used for decoration.

Pierced Ears - have holes in the ear lobe to hold earrings.

Pierced-in Ears - have holes pierced into the interior of the doll's head, not just through the ear lobes.

Pin Cushion - also called half-dolls, used with skirt and stuffing to form a cloth pincushion for the bottom part of the doll.

Play doll - this is a plaything usually mass-produced, meant and sold for children. Some play dolls are also collectible.

Portrait Doll -a doll that has facial features of some particular person.

Pottery Doll- a doll of low-fired ceramic which is usually fairly thick and somewhat heavy. They may be glazed or unglazed.

Poupee - name of a French fashion type doll.

Poured Wax Doll - doll with head or entire doll made of wax. The wax is poured into a mold and when the coated portion is hardened the rest of the wax is poured off. The wax can be beeswax, spermacetti or parrafin wax.

Pouty - doll with closed mouth, "kissable" expression.

Primitive Dolls - dolls of any material created by craftsmen, sometimes crude and can be commercially sold.

Provenance - this is a written description of the dolls origin, period, type and if possible who has owned the doll.

Queen Anne Dolls - dolls of the Georgian Period of English history, circa 1720-1840, usually made entirely of wood, usually painted features, but sometimes glass eyes. May have flax, hair or hemp wigs.

Real lashes - lashes made and added to lids to give more realistic look to dolls.

Regional costume - clothing for dolls that reflects the nationality or a particular region. Some costumes may have much detail while others only a general likeness of the real clothing.

Reproduction - doll is made from mold of original doll.

Rub - lighter spot where paint has worn away.

Set eyes - eyes that are fixed to hold in one position rather than open and close.

Shoulder head - head and shoulder are molded together in one piece and then sewn or glued to a body.

Shoulder plate - a shoulder piece is molded separately and used with a head and then is then sewn or glued to a body. When there are two pieces the head may swivel.

Socket head - the head has a neck that will fit into a shoulder plate or composition or other type of firm body.

Solid dome - the head is molded with no opening in the crown. It may have molded and painted or painted hair or take a wig.

Sonneberg Taufling - a method of doll body construction where hard parts of the torso and limbs are interspersed with composition or some hard material. Wood tubes may be used for limbs giving a floating joint. Some criers were in the torso and these dolls originally were mostly dressed as babies.

Snow Babies - dolls named after Admiral Peary's daughter, Marie, whose mother, Josephine D. Peary wrote a book, The Snow Baby in 1901. Snow babies are often one-piece bisque miniature dolls rolled in bits of crushed porcelain to represent snow. They were popular during the early part of the century.

Stiff neck - the head is joined to the torso.

Stone bisque - is bisque of a coarse more porous quality.

Toddler - has stocky legs mounted at hips sometimes with a slanted fit at the joint.

Topsy-Turvy - a doll with two heads, in the past it usually referred to a doll with one black and one white head - with one head hidden under the skirt. Turn it upside down and you see the other doll.

Turned shoulder head - the head is positioned on the shoulder turned slightly away from the center.

Vinyl - this material was developed after hard plastic and the end product could be either soft and pliable or rigid. It was used in doll making in 1959 through the end of the century.

Watermelon Mouth - is a closed smiling mouth.

Wax-over dolls - dolls with the composition , wood, bisque or other material head is dipped in wax.

Weighted Eyes - use weights to help the eyes to open and close.

Woodpulp Composition - made from wood pulp or wood "flour" and mixed with glue to form composition. Each company had their own recipe for this product.

Chapter 8

Bibliography

Anderton, Johana
1. 📖　Twentieth Century Dolls, Trojan Press, 1971
2. 📖　More Twentieth Century Dolls, Athena Publishing Co. 1974

Angione, Genevieve
3. 📖　All-Bisque & Half-Bisque Dolls, Schiffer Publishing, 1981

Augustyniak, J. Michael
4. 📖 Thirty Years of Mattel Fashion Dolls 1967-1997, Collector Books, 1998

Avery, Kim
5. 📖　The World of Raggedy Ann Collectibles, Collector Books, 1997

Axe, John
6. 📖 Effanbee, A Collector's Encyclopedia 1949 through 1983, Hobby House Press, 1983
7. 📖The Encyclopedia of Celebrity Dolls, Hobby House Press, 1983

Bach, Jean
8. & Dictionary of Doll Marks, Sterling Publishing Co., Inc., 1990

Bitman, Joe
9. 📖　Francie & her Mod, Mod, Mod, Mod World of Fashion, Hobby House Press, 1996

Borger, Mona
10. 📖　Chinas, Doll for Study and Admiration, Borger Publications, 1983
Casper, Peggy Wiedman
11. 📖　Fashionable Terri Lee Dolls, Hobby House Press, 1988
Cieslik, Jurgen and Marianne
12. 📖　German Doll Encyclopedia 1800-1939, Hobby House Press, 1985
Coleman, Dorothy S., Elizabeth Ann and Evelyn Jane
13. 📖　The Collector's Book of Dolls Clothes, Crown Publishers,

1975

14. 📖 The Collectors Encyclopedia of Dolls, Vol. I & II, Crown Publishers, 1968, 1986

Cook, Carolyn
15. 📖 Gene, Hobby House Press, 1998

Corson, Carol
16. 📖 Schoenhut Dolls, A Collector's Encyclopedia, Hobby House Press, 1993

Crowsey, Linda
16. 📖 Madame Alexander Store Exclusives & Limited Editions, Collector Books, 2000

DeWein, Sibyl and Ashabraner, Joan
17. 📖 The Collectors Encyclopedia of Barbie Dolls and Col lectibles, Collector Books, 1977

Edward, Linda
18. 📖 Cloth Dolls, From Ancient to Modern, Schiffer, 1997

Fainges, Marjory
19. 📖 Celluloid Dolls of the World, Kangaroo Press, 2000

Foulke, Jan
20. 📖 Blue Book Dolls & Values, 14 Ed. Hobby House Press, 1999
21. 📖 Kestner, King of Dollmakers, Hobby House Press, 1982
22. 📖 Simon & Halbig Dolls, The Artful Aspect, Hobby House Press, 1984

Garrison, Susan Ann
23. 📖 The Raggedy Ann & Andy Family Album, Schiffer Publish ing, 1989

Holland, Thomas W.,
24. 📖 Girls' Toys of the Fifties & Sixties, Windmill Press, 1997
25. 📖 The Doll & Teddy Bear Department, Windmill Press, 1997

Hoyer, Mary
26. 📖 Mary Hoyer and Her Dolls, Hobby House Press, 1982

Izen, Judith
27.📖 A Collector's Guide to Ideal Dolls, 2nd Edition, Collector Books, 1999

Izen, Judith and Stover, Carol
28. 📖 A Collector's Encyclopedia to Vogue Dolls, Collector Books, 1998

Judd, Polly and Pam
29. 📖 Cloth Dolls, Identification & Price Guide, Hobby House Press, 1990
30. 📖 Composition Dolls, 1928-1955, Hobby House Press, 1991
31. 📖 Composition Dolls, 1909-1928, Hobby House Press, 1994
32. 📖 European Costumed Dolls, Identification & Price Guide, Hobby House Press, 1994
33. 📖 Hard Plastic Dolls, Hobby House Press, 1987, 1994
34. 📖 Glamour Dolls of the 1950s & 1960s, Hobby House Press, 1988
35. 📖 Santa Dolls & Figurines, Hobby House Press, 1992

Karl, Michele
36. 📖 Baby Boomer Dolls, Portfolio Press, 2000

Langford, Paris
37. 📖 Liddle Kiddles, Collector Books, 1996
Lewis, Kathy and Don
38. 📖 Chatty Cathy Dolls, Collector Books, 1994

Mandeville, A. Glen
39. 📖 Ginny, An American Toddler Doll, Hobby House Press, 1994

Lindenberger, Jan and Morris, Judy D.
40. 📖 Encyclopedia of Cabbage Patch Kids, the 1980s, Schiffer, 1999

Mansell, Colette
41. 📖 The Collector's Guide to British Dolls Since 1920, Robert Hale - London, 1983

Melillo, Marcie
42. 📖 The Ultimate Barbie Doll Book, Krause Publications, 1996

McGonagle, Dorothy A.
43. 📖 The Dolls of Jules Nicolas Steiner, Hobby House Press, 1988

Mertz, Ursula

44. 📖 Collector's Encyclopedia of American Composition Dolls, 1900-1950, Collector Books, 1999

Morris, Thomas G.
45. 📖 Carnival Chalk Prize I, II, Prize Publishers, 1985, 1994

Moyer, Patsy
46. 📖 Doll Values 1st, 2nd, 3rd, 4th 5th Eds. Collector Books, 1997, 1998, 1999, 2000
47. 📖 Modern Collectible Dolls, Vol. I, Collector Books, 1997
48. 📖 Modern Collectible Dolls, Vol. II, Collector Books, 1998
49. 📖 Modern Collectible Dolls, Vol. III, Collector Books, 1999
50. 📖 Modern Collectible Dolls, Vol. IV, Collector Books, 2000
51. 📖 Modern Collectible Dolls, Vol. V, Collector Books, 2001
52. 📖 Patsy & Friends Newsletter, 1987-2001

Niswonger, Jeanne D.
53. 📖 That Doll Ginny, Cody Publishing, 1978

Osborn, Dorisanne
54. 📖 Sasha Dolls, Through the Years, Gold Horse Publishing, 1999

Outwater, Myra Yellin
55. 📖 Advertising Dolls, Schiffer, 1997

Pardella, Edward R.
56. 📖 Shirley Temple Dolls and Fashions, Schiffler Publishing, 1999

Perkins, Myla
57. 📖 Black Dolls, 1820-1991, An Identification and Value Guide, Collector Books, 1993
58. 📖 Black Dolls, Book II, An Identification and Value Guide, Collector Books, 1995

Richter, Lydia
59. 📖 Huebach Character Dolls and Figurines, Hobby House Press, 1992

Robison, Joleen Ashman & Sellers, Kay
60. 📖 Advertising Dolls, Collector Books, 1992

Sabulis, Cindy

61. 📖 Collector's Guide to Dolls of the 1960s & 1970s, Collector Books, 2000

Schoonmaker, Patricia N.
62. 📖 Effanbee Dolls: The Formative Years, 1910-1929, Hobby House Press, 1984
63. 📖 Patsy Doll Family Encyclopedia, Hobby House Press, 1992
64. 📖 Patsy Doll Family Encyclopedia, Volume II, Hobby House Press, 1998

Seely, Mildred
65. 📖 The Complete Book of All-Bisque Dolls, Scott Publications, 1992

Smith, Patricia R.
66. 📖 Madame Alexander Collector Dolls, Collector Books, 1978
67. 📖 Modern Collector's Dolls, Series 1-8, Collector Books

Strahlendorf, Evelyn Robson
68. 📖The Charlton Standard Catalogue of Canadian Dolls, The Charlton Press, 1997

Tabbat, Andrew
69. 📖 The Collector's World of Raggedy Ann and Andy, Vol. 1, Gold Horse Publishing, 1996
70. 📖 The Collector's World of Raggedy Ann and Andy, Vol. 2, Gold Horse Publishing, 1997
71. 📖 Raggedy Ann and Andy, I.D. Guide, Gold Horse Publishing, 1998

Tarnowska, Maree
72. 📖 Fashion Dolls, Hobby House Press, 1986

Theimer, Francois
73. 📖 The Bru Book, Gold Horse Publishing, 1991

Theimer, Francois & Theriault, Florence
74. 📖 The Jumeau Book, Gold Horse Publishing, 1994

Van Ausdall, Marci
75. 📖 Betsy McCall, A Collector's Guide, Hobby House Press, 1999

Whitton, Margaret
76. 📖 The Jumeau Doll, Dover Publications, 1980

Chapter 9

Indexes

Mold Numbers — page

199	97	242	133, 166, 167	300	99, 133, 165
200	74, 82	243	63, 123	301	165, 166, 169
201	74, 82, 165, 192	244	133	302	99
202	126	245	37, 123, 167	306	116
203	116, 117, 128	246	78, 133, 167	307	97
204	78, 128, 165	247	78, 123, 166,	309	78
205	117, 128		167,169	310	133, 134
206	117, 123, 128	248	166	320	99
207	82	249	123	321	99
208	82, 116, 118, 123			325	78, 125, 126
209	82, 118	250	99, 125, 126, 133,	326	133
210	82, 118, 123	166		327	133
211	118, 123	251	99, 133, 169	328	133
212	82	252	78, 165, 166	329	133
213	118	253	133	332	78
214	120, 123	255	123	333	133
215	82	256	133	338	99
216	128	257	124, 133	339	99
217	118	259	133	340	78, 99, 133
218	82, 118	260	124	341	133
219	82	262	82, 124	342	99
220	82, 123	263	82, 124	345	133
221	116, 118	264	82	348	99
223	118, 128, 167	266	125	349	99
224	78	267	99	350	133
225	118, 132	269	163	351	133
226	123, 166	270	82	352	133
227	166	273	78	353	133
230	116, 128, 132,	274	78	360	133
	166	275	78, 82, 99	370	126, 133
231	132	277	78	371	133
232	128, 167	281	125, 126	372	126, 133
233	166	283	97	377	126
234	123	285	82	379	78
235	123, 166	286	78, 97	390	133
236	166	287	97	394	78
237	123, 166	289	78	395	167
238	166	291	97	399	56, 99
239	78, 123, 166	292	125	400	133
240	133, 167	293	78, 163	401	133, 167
241	123	297	78	402	120

403	120	698	71	971	134
414	133	700	134	972	134
444	99	701	134	973	134
449	18, 133	710	134	975	134
450	79, 133	711	134	979	166
451	133	719	166	980	134
500	133, 163	720	166	985	134
520	78, 125, 133	728	39	990	71, 134
521	96	729	166	991	134
525	125	739	166	995	134
526	125	740	166	1000	71, 167
529	163	749	166	1005	75
530	166	750	134	1008	71
531	125	758	166	1009	166
537	163	759	166	1010	166
539	163	760	134	1019	166
540	166	769	167	1028	71
546	125	784	72	1032	71
549	125, 126	790	135	1039	166
550	133, 166	800	135	1040	166
554	125, 126	810	135	1044	71
560	133	852	167	1046	71
567	125	886	166	1049	166
568	125, 126	890	71	1059	166
570	133, 166	900	134	1064	71
585	78	905	166	1069	166
586	78	911	71	1070	124, 128, 166
587	78	912	71	1071	163
590	134	914	164	1078	166
600	134, 166	915	71	1079	166
602	78	916	71	1080	166
604	78	919	166	1099	166
619	78	927	134, 163	1100	82
620	134	929	166	1109	166
624	78	939	166	1123	71
630	71, 78, 134	940	166	1127	71
639	71	949	166	1142	71
641	78	950	166	1148	166
642	78	951	144	1159	15, 166
678	78	969	166	1160	166
680	125, 126	970	144	1180	163

1200	82	1361	71	4700	155
1210	71	1362	71	4900	155
1234	71	1367	71	5500	164
1235	71	1368	71, 75	5636	100
1246	166	1376	165	5689	100
1248	166	1388	166	5700	164
1249	166	1428	166	5730	100
1250	163	1448	166	5777	100
1253	163	1469	86	5800	164
1254	71	1478	166	6688	100
1259	163	1488	166	6692	100
1260	163	1489	166	6736	100
1262	163	1498	166	6789	173
1263	163	1890	134	6894	100
1266	163	1892	134	6969	100
1267	163	1893	134	6970	100
1269	166	1894	134	6971	100
1270	163	1897	134	7246	100
1271	163	1898	134, 166	7247	100
1272	163	1899	134	7248	100
1274	163	1900	99, 134	7268	100
1279	166	1901	134	7345	100
1293	163	1902	134	7407	100
1294	166	1903	134	7602	100
1295	163	1906	164	7603	100
1296	163	1907	116	7604	100
1297	163	1909	134	7622	100
1298	163	1909	164	7623	100
1299	166	1912	86	7644	100
1303	166	1914	86	7681	100
1304	71, 166	2023	163	7711	100
1310	163	2033	163	7759	100
1322	71	2048	163	7847	100
1329	63	2072	163	7850	100
1342	71	2094	163	7911	100
1346	71	2095	163	7925	100
1348	86	2096	163	7926	100
1349	86	2097	163	7972	100
1352	71	3200	134	7975	100
1357	71, 82	4000	164	7977	100
1358	71	4600	164	8191	100

8192	100	8774	100
8221	100	8819	100
8226	100	8950	100
8316	100	9027	100
8413	100	9055	100
8420	100	9355	100
8429	100	9457	100
8661	132	9746	100
8662	132	10532	100
8686	100	11010	100
8724	100	11173	100

Name Index
Name – Page Number

Ways to Sell a Doll

Now that you know what you have, the question is - "do you keep it or sell it"? No one can make that decision for you, but if you decide to sell here is some helpful information.

Several options are open to you - (1) sell direct to a dealer; (2) sell at a show; (3) place them on consignment at a shop; (4) sell via newspaper; (5) Ebay; or, (6) sending them to an auction.

Dealers usually must buy at 50 percent or less of what they hope to sell the dolls for to regain their investment and make a profit. They must buy with the reality of having to hold a doll for a period of time thus typing up their money with no return until the doll sells. Experienced dealers and those with deep pockets who know their market can be very successful. The person who sells as a sideline or hobby may have a slower time recovering their money as they are waiting on the right buyer to come their way. Dealers must make a profit if they are spending the time, energy and cash to buy your dolls.

Doll shows offer an opportunity to be face to face with the buyer and to be able to answer questions about the doll's condition, originality and rarity. It does require having to ready the dolls, price them, box them up, cart them to the show and then having to dismantle the display when you go home. You are dependent on the show operator to provide adequate advertising, fate to have wonderful weather, a strong economy and buyers who want to buy your dolls.

Placing them on **consignment** also requires you to prepare your dolls, price them, haul them and then wait to see if the shop has lots of customers who are looking for what you have to offer.

Selling through the mail requires you to prepare your dolls, take clear in-focus photographs to send to prospective buyers and deal with checks from people you do not know and then boxing the doll up and carting it to the post office or UPS.

Ebay auction on the Internet requires you to register, post a photo taken with a digital camera and if the auction meets your reserve bid, you still have to collect the money, box and ship the doll.

Two people I know recently went through the auction experience. One of the people had inherited a collection. While she was aware of the identity of the dolls, she was not a member of a doll club and had no current ties to the doll world. She chose an out-of-town reputable auction house in a smaller but remote community that specialized in antiques. The attendance was poor and the few dealers who attended had a bonanza buying dolls at bargain prices for their resale inventory. The owner of the collection shed tears throughout the day as the sale progressed.

The other person thought long and hard about the best solution and realized she did not want the hassle or exertion of dealing doll by doll with buyers and having to pack and ship each one to a different buyer. She contacted the better-known auction houses that specialized in dolls and asked her friends for their recommendations. The auction house *McMaster's Doll Auctions* received favorable reviews. She decided to trust them. Their sales were not hurried or rushed but deliberately spaced. The auction brought record prices. The owner was delighted that her dolls were transferred into the hands of eager new collectors who would be able to enjoy them while she enjoyed the money she received.

Because *McMaster's* specializes in dolls, they have an established customer base from their years in the business that they can alert when an auction is coming.

They auctioned some of the dolls pictured in this book. Below are some of the dolls and the prices they brought at the auction.

Page 33 10" bisque Kestner Kewpie Googly, $6,400.00
Page 35 10" all-bisque Kestner, $875.00
Page 36 26" bisque Portrait Jumeau, $3,900.00
Page 36 23" bisque Schmitt & Fills $18,000.00

Page 37 16" bisque Kammer & Reinhardt "Max" $14,500.00
Page 37 25" bisque Kestner "Hilda" baby, $3,900.00
Page 39 18" Celluloid Kammer & Reinhardt $215.00
Page 40 25" China $1,200.00
Page 42 Set of 8" composition Alexander Quintuplets $2,300.00 and Dr. Dafoe, $1,600.00
Page 46 17" German Papier Mache Milliner's Model $900.00
Page 47 15" rubber Effanbee Dy-Dee Baby, $400.00
Page 50 21" poured wax baby, $1,300.00
Page 50 16" wooden Schoenhut, $2,100.00
Page 54 21" Simon & Halbig Automaton, $2,700.00
Page 55 No. 1 Ponytail Barbie, $7,000.00
Page 55 No. 2 Brunette Barbie, $2.600.00
Page 56 7 1/2" black bisque Ernst Heubach baby, $325.00
Page 57 21" composition Ideal Deanna Durbin, in box $1,700.00
Page 58 14" cloth Georgene Averill "Little Lulu," $500.00
Page 62 18" bisque French Fashion, $1,900.00
Page 63 13" bisque Kestner 243 Oriental baby, $4,700.00

My thanks to McMasters for allowing us to use the beautiful photos from their catalogs. If you would like to talk with them about selling your doll or dolls, give them a call at (800) 842-3526. The call is free and so is their estimate of what your doll might sell for at their auction. Send photographs to: *McMaster's Doll Auctions*, P. O. Box 1755, Cambridge, Ohio 43725. You can also check out their web site at: mcmastersauctions.com.

Look for these exciting additions to the
Antiques Detectives **"How to"** series:

The Jewelry Detective
The Glass Detective
The Pottery Detective
The Furniture Detective
The Stamp Detective
The Silver Detective
The Oriental Rug Detective
The Coin Detective
The Pocketwatch Detective
The Antique Toy Detective
The American Indian Jewelry Detective
The Military Collectables Detective
The Art Detective
The Wristwatch Detective
The Clock Detective
The Vintage Clothing Detective
The Laces & Linens Detective
The China & Porcelain Detective

To Order Call:
800-516-8656
Fax: 800-515-3289

Doll Detective Supplies Order Form

The Skinny
Little Lumifer $19.95+$2.50 S&H

Easy reading goes wherever you go. Slip the Skinny Little Lumifer into your pocket or purse, attach it to your key ring, or wear it around your neck. Small type magnified 2.5 times, becomes easy to read. The bright red beam allows the eye's pupils to remain open for the best legibility in dim light or no light at all.

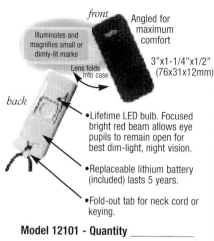

front

Angled for maximum comfort

Illuminates and magnifies small or dimly-lit marks

3"x1-1/4"x1/2" (76x31x12mm)

Lens folds into case

back

- Lifetime LED bulb. Focused bright red beam allows eye pupils to remain open for best dim-light, night vision.
- Replaceable lithium battery (included) lasts 5 years.
- Fold-out tab for neck cord or keying.

Model 12101 - Quantity _____

Micro Fluorescent
Lantern $25.00+$5.00 S&H

A powerful fluorescent lantern with a superbright flashlight. Now you can have the world's smallest and brightest fluorescent lantern teamed up with a high intensity flashlight. The folding Micro is able to switch from lantern to flashlight with the touch of your finger. The shielded fluorescent tube unfolds from its case from 0 to 180 degrees to become a wand for area lighting, and gives 360 degrees of light exposure. The Micro compactly stores back into itself. When you need the concentrated beam of a flashlight, simply slide the switch for a brilliant beam.

- Lifetime, powerful fluorescent tube never needs replacing.
- Flashlight's tungsten bulb provides high-intensity beam.
- Includes wrist strap.
- Folds down to compact size, 5-3.4" x 1-3/4" (146mm x 44mm)
- Requires 4 "AAA" batteries (not included)

Model 10018 - Quantity _____

Books:

How to be a Doll Detective,
by Patsy Moyer, $18.95
Quantity _____

Doll Values, by Patsy Moyer, $12.95
Quantity _____

How to be a Jewelry Detective,
by C. Jeanenne Bell, $18.95
Quantity _____

Fill this form & send a check or money order to:

A.D. Supplies & Tools
7325 Quivira Rd. #238
Shawnee, Kansas 66216

Or call 1-800-516-8356
(orders only)

Or fax 1-800-515-3289

Allow 1-2 weeks for delivery.

Check, Money Order, MasterCard or Visa
Credit Card Information:

MC/Visa # _____

Exp. Date _____

Name as on Credit Card:

_____

Signature: _____

Pocket Fluorescent Lantern
with Ultra Violet Tube

$29.95
+$5.00 S&H

The Pocket Fluorescent Lantern that sees things the naked eye can't. Because ultraviolet light has a wave length shorter than visible light, it can pick up things the naked eye is not able to see. it causes certain substances (like inks) to either glow or change their color. Some of it's uses are checking a doll for cracks or restoration work. Battery operated, this lightweight lantern is small enough to fit in your pocket. The Pocket Fluorescent Lantern is in the permanent collection of the Museum of Modern Art.

2" x 6-1/2" x 3/4"
(50 x 165 x 19mm)

Requires 4 "AA" batteries.
(not included)

Model 10016 - Quantity _____

No. 25 248 Sonja Henie   No. 25 247 Sonja Henie

No. 25 246 "Madeline" Doll (two sizes)

Wardrobe for either size "Madeline" Doll

No. 26 63 Sonja Henie Trousseau   No. 25 46 Baby Doll   No. 26 61 Sonja Henie Trousseau

"MADELINE" AN EXCLUSIVE DOLL—SONJA HENIE IN ALL HER GLORY

No. 25 248—Sonja Henie— An excellent likeness of the internationally known and popular skating champion; he is 18" tall with a fully jointed composition body, blonde curly hair, brown (sleeping) eyes with lashes, smile and dimples too. She is wearing a genuine skating outfit of a short blue jacket, trimmed with gold braid, a very short full skirt with short blue panties, and a cert little flower-trimmed hat, placed well forward on her head. Her high white skating shoes have skates attached. $5.00

No. 25 247—Sonja Henie— Same doll except this skating costume consists of a short red velvet dress with glazed shoulder straps over a white rayon blouse, and the white tasseled red velvet skating cap completes the outfit. Her high white shoes have skates attached. $5.00

No. 25 246—Madeline Doll— This 22" fully jointed doll has been especially created to meet our most exacting specifications; we take pleasure in presenting her, knowing with what special pride her future parents will present her to her friends. Her features are beautiful with real hair, and sleeping eyes with lashes, while her limbs are smooth and graceful with carefully moulded hands and fingers. Her peach colored organdie dress is trimmed with lace and black velvet ribbon. She wears black slippers and a black straw hat trimmed with flowers. Exclusive with F. A. O. Schwarz $8.75

No. 25 245—"Madeline" Doll— As above but in a smaller size, 18". $6.75

A complete wardrobe for either size "Madeline" Doll as per list below:

For No. 25 245—18":	For No. 25 246—22":	
No. 55 18 $1.50	No. 55 22 $1.75	
Nightgown with Bed Jacket, pink		
No. 56 18 $2.00	No. 56 22 $2.25	
Housecoat, white with flowers		
No. 57 18 $2.00	No. 57 22 $2.25	
Taffeta Cape, rose		
No. 58 18 $3.75	No. 58 22 $4.00	
Taffeta Flowered Dress, pink		
No. 59 18 $2.75	No. 59 22 $3.00	
White Organdie Dress, pink trim		
No. 60 18 $5.75	No. 60 22 $6.00	
Taffeta Coat and Hat, red		
No. 61 18 $2.75	No. 61 22 $3.00	
Flowered Dimity Dress		

No. 26 61—Sonja Henie Trousseau— Much of the natural charm of this international favorite has been portrayed in this 13" fully jointed doll. Her happy, slightly rounded face with dimples and round eyes and lots of curly blonde hair, and lots of what she

wears in this 12 x 24" suitcase, is somewhat on the athletic side and consists of a black and white skating outfit with white shoes and skates attached, a fancy skating costume, a ski outfit of blue pants and red coat with skis and poles too, a flowered play suit, a white sport suit, a pink dress, Chinese lounge outfit and many accessories $10.75

No. 25 46 1—Baby Doll— This doll is almost life size being 22" tall. Her soft body contains a voice and has composition arms, legs and head with sleeping eyes and eye lashes. She wears a pink rayon coat with a lace trimmed bonnet, a pretty white dress with white shoes and socks and of course rubber panties and white cotton undies $5.00

No. 25 46 2—Baby Doll— Same as above but with Blue coat and hat $5.00

No. 26 63—Sonja Henie Trousseau— With much of the charm of her famous namesake, she has met with immediate popularity—her faint smile, dimples and blonde curly hair all contribute towards a good likeness. Her jointed body is 18" tall and she wears a skating outfit of white velvet skirt, white rayon blouse, with skates attached to white shoes. Besides another skating outfit of white with a light jacket and a fur trimmed full skirt, there is a blue and red ski outfit with skis and poles, a Chinese pajama set, a lounging robe and accessories all carefully arranged in this large 25 x 30" box $16.75

6

F. A. O. SCHWARZ

Above: 1939 F.A.O. Schwarz Christmas Catalog page

Dressed Babykin

Dydee Trousseau

Suzanne Trousseau

Musical Baby Doll

Patriciakin Trousseau

No. 25 250 Portrait Doll

Tousle Head

No. 25 243 Portrait Doll

EXCEPTIONAL DOLLS

No. 25/220—Dressed Babykin—An excellent likeness of a plump healthy baby. Made entirely of a durable composition, measuring 10" tall, with head, arms and legs jointed at the body. Her big round eyes have lashes and close when she sleeps. She wears a voile dress, lace trimmed, with white undies, shoes and socks with a taffeta coat and bonnet to match. Dressed in our workroom **$5.00**

No. 26/57—Dydee Trousseau—Here is Dydee in a 14" size, dressed only in a cotton undershirt, diapers, rubber panties, white shoes and socks. Her pretty pink dress and bonnet to match are all ready to put on. Nor much need be said about Dydee. Most children know her well, that she drinks from a nursing bottle and needs the intimate care a child will give her, adding much to the joy of playing with her **$6.75**

No. 26/62—Suzanne Trousseau—Dolls must have clothes and a place to put them. Here one can have both with a very pretty 13" jointed doll with sleeping eyes besides. In addition to the white rayon, red trimmed, dress she wears, there is a short velvet dress, sport suit, lounging robe, night clothes and undies, a dark blue coat and hat, extra shoes, handkerchief, pocket book and wrist watch **$10.00**

No. 25/249—Musical Baby—The soft body of this 16" doll contains a music box which plays "Rock-a-Bye Baby." Her arms, legs and head are composition with sleeping eyes and lashes. She wears an extra long dress (all well-dressed babies do) lace and ribbon trimmed with bonnet to match. **$5.00**

No. 26/55—Patriciakin Trousseau—A combination of a popular doll, a fine trunk and an assortment of pretty clothes. The sturdy blue trunk measures 7 x 8 x 14". It has heavy brass corners, hinges and lock and is covered with travel stickers. The doll "Patriciakin" dressed in red with white dots, shoes and socks, measures 11" tall, and is fully jointed. Has sleeping eyes and curly hair. In the trunk and tray is a flowered dress, pink pajamas, play suit, party dress, coat, a hat and bonnet, handkerchiefs, towels, soap, brush and comb and perfume. Exclusive with F. A. O. Schwarz **$15.00**

No. 25/243—Portrait Doll—Modeled after a typical 8 to 10 year old girl. Her face has lost the baby roundness, her arms and legs are slenderized and her artistic hands have rather long tapering fingers. Because of her older appearance, her clothing can be more sophisticated and follow fashion trends. She measures 16" tall, and has fully jointed composition body. Her sleeping eyes have eye lashes. She wears a white cotton dress with red stripes, trimmed with blue, also white shoes and socks. **$7.50**

No. 25/250—Portrait Doll—Same 16" doll but wearing a pink dress, edged with maroon, to match the pink lined maroon coat and hat with gloves to match. This color combination is very unusual, is a perfect blend and is made even more stylish but smart. The coat has a white collar and cuffs, and she wears black shoes and white socks. **$10.75**

Tousle Head—A mass of curly locks——hence the name—just the softest, silkiest locks imaginable because the wig is the finest lamb's wool. It is washable—to little mothers an added pleasure. Sleeping eyes with lashes, soft body with arms and legs jointed at the body. She is dressed in pink or blue rompers with moccasins and socks. State color.
No. 25/18—in 17" size **$5.75**
No. 25/20—in 20" size 7.50
No. 25/19—in 22" size 10.00

F. A. O. SCHWARZ

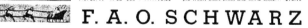

Above: 1939 F.A.O. Schwarz Christmas Catalog page

Above: 1931 Spring and Summer Montgomery Wards Catalog